Praise for *Future Ready*

"This book comes at a crucial time to help business leaders and decision-makers better understand the scope and scale of the climate challenges we are all facing, and the tools that are available to develop successful climate, resilience, and sustainability strategies. The authors channel their extensive experience in projects across multiple markets and sectors, bringing a unique understanding of effective solutions to create measurable, long-lasting sustainable impact. The book helps readers learn more about the risks and opportunities when developing resilient and sustainable projects, and how these are addressed in practice through a rich set of real-world examples. A practical guide covers effective pathways and strategies for organizations to jump-start their sustainability programs and measure, quantify, and improve their long-term sustainability performance. Overall, the book provides a guiding compass for organizations to rise to the climate challenge and help deliver a more resilient and sustainable world. It is highly recommended for executives, professionals, public officials as well as members of the public who want to learn more about how to make a difference."

—**Dr. Andreas Georgoulias**
Director of Sustainability and ESG,
The Environmental Financial Consulting Group

"This literary work is a powerful and perfect primer combining all the tools needed for those just beginning to explore sustainability and resilience as well as a roadmap for seasoned and veteran pros in their journey for the world to be Future Ready. As the Executive Director of the Disaster Recovery Coalition of America (DRCA), whose members are the largest U.S. organizations leading pre- and post-disaster response and recovery, I have had the privilege to work with resiliency expert and inspirational leader Tom Lewis and his co-authors for the past 20 years on the urgent necessity of building more resilient and sustainable infrastructure. This book demands that we rethink and change our approach to the unequivocal and increasingly clear risk all Americans face because our planet is warming in an unprecedented way, driving more extreme weather. Towns, cities, states, the federal government, and private sector all have to take a more future-focused approach to close the gap in understanding what "doing better" means to address climatic deviations from what used to be considered normal. This book puts in your hands the geographical reality of the future."

—**Casey A. Long**
Managing Director, The Disaster Recovery
Coalition of America (DRCA)

"Tom Lewis and co-authors Alastair MacGregor explore the job of confronting climate change and detail what is happening right now with stirring new innovations that have emerged in the battle against an ever-changing climate. Their book *Future Ready: Your Organization's Guide to Rethinking Climate, Resilience, and Sustainability* is an amazing compilation of how organizations and professionals can begin or continue to better prepare the world to tackle this intimidating challenge."

—Thomas Abdallah
P.E. LEED AP, Vice President and Chief Environmental Engineer,
MTA Construction and Development, New York City
Professor Columbia University—Sustainability Management
Graduate Program, SPS
Author of *Sustainable Mass Transit: Challenges and Opportunities in Urban Public, Transportation*

"The world faces both a climate and a social emergency, yet for the most part, organizations are sleepwalking into a dystopian future, and at best, making incremental changes to their strategies. *Future Ready* challenges us, with real-world examples, to make a mindset shift, rethink everything, and embrace transformational change in the infrastructure systems that underpin our societies. Read, be inspired, and act before it is too late."

—Richard Threlfall
Chair, International Coalition for Sustainable
Infrastructure, and KPMG Global Head of
Infrastructure, Government and Healthcare

"*Risk* and *vulnerability* are terms that we often hear when discussing the impacts of extreme weather events on infrastructure. We hear of many global projects illustrating how solutions are developed and implemented. In *Future Ready: Your Organization's Guide to Rethinking Climate, Resilience, and Sustainability*, Lewis and MacGregor not only brought into one place some of these stories, but also took on a different meaning of risk and vulnerability. There is the risk of not providing enough detail or context to illustrate how they came up with the strategies they offer in the book. There is also the vulnerability of opening up their organization's project portfolio and letting others critique the "why" of those strategies' applications. I applaud the authors' boldness in leveraging their vulnerability to ensure that the infrastructure industry learns from their experience in planning, designing, building, and maintaining sustainable and resilient programs and infrastructure. Part history and part best practice, the book balances the need to address the moment's challenges, strategic solutions, and how one organization is making a difference: achieving innovative outcomes in often the most challenging circumstance. There is no one-size-fits-all strategy to combat the unique issues of the complex ecosystem of climate-related impacts. *Future Ready: Your Organization's Guide to Rethinking Climate, Resilience, and Sustainability* provides a menu of strategies that, at the time, may only apply to the circumstances of a city or a region. But a better picture emerges when combined with the lessons learned from other locations. We need an ecosystem of players and strategies to optimize solutions. Lewis and MacGregor challenge us to think about the future differently. Not only to be ready, but also to further minimize the increasing risks and vulnerabilities of infrastructure to the growing impacts of the climate status quo. We need to continually use the built infrastructure using the paradigms of the past. Through this collection of projects and the book's advice, this time, we're in a better place to succeed in doing the 'right project.'"

—Dr. Cris B. Liban, P.E.
2020 Engineering News-Record Award of Excellence Winner; Distinguished Member, American Society of Civil Engineers Fellow; American Society of Civil Engineers Chief Sustainability Officer LA Metro

"*Future Ready* is more than the usual "how-to" guide for resiliency professionals. By advocating for equity and community empowerment as core project deliverables, this book provides a vision for *doing resiliency right*—and for the people who need it most."

—Paul Gallay
Director, Resilient Coastal Communities Project, Columbia Climate School

"A must read for those responsible for building or retrofitting in our private sector as well as infrastructure and built environment owners and operators in local, regional, and federal government. With a perspective firmly anchored in the future, this book lays out in clear terms what the opportunity cost will be if we don't build with a focus on both sustainability and resilience. Put simply, it's not about the short-term cost of building efficient sustainable buildings and infrastructure, it's about the much greater long term cost if we don't! The authors are not only subject matter experts, but they advise and design for newly built as well as pre- and post-disaster sustainable and resilient solutions around the globe for both the private and public sectors."

—David R. Soares
President & CEO of Lexden Capital, LLC, a New York real estate and infrastructure investment company

"A compelling account for an organization's journey to rethink everything and coalesce around the idea of becoming Future Ready. Plenty of useful advice and tangible examples for those who are striving to bring sustainability, resilience, and climate action at the heart of their organizations. Embarking on a similar journey is urgent and necessary for all built environment professionals if we are to tackle the most pressing challenges of this decade and build a just, sustainable, and resilient future for all."

—**Savina Carluccio**
Executive Director, International
Coalition for Sustainable Infrastructure

"In an era of an escalating human-based impact on climate change and runaway destruction of the environment and biodiversity, this timely book emphasizes the urgency for the client to seek the advice of engineers and other experts on selecting suitable projects with future-focused solutions."

—**Spiro Pollalis**
Professor of Design Technology and Management at the
Graduate School of Design, Harvard University

FUTURE

READY

TOM LEWIS | ALASTAIR MACGREGOR

FUTURE
READY

YOUR ORGANIZATION'S GUIDE TO RETHINKING
CLIMATE, RESILIENCE, AND SUSTAINABILITY

WILEY

Library of Congress Cataloging-in-Publication Data is Available:

ISBN 9781119894568 (Cloth)
ISBN 9781119894636 (ePDF)
ISBN 9781119894629 (ePub)

Cover Design: WSP
Cover Images: © Irina Strelnikova/Shutterstock, © Julien8001/Shutterstock, © vi73/Shutterstock

SKY10044244_031023

To
Christina, Alexa, Abigail, James, and Holly Lewis
Christine, Abigail, and Alexander MacGregor

And to our WSP
colleagues, clients, and partners
for challenging and inspiring us to be innovative, resilient, sustainable,
and Future Ready®

Contents

Foreword

CHRISTIAN MENN, THE famous Swiss engineer and bridge designer, approached bridge design with safety being his utmost objective while designing beautiful bridges perfectly blended in the mountainous landscape. Safety in the 1970s and 1980s was simpler to understand and handle. The bridge should safely fulfill its intended use for pedestrians and vehicular traffic, designed according to code. But what would be "safety" today? Is it only about the bridge, the construct?

Expanding on the traditional definition of safety, which generations of engineers have inherited, we can include the prevention of the adverse effects of climate change on our own current and future projects. The utmost objective becomes the safety of the users and the safety of many more people who may live thousands of miles away.

Our projects impact nature, leading to ever-increasing loads on our constructs. Our designs should address how our constructs will continue withstanding natural phenomena, which will exceed the requirements of today's codes. Our designs should be sustainable, that is, built within the capacity of our ecosystems, preventing the increase of extreme phenomena. The designs should be resilient to withstand the impact of future extreme phenomena, unavoidable to be completely contained. In a nutshell, today's engineers, designers, environmentalists, and construction professionals should also be concerned about how their projects affect the climate and how their projects protect the planet. Addressing the broader impact of projects in unchartered territories requires professionals to cross the boundaries of their own silos. Interdisciplinary collaboration is necessary for analyzing and understanding the issues, convincing the stakeholders to make the necessary decisions, and building meaningful future-oriented projects.

The authors have a good understanding of these issues. They quote that "climate change is now and tomorrow. It's local and global. It's risk and opportunity." They are members of a large engineering company, which identified early the need to act responsibly on the environment. They have participated in different fora researching the impact of engineering work on the environment. So, they undertake the responsibility to reach a wider audience. First, to share their knowledge. Second, to emphasize the imperative need for a broader and coordinated collaboration of the experts with the clients and the policymakers to have an impact on mitigating and adapting to climate change.

The book is not a traditional engineering textbook. Instead, it follows a different approach to engage the audience effectively. Based on case studies accompanying a narrative, the book attracts the reader's interest, whom the authors consider their future collaborators in selecting and implementing suitable projects fulfilling the client's needs and meeting this society's expectations at large. The approach is convincing as the book presents cases known to the reader that can be repeated soon, like the Superstorm Sandy in New York. However, although the book uses examples familiar to most, they do it with the authority of having been engaged in addressing them as experts.

The narrative follows a carefully planned thread. It starts with the need for safety, as any responsible engineer would do, and very quickly introduces the concept of risk. In the past, the risk was addressed straightforwardly. Although the future cannot be predicted, analyzing the past leads to informed decisions about what is expected to happen in a probabilistic way. The assumption is that the external parameters remain the same. However, nowadays, it is more complicated to be based on past data. Extreme phenomena with unprecedented frequency have become the norm. What used to be the 100-year phenomenon may occur more than once in a decade. The risk becomes a climate risk, which requires equal attention to adapting practices and mitigating future climate risks by selecting the proper projects.

Then, the transition risk is introduced, defined by international multilateral and nonprofit organizations as the risk of adapting practice to new conditions. The transition risk also includes leaving parts of the population and entire countries out of climate mitigation and adaptation benefits. Equity and the social dimension are essential to ensure the success of climate action. A step further, reflecting realism, the low-profit margins of the construction industry are emphasized. The industry is fragmented with too many players and mature technology, leading to price competition that leaves little room for research and innovation. The intervention of government and society fills the gap. At the government level, executive orders in the United States, like ARRA (American Recovery and Reinvestment Act, 2009) and IRA (Inflation Reduction Act, 2022), funnel large amounts of money to sustainable and resilient projects. These funds do not last forever, but the changes have a long-lasting effect, especially when pursuing sustainability and resilience proves less expensive than initially thought. If the right project is selected from the beginning, and if the proper steps are followed from the very beginning, the cost of the sustainable project may be a little higher in the short term, but cheaper in the long term. Sustainable projects have a higher risk-adjusted return on investment when considering future regulations and their societal acceptance of continuing operating. Furthermore, informed forward-looking communities authorize additional funds for sustainable projects that impact the daily life of their citizens and boost the local economy, with a primary example being the cleaning of the Santa Monica beach in California.

The authors look for alliances in calling for action on sustainability and resilience and identify three megatrends. The first megatrend is the extreme climate phenomena, evident everywhere on the planet. The reaction and demand of society in the most affluent countries is the second megatrend. Technology development and use of technology is the third megatrend, an enabler of effectively addressing climate change within the cost afforded by society.

Through examples, the book presents the issues effectively and powerfully and requires action. The authors' own firm demonstrates how action can be taken. Sensibly, they recommend flexibility to address low-hanging fruits, paving the path for bold action. Quoting the book, "getting early wins is essential to building momentum and buy-in. Once employees see that establishing a new and better solutions-oriented framework produced results—being selected by key clients for large and high-profile projects—even skeptics will likely become converts." They also strongly recommend working with nature and learning from nature, discounting the attitude of many years that human intervention can tame nature.

The effectiveness of developing sustainable projects depends on being next to the client when making decisions about which project to undertake to address specific needs. It also depends on the policymakers, who respond to societal demands, and provide the framework to select and develop sustainable and resilient projects. Design professionals have always desired to be the first to advise clients and policymakers, with fluctuating success throughout the years. Today, though, it is imperative for clients to seek the expertise necessary to select future-looking projects. The role of experts is more than executing the program of requirements of the client; the role of experts is to develop the program of requirements to fulfill present and future needs effectively, and equally importantly, efficiently with limited resources. It is desirable for the experts developing the program of requirements to execute it.

The book provides the opportunity for the clients of engineering works to comprehend the complex concepts of sustainability and resilience. The book is equally valuable for policymakers to act, following the advice of those who execute the projects and have demonstrated a commitment to serving society at large. Policies should effectively address climate mitigation and adaptation without overtaxing society.

In an era of an escalating human-based impact on climate change and runaway destruction of the environment and biodiversity, this timely book informs and emphasizes the urgency for the client to seek the advice of engineers and other experts on selecting suitable projects with future-focused solutions.

—**Prof. Spiro N. Pollalis**
Harvard Design School

—**Anthony Kane**
Institute for Sustainable Infrastructure

Introduction: Superstorm Sandy

ON THE NIGHT of October 29, 2012, Superstorm Sandy was everywhere. I had a hard time keeping my eyes off the TV, flipping back and forth between the Weather Channel and CNN's beachfront reporters, who were on the verge of being blown over or swept away by water. I was also getting first-hand reports of the flooding in lower Manhattan. At the time, I was the U.S. company lead for Louis Berger, the global professional services firm that is now part of WSP. Louis Berger was responsible for managing the Downtown Recovery Program where rebuilding work at the World Trade Center site was continuing over a decade after the September 11 terrorist attacks. That job had expanded my environment and sustainability technical focus to include disaster management, of which Superstorm Sandy would become an extreme example. The wall of water that was pushing in from the mouth of New York Harbor was threatening all the progress that had been made at the site.

Sandy also hit closer to home. Right outside my window, trees were bent parallel to the ground in 70-mph blasts of wind. My family lived in a small town in New Jersey, just outside New York City—and directly in Sandy's path. By midnight, the gusts weakened to 50 miles

1

an hour, but it took me another two hours to finally crawl into bed. It was a short night's sleep.

At approximately 4:00 a.m., an employee of New York City's Department of Citywide Administrative Services called my cell phone. He thanked me for picking up before moving straight into his early-morning pitch. "I'm making all kinds of calls because we need heroes right now. I'm having a hard time finding heroes. I'm hoping Louis Berger can be a hero."

"Absolutely," I said, walking out into the hallway. The wind was still hammering the south side of my house. "What do you need?"

"Everything."

"Let's start with the priorities," I said.

"We need pumps. We need generators. We need fuel. We need trucks. Whatever you can get me, I'm pretty sure I'll take it."

I was full of adrenaline as I marshalled together the initial equipment supply with my emergency management team. Over the next few days, I dove into the seemingly endless additional requests for emergency response support and materials coming our way. At the same time, our house had no power except a small gasoline-powered generator, so I was taking calls in my car with the phone plugged into the cigarette lighter.

Outside, the neighborhood had been transformed into a surreal landscape of downed powerlines and toppled trees. On Halloween, two days after the storm blew through, I drove across my neighbor's front lawn to get out to the main road and buy gas for our generator—it was the only way to get around the debris blocking the street. Once I got onto major roads, I searched for gas stations that still had fuel, but they often had hours-long wait times.

Yet, even as I drove past the wreckage around me, I knew we were lucky. We were alive—the storm killed close to 100 people in New Jersey and New York alone—and in a relatively undamaged house. Thirty miles away in Queens, a whole neighborhood had been inundated by flooding and then, after a flood-related electrical accident, burned to the ground. Down at the Jersey Shore, houses in expensive beachfront communities collapsed into the sand, while the streets surrounding them were reclaimed by the ocean. In just a few hours, one of the wealthiest parts of one of the wealthiest countries in the world had been devastated and humbled. It was clear that we needed to do better, and my career and business focus expanded again to include a stronger and more direct blending of climate resilience and sustainability.

Arguably, 2005's Hurricane Katrina should have been the definitive wake-up call across the United States about the urgent necessity of building more resilient and sustainable infrastructure. The event's sobering death toll, around 1,800 people, the widely criticized local, state, and federal response, and the horrible inequity in who suffered the most—like many disasters, a disproportionate number of the dead were poor, Black, and elderly—were all shocking. I saw the inordinate toll on already underserved communities from the storm's damage and the subsequent, lagging rebuilding efforts first-hand in 2007, when I spent time in New Orleans supporting the long-term recovery. But for many people—and I was one of them—it was also easy to put a few asterisks next to Hurricane Katrina's impact. Unlike New Orleans, most U.S. cities don't sit on the hurricane-heavy Gulf of Mexico, surrounded by water, below sea level (and sinking), and reliant on an extensive system of pump stations and levies to stay dry and habitable.

In that sense, Sandy was different. First, it made climate change very personal to me by putting family at risk. But, more broadly, it was irrefutable evidence of how much more of the United States was at risk. If New York City could effectively be paralyzed for weeks, nowhere along the densely populated East Coast of the United States could be considered safe. However, by the time Sandy hit in 2012, the science on climate change was unequivocal and the risk increasingly clear. Over 90% of climate scientists agreed that the planet was warming in an unprecedented way, the warming was largely driven by human activity, and the changing climate was driving more extreme weather. Thousands of scientists around the world contribute to the Intergovernmental Panel on Climate Change's (IPCC) climate modeling, but the basic dynamic behind global warming is high school physics. Putting more heat in the atmosphere and oceans means they also contain more energy. This additional energy will, in turn, be released in larger and more anomalous storms and other climatic deviations from what used to be considered normal.

Predicting exactly what types of weather events global warming will produce is trickier. No single event can be ascribed to climate change. In fact, explaining any one weather event at all is complicated since they are all the result of numerous, complex interrelated dynamics acting across a spatiotemporal scale. However, we do know what *kind* of storms will be more frequent and severe as a result of climate change. Sandy, an extreme storm and huge flooding event, fit that profile—we'll dig into some specific details later.

However, for anyone waffling on whether climate change was "their problem," getting walloped by Sandy put an exclamation mark on it. The extreme weather predicted in the relatively dry and dense IPCC reports that span thousands of pages is happening now. Sandy gave the New York metro area a peek into what life in the era of climate change looks like—flooded subway tunnels, destroyed neighborhoods, and millions of people without power or heat as winter approached.

The good news was that many people in businesses, government, and other organizations got the message. In the years following Sandy, I met hundreds of very smart, capable people working passionately on innovative solutions. They were climate scientists and modelers, architects, planners, engineers, and project managers at state and federal infrastructure agencies and environmental departments, logistics experts and disaster preparedness specialists at the Federal Emergency Management Agency (FEMA), and sustainability executives at corporations across the spectrum. We all shared a conviction that climate change is humanity's most urgent issue and that we need to make better choices, and tens of millions of other Americans agree with us.

At a fundamental level, there is no great mystery about what "doing better" means. Towns, cities, states, the federal government, and the private sector all have to take a more future-focused approach and do two specific things better. First, we must reduce our greenhouse gas (GHG) emissions and consider full life-cycle costs and impacts by enacting sustainability measures. Second, we should limit our short- as well as long-term vulnerability to extreme weather through climate adaptation and resilience measures. These goals are deeply interrelated. If we don't rapidly reduce our GHG emissions, we'll never be able to build barriers that are high, wide, and strong enough to be resilient. Similarly, if we don't improve stormwater management and integrate naturally adaptive measures, our cities will repeatedly flood and/or run short of critical resources like clean water before our sustainability measures are able to bend the curve of emissions.

If we had started two or three decades ago, arguably, rapidly reducing GHG emissions would have been sufficient to avoid the need for massive climate adaptation and resilience measures. That moment has passed. Today, the pace and advanced state of climate change means there is no either/or option—we need to reject false choices and build a resilient *and* sustainable future. There was also little doubt about what we *didn't* need after Sandy: a return to business as usual. That was what got us into this mess in the first place.

Since then, I've worked on countless projects in New York and New Jersey and across the United States that focused on resilience and sustainability. Yet, even as I could feel a shift toward these aims, it was clear we weren't all aligned. Some people had short memories about the last flood or drought or wildfire, or simply tuned out when faced with a phenomenon as complex and massive as climate change. Other times, I encountered some of the same old false choices and unsustainable leadership mindsets that create systemic blocks to building resilience. I also heard well-intentioned experts say that we should focus our attention and resources on climate mitigation alone rather than climate adaptation and resilience at the same time.

Engineers are ethically bound to look for solutions that will endure, so they can't focus on only one condition at a time. That meant that, post-Sandy, when I was driving on my neighbor's lawn to avoid the dangerous, downed powerlines, I was also thinking "This is crazy! We've got to get those things underground." It turns out, however, that the poles are owned by the town, which rent them to the utilities. If the utilities buried their wires, the town would lose the income stream. Just like that, a relatively cheap and easy way to save human lives and protect part of our infrastructure becomes a nonstarter in many locations.

Despite these headwinds, I knew I was in the right sector to make a difference. Infrastructure including in what is also referred to as the built environment—hospitals, schools, offices, airports, railroads, water, sewers, power, housing—accounts for a full 70% of the GHG emitted in the United States every year. It's easier to visualize the pollution coming from a large truck rumbling by than the apartment building it's passing, but we need to pursue the decarbonization across our infrastructure. Even if everyone in America switched to electric vehicles (EVs) overnight, we'd still be a long way from meeting our long-term climate goals and truly doing our part globally. Until we rethink the roads we're driving on—and the rest of the built environment around us and the associated role that different organizations and sectors play in that environment—we don't have a chance of overcoming the climate crisis that threatens our planet and our collective future.

In the aftermath of any disaster, there are thousands of heroes—paramedics, firefighters, police, and ordinary citizens—who ignore political and ideological differences and go out of their way to save the lives of strangers and protect their neighbors. But, between storms, we need dedication to the same goals every day. This kind of quiet heroism and selflessness requires different skills, like persistence, flexibility, curiosity, collaboration, and diplomacy.

The climate, as well as other future conditions, are changing rapidly, so building just like we did (and sometimes even where we did) last time is reckless. The challenge is urgent, so exploring new technologies, materials, and processes is essential. Innovation is vital, so integrating people and their expertise in unprecedented ways is imperative.

In a way, the journey that was kicked off by that 4:00 a.m. phone call never ends. In this book, my co-authors, Alastair MacGregor, and I explore why it's taken the planet so long to begin the job of confronting climate change in earnest—and what is finally moving the needle. We discuss some of the most exciting innovations that have emerged since Hurricane Sandy tore through New York and New Jersey. We help you and organizations like yours avoid the false choices, maladaptation, and perverse incentives that stymy efforts to plan and design for a very different future. We share our commitment to climate action and creating better infrastructure that blends sustainability, resilience, and a just transition to a green economy. Most importantly, we want to inspire other people and organizations to rethink what is possible on their journeys toward truly Future Ready® cities, communities, and companies.

1

Rethink Everything

ON OCTOBER 22, 2012, meteorologists at the National Hurricane Center (NHC), a cement fortress in Miami, Florida, registered Tropical Depression 18 in the southwestern Caribbean Sea. The event was then just a line of thunderstorms moving across the turquoise water, but it represented a serious potential risk. Hurricanes and other weather-related events kill an annual average of hundreds of people and cause hundreds of billions of dollars in damages in the United States alone.

The NHC, which is tasked with predicting the future risk of these low-pressure systems across the United States, jumped into action. It dispatched one of the Air Force's Lockheed Martin Super Hercules aircraft for observation. Despite all the data that streams in from geostationary satellites, as well as other land- and water-based weather stations, flying an 80-ton airplane into a furious windstorm is currently still the best way to gather some information.

In Miami, experts in meteorology, satellite data, and remote sensing poured over the reports and fed it into multiple hurricane forecast models that predicted the event's future direction and destructive potential. Many tropical depressions fizzle out, but the environment surrounding Number 18—including warm waters and local atmospheric conditions—caused it to intensify rapidly with a defined circulating pattern and winds above 38 miles per hour (61 kmh), thus earning it a name: Tropical Storm Sandy. Over the next few hours,

Sandy's increasing wind speed and structure quickly took it to hurricane-strength. The NHC issued warnings to Jamaica, Cuba, and other Caribbean islands in its likely path, saving lives and reducing damage, while keeping an eye on potential risk to the United States.

Well before Sandy made landfall in New Jersey on October 29, the NHC had released a continual stream of updates and warnings for areas likely to be impacted, the National Weather Service had issued watches, governors had declared states of emergency—and even mandatory evacuation orders for certain areas. All these advisories were picked up and spread by local police and emergency officials, television, newspapers, and social media. However, even mandatory evacuations are rarely enforced. Once the expert advice about Hurricane Sandy's risks reached residents, it was up to them to decide what to do. Many chose not to heed the warnings; 186 Americans died in the storm.

A later Center for Disease Control and Prevention (CDC) report detailed the fatal consequences of ignoring official advice. The leading cause of death related to Sandy was drowning due to the storm surge and associated flooding, which accounted for nearly half of the fatalities. Of those drowning deaths, over half were people who died in homes located in primary evacuation zones. The result was that, in 2012, more Americans drowned in their own homes than were killed during violent home invasions, sexual assaults, or carjackings.

A decade later, on September 28, 2022, category 4 Hurricane Ian tore into the southwest coast of Florida. Governor Ron DeSantis had declared a state of emergency four days earlier and mandatory evacuation orders covered all or part of 12 counties. Once again, though, many people did not evacuate. Nearly 130 people died in Florida, many of whom, again, drowned near or in their houses located in evacuation zones.

There is a wide range of circumstances that make it harder for certain people to evacuate—some have physical or mental disabilities, some don't have transportation, others simply can't afford to leave. But there are also large numbers of people who remain in the path of storms by choice. Hurricanes are known killers, so what leads those in mandatory evacuation zones to decide against following the expert advice intended to save their lives?

We could ask similar questions about our historic lack of urgency around climate change. The accelerating buildup of greenhouse gases and resultant increase in heat energy trapped in our planet's atmosphere represents a destructive and global threat that causes billions of dollars in damages and directly or indirectly kills thousands of people a year. It is also a phenomenon we have been publicly and repeatedly warned about by scientists since the 1980s. So why have most of us routinely ignored expert advice and downplayed this accelerating threat?

It turns out that our stuttering responses to both specific events like hurricanes and the global phenomenon of climate change are deeply interrelated—both largely determined by human risk perception. Though risk is one of our greatest motivating forces, we also evaluate risk in deeply inconsistent ways that are poorly attenuated to recognizing certain threats. For example, humans tend to react more urgently to near-term, immediate risks—even if the future risks are ultimately much greater. Of course, from an evolutionary standpoint, prioritizing "avoiding hungry tigers" makes a lot of sense. However, the same life-saving perception of immediate risk also introduces a tendency to discount the future. Likewise, we tend to react more urgently to threats with which we've had negative personal experience. Again, deciding not to eat mushrooms of a certain color has distinct evolutionary advantages. But privileging personal experience also tends to reduce the importance of potentially life-saving advice from other people, including those with scientific expertise.

Today, the biggest threats humans face have changed dramatically, but our risk perception is still saddled with evolutionary baggage that gives primacy to risks that are immediate, near-term, and personal. For many people, neither hurricane forecasts nor climate change make that list. However, climate change faces additional obstacles to being perceived as a serious risk. For one, the phenomenon is complex and described most accurately in nuanced scientific terminology—language that doesn't register climate change as a dire threat for many people. Accepting the broad scientific consensus around climate change has also become deeply politicized in the United States, forcing people to "choose sides" rather than dispassionately evaluate risks. The cumulative result of these factors is that, for decades, humans haven't responded appropriately to a potentially existential threat largely because so many of us didn't perceive climate change as carrying meaningful risks.

Making Climate Risk Real

In 2022, the United Nations' Intergovernmental Panel on Climate Change (IPCC), the most authoritative source of scientific data on climate change, issued its sixth assessment. Hoesung Lee, the Chair of the IPCC, described the report as "a dire warning about the consequences of inaction."[1] António Guterres, the United Nations (U.N.) secretary general, added that the assessment represented "an atlas of human suffering and a damning indictment of failed climate leadership."[2]

The only good news was a notable shift in how the report was received. In parts of the private sector, there was an urgency around the issue of climate change that hadn't existed even five years previously. After decades of collective foot dragging—amid increasingly specific and stark warnings from the IPCC—what has changed? Why have organizations finally decided to take climate action seriously?

Once again, the primary driver is risk perception. Decades of resistance to taking climate change seriously is rapidly dissolving as more people believe it poses a near-term, personal, material risk. As investors, shareholders, and business leaders rethink the threats—and opportunities—climate change represents, climate action is finally emerging as a mainstream priority.

Climate-related risk is certainly not hard to find—nor is it new. But while deadly and destructive climate-linked extreme weather used to be viewed more like a black swan event, it is now an annual inevitability. Every year, wildfires, droughts, hurricanes, and other extreme weather will exact a toll—the only questions are exactly how many human lives or billions in dollars. Take, for example, the cumulative financial damage from climate-related events in 2021. Wildfires in the western United States cost roughly $11 billion, a pervasive drought and record-setting Pacific Northwest heatwave cost $9 billion, a historic winter storm cost $25 billion, and Hurricane Ida cost $78 billion. Globally, the losses were even higher—flooding alone hit $90 billion.[3] In short, the massive losses caused by extreme weather were finally making climate risk unignorable.

In the past five or so years, however, a whole new dimension of climate risk has also emerged. Physical risk refers to disruptive, costly events like buildings flooded by hurricanes or supply chains disrupted by wildfires. In contrast, transition risks result from the transition to a lower-carbon economy, and are related to policy and legal actions, technology changes, market responses, and reputational considerations. For example, governments at all levels are introducing and tightening regulatory mechanisms like energy efficiency mandates or requirements on greenhouse gas (GHG) reductions. Companies that don't transition quickly enough risk experiencing severe reputational and brand damage, or being excluded from certain markets. Changing expectations about future profitability within carbon-intense industries can lead to significant loss of asset value. Similarly, changed water conservation policies could negatively impact agricultural companies.

Transition risk also refers to missed opportunities—the new markets and growth that are open to leaders in decarbonization efforts, as well as those organizations that are more progressive with regard to the mainstreaming of resilience and sustainability approaches and technologies. Tesla, for example, is a massive beneficiary of national GHG emission reduction goals. The United States, Europe, China, and other countries offer automakers that can't meet mandated emission reductions the option of buying credits from car companies that have surpassed regulatory goals. Tesla, which primarily sells electric vehicles, has been able to maintain its profitability in the U.S. market largely because it sells so many carbon credits to other carmakers—$1.5 billion worth in 2021.[4]

The third factor driving awareness of climate risk is coming from investors, shareholders, and other company stakeholders. Over the past few years, investor demand for Environmental, Social, and Governance (ESG) reporting—in which companies account for their GHG emissions and climate resilience, and other Environmental, Social, and Governance (ESG) metrics—has soared. ESG assets, like companies that issue annual ESG reports and employ corporate policies to act more responsibly as environmental stewards and community partners, were a relatively niche category 10 years ago. Today, they are on track to reach $53 trillion assets under management (AUM) by 2025, or a third of the global total AUM.[5,6] Though there is no universal framework for ESG declarations nor legal requirement for action, even the process of reporting on GHG emissions has created a whole new driver—as well as a growing industry—for taking climate action seriously.

The meteoric growth of ESG reporting and as a class of investment is also creating a sort of virtuous ecosystem. When companies elect to voluntarily disclose their climate-related financial risks and other ESG criteria, it sends signals to the broader marketplace that these issues are important for organizational decision-makers, employees, customers, and investors of all types.

Increases in ESG reporting also drive more consistent understanding of ESG risks over time. (Although that understanding is still quite inconsistent and messy today—a topic we explore in the second section of the book.) Improving literacy around ESG reporting, in turn, encourages changes in the regulatory landscape to meet investor needs. The European Union (EU) already requires corporate sustainability reporting from a growing number of companies.[7] The U.S. Security and Exchange Commission (SEC) is also expected to require publicly held companies to disclose climate-related information as well as other ESG data.[8] As these disclosures become expected by more consumers and the public, privately held companies are also more likely to voluntarily release information. These reactions, in turn, send additional signals to the marketplace, further accelerating the cycle of normalizing and expanding ESG disclosures.

The public sector is also moving to limit its exposure to climate risk. Not surprisingly, the areas in the United States that are most at risk of experiencing loss are often among the leaders in building sustainable and resilient infrastructure. For example, Florida and California—on opposite coasts and sides of the political spectrum—are two of the states with the highest climate risk. However, cities, counties, and other stakeholders in both states have invested heavily in sustainable and resilient infrastructure.

Driving toward Zero

One of the most common goals to combat the risk of climate change is what's called "net zero." Net zero effectively means cutting an organization's GHG emissions to as close to zero as possible, with any remaining emissions reabsorbed from the atmosphere—for instance, by forests that naturally store carbon dioxide or by technological means of carbon sequestration.[9] To date, over 70 countries—including the United States, China, and the European Union—have set net zero targets, along with over 1,000 cities, 1,200 companies, and 400 financial institutions.

In practice, though, net zero is often used inconsistently and many organizations definitively count only a fraction of their carbon emissions. We dive deeper into net zero in the second section, along with more detail about what ESG disclosures, sustainability roadmaps, and climate action plans look like and how they are developed. At this point, it's sufficient to know that "decarbonization" and "reducing GHG emissions" both refer to the many processes and technologies used to reach the goal of net zero. The most common timeframe for reaching net zero—and the one supported by the best climate science—is 2050, at the latest.

It's also important to note that reaching net zero is not enough to build a thriving and sustainable future. First, our decarbonization efforts must be grounded in equity—a sustainable future is inherently one in which all people and countries can prosper. Second, we need to reduce the amount of GHG released into the atmosphere in ways that support our planet's diminishing biodiversity and help maintain and rebuild critical ecosystems.

We still aren't moving nearly fast enough to meet the challenge of climate change, but the combination of increasing engagement and focused action from the private and public sectors is promising. It is also being supported by unprecedented government spending on climate action, investments in technology, and building resilient, sustainable infrastructure. The European Union's 2021–2027 budget calls for spending over €2 trillion ($1.9 trillion) to fight climate change and build a more sustainable Europe.[10] In the United States, 2021's Bipartisan Infrastructure Law includes $550 billion to combat climate change and reduce GHG emissions through a variety of initiatives.[11] In 2022, the Inflation Reduction Act included more than $360 billion in additional funding to fight climate change and incentivize sustainability in the United States.

This overdue, but rapidly growing, commitment to combat climate change is inextricably linked to our changing perception of climate risk. As more companies, consumers, leaders, investors, politicians, and citizens come to understand the enormous risks—and rewards— associated with climate change, the faster our transition to a low-carbon economy will be.

System Failure

However, even as climate risk spurs an expanding number of companies and cities to report on their GHG emissions, set net zero goals, and lay out climate action plans, significant challenges to planning and designing infrastructure for a very different future remain stubbornly entrenched. As organizations work toward a more sustainable, resilient, and equitable future, there are a number of recurring, systemic obstacles to these goals.

For example, the necessity and commitment to decarbonize our economy often runs head-on into perverse incentives to *not* build sustainably and resiliently. The traditional economics of the insurance industry, for example, are one such stumbling block in efforts to design resilience into buildings. Following hurricanes that devastate beachfront properties, many homeowners build right back on ground zero. Sometimes they take measures like elevating their houses on stilts, but, whether they built back better, they very often built back bigger and more expensively. Were these homeowners, who had recently experienced a major material, personal loss, all pretending that the last storm was a one-off? Perhaps, but in many cases, they built back the way they did because their homeowner's insurance and/or government-subsidized flood protection programs paid to replace what was damaged—in whole or in large part—not what would be smarter for a future that includes accelerating sea level rise and more intense storms.

This is even more curious because insurance companies are large organizations staffed with smart people who have all the data on climate change. They understand the science and the vulnerabilities of assets around the world very well; mapping climate risk is even a product line. So why aren't insurers world leaders in building resiliency, at least for the assets they cover?

Part of the reason is that insurers operate in a unique industry. Just about every bank requires a homeowner to have insurance before it will sign off on a mortgage. So, homeowners with mortgages have no choice but to buy insurance, while those who do not have a mortgage can afford and often choose to purchase insurance as a hedge on risk. What's more, insurers can tightly define the risks they cover and for how much, which can be adjusted based on likely climate risk. For example, a policy might cover 70% of the cost of repairing flood dam-age, but only 50% of wind damage repairs to the same house.

The issue of time also looms large. Policies expire and require renewal every 12 months, so insurers can regularly adjust the premi-ums they charge. As a result, there is little incentive for insurers to share risk assessments—in the form of risk-adjusted premiums—with consumers beyond one year out. Many states do regulate premium increases, but insurance companies always have the option of getting out of a market altogether. Ultimately, the business of insurance under-writing is to sell risk transfer, not to educate consumers—at least not yet.

These dynamics are playing out dramatically in Florida, a state with very high climate risk. The insurance market had been in turmoil for years, with insurers regularly exiting the state or liquidating—six companies became insolvent in 2020, even before Hurricane Ian hit the state. Floridians' premiums have also been rising at a much faster rate than other Americans. In 2022, premiums increased roughly 33% in Florida versus 9% for the United States as a whole.[12] To date, how-ever, all this turmoil and financial pain has done very little to design for and properly adapt to climate change. The economics of this sector provide little incentive to invest in long-term resilience and to truly adapt to the climate that will prevail several decades from now.

A system that encouraged people to rebuild where and how they did before is frustrating not just from a problem-solving, engineering per-spective, but a basic financial one. In the United States, Federal Emer-gency Management Agency (FEMA) statistics show that every dollar spent on pre-disaster hazard mitigation returns $6 the next time a similar storm comes to town.[13] You'd think that a 6-to-1 return on investment would encourage a wholesale rethinking of resilience spending, but only about 10% of FEMA's government post-disaster resources are spent on reducing the impact of extreme weather before disaster strikes again. Resilience requires modern codes and economic incentives to be better aligned with proactively building, or rebuilding, for a different future.

Full Costs

The economics of the traditional construction business is also not con-ducive to rapid innovation. Historically, the industry has operated on very low margins and decisions have been made on the basis of lowest upfront capital costs—not on innovations that could add long-term value. This model has long discouraged investment in—as well as uptake of—newer, more resilient and sustainable technologies and processes.

Confronting climate change means rethinking this capital cost-driven approach to planning, design, and procurement across every sector. Upfront cost considerations should be part of any decision. But the costs and benefits of integrating innovative materials, processes, and techniques needs to be viewed across the whole life cycle of a product. This includes everything from the product's initial funding and planning studies through to design, manufacture, and end of life, usually either reuse, recycling, or landfilling. While these full life cycle costs are important for evaluating consumer goods like a laptop or an EV, the extremely long useful lives of buildings and other infrastructure elements that make up the world's built environment amplifies the importance of full life cycle assessments and accounting, and more broadly the concept of circularity.

Investing in sustainability and resilience at the planning and design stage of a school, apartment, or pretty much any type of building, will provide multiple rewards, which could include lower GHG emissions, construction waste, and build time. Picking a better location and designing in resilience and sustainability will produce other benefits too. Owners and landlords' assets will retain their value longer. Occupants will breathe cleaner indoor air or pay less for heating and cooling. But building more sustainably and resiliently requires life cycle cost accounting and a circularity mindset instead of focusing primarily on the upfront capital cost of construction.

So, given all of these advantages, why aren't more buildings designed with these resilience and sustainability goals front and center? In many cases, it's because the assets don't have a consistent owner across the life cycle of the asset. For example, the owner of the initial design and construction budget is different from the owner of the asset's ongoing operation, and each owner brings their own budgets, priorities, and goals to the decision-making process. While the real estate and construction industry is much more likely to invest in greener, more climate-resilient buildings today, this lack of continuity in ownership is a drag on rapid adoption.

Solutions Everywhere

Designing one-purpose solutions that don't consider the whole impact of infrastructure projects and programs can also have unintended negative consequences. In contrast, holistic solutions that deliver multiple co-benefits are more likely to be widely embraced—even by people who aren't particularly interested in reducing GHG emissions. Low-emission transportation options, including cycling lanes, pedestrian-friendly urban design, and electrified transit, will reduce carbon emissions, while also reducing inequality by providing mobility to lower-income and non-licensed drivers, improving health by cleaning toxins out of the air, and reducing cardiovascular disease by encouraging cycling and walking. Green roofs provide multiple benefits, such as mitigating flooding, cooling the areas around them, providing aesthetic benefits, and can be combined with solar to accelerate decarbonization.

Multiple benefits solutions also offer an answer to the human tendency to discount the future. Convincing people to give up something now—flying, consuming meat, using air conditioning—in exchange for a future payoff is a losing argument. However, offering a program or project that directly benefits people in a community right now, while also mitigating future climate change risk, has a much better chance of success. Instead of sacrificing today to mitigate a future risk, multi-benefit climate action is an opportunity to improve the world today.

This approach might even help people suffering from eco-paralysis, or an inability to process the worst potential climate change scenarios. One clinical therapy encourages patients to focus on one small thing that makes a difference. People with a passionate commitment to climate action might have more long-term success—and better mental health—building local support for an EV hub than advocating for a long-shot global phase out of fossil fuels within three years.

By delivering multiple benefits as soon as they are completed, additional stakeholders will come on board because they appreciate the short-term advantages of sustainable infrastructure—even if they aren't convinced of the need to act on climate change. In the United States, for example, the last three presidential administrations were a rollercoaster in terms of the politics and communication around climate change. Nonetheless, the sustainability and resiliency efforts were bundled and remained essentially unchanged while the overarching "strategy" changed from energy to mission resiliency to carbon. However, teams that design and deliver infrastructure projects as win-win-win solutions need to be highly connected and have deep expertise across the entire life cycle of a project. These are values and capacities that are consistent with a Future Ready mindset and at the core of WSP's Climate, Resilience, and Sustainability practice.

Planning for an Uncertain Future

In February 2008, a group of water engineers published an article in *Science* magazine entitled "Stationarity Is Dead: Whither Water Management?" "Stationarity" refers to the limited range of variability within a natural system and is used to create a statistical average around which engineers can plan. For example, water engineers use statistical averages like local rainfall to plan dams or stormwater pipes or municipal drinking water systems. By 2008, however, the authors believed these averages were hopelessly outmoded. The risks to water supplies, waterworks, and floodplains could no longer be calculated as they had been for decades, or even centuries. Stationarity was dead, they concluded, and hydroclimatic change had killed it.

The article has since had impacts far beyond the "Policy Forum" section of *Science*, in part, because the engineers' predictions have repeatedly been borne out. In 2015, 2016, and 2017, for example, the Houston area experienced three consecutive 1-in-500-year rain events, each creating devastating flooding. The events couldn't be written off as a trio of rare historic anomalies—in 2019, another 24–36 inches (61–91 cm) of rain fell in a three-day period between Houston and Beaumont, Texas. When an area gets four deluges of that size in five years, they are no longer 1-in-500-year events. However, the events didn't mean that Houston should be designing for epic flooding every four out of five years either. So, what did it mean? For water management engineers, it meant that the existing codes and flood maps were not as reliable as they once were.

The summer of 2022 also saw dramatic variations from historic means in water resources across the United States. A persistent western drought dropped Lake Mead, the largest reservoir in the United

States, to its lowest level since it was filled in the 1930s. Soon thereafter, the nearby Las Vegas strip was inundated by flash flooding, St. Louis set a new 24-hour record for rainfall, and both eastern Kentucky and Death Valley, California, experienced 1-in-1,000-year flood events.

However, the reason that the water engineers' 2008 article has gained currency outside of hydrology circles is because the phenomenon is not limited to any one field. In a hotter world, stationarity is losing its meaning everywhere. Wildfires in the western United States and Australia, for example, haven't just reached historic sizes, they have begun acting in fundamentally different ways. There are fewer fires per season, but, aided by heat waves and parched landscapes, fires are burning hotter and faster. As a result, even compared to fires of similar size, recent fires cost up to twice as much to fight per acre. They are also, in some cases, creating their own weather, like pyrocumulonimbus clouds and "fire tornadoes."[14] Many veteran firefighters and researchers report that the behavior of fires in the past few years is virtually unrecognizable from what was once normal.

This departure from stationarity creates a real challenge for designers, planners, and engineers on any infrastructure project. Structural engineers, for example, work off building codes that tell them how thick the reinforced concrete in an apartment building needs to be to withstand the sheering impact of wind or how high a bridge must be to resist floodwaters. But if the speed of wind or height of floods are no longer readily predictable over a long period of time, the codes aren't as useful. Engineers are more likely to run the risk of either under-designing or over-designing infrastructure—as well as misjudging or not anticipating the impacts of failure or some other aspect of the potential future.

Adding to these complications is that infrastructure is often expected to last for decades, and even as much as 100 years in the case of high-cost, high-criticality infrastructure like long bridges and deep tunnels. As planning projects further into the future, the variabilities, contingencies, and unknowns increase. Engineers or urban planners in 1930 could use the storm records of the previous 100 years to plan for, say, 1980 with relative confidence. Today, an engineer wouldn't have nearly the same amount of confidence about predicting the climate in the 2070s because of how rapidly climate and weather is changing, in a way that makes storm records from the past essentially useless as a predictor of the future. In other words, we're moving from an era of high-confidence decision-making to one of low confidence. That doesn't mean we don't make decisions, or that we accept that we're likely to make bad ones. It means the future requires operating in a more nimble and adaptive fashion.

One possibility would be to design buildings and infrastructure that are more adjustable and flexible over their lifespan. For example, a British station in Antarctica was designed to "step out" of the massive snow drifts—4 feet (1.2 m) falls annually—that regularly bury and crush buildings. The units are each fitted with 13-foot (4-m) hydraulic legs that sit on skis, allowing the units to be relocated outside of existing snow drifts and extend their useful lives.[15] A similarly transformative approach to more conventional, fixed infrastructure might include designing ground floors of buildings as collateral damage—areas with low-value functions that could be quickly repaired post flood. In some cases, buildings could also be designed to be permeable to high winds, thus avoiding the risks of major structural damage or failure.

Megatrends and Being Future Ready

Designing infrastructure that meets today's codes as well as the challenges of tomorrow's world requires rethinking many of our assumptions. First, we need to get comfortable with the idea that there is no *one* answer. In a previous era, engineers might have consulted the current building codes, technologies, materials, conditions, and equipment and made the "single best current choice." This best choice often looked very much like the previous best choices in any given infrastructure agency jurisdiction. Then the engineers would walk away to their next project, which was also likely to look like earlier versions of the "best choice." There are multiple reasons why this mindset was so prevalent, but, even decades ago, it also received a fair bit of justifiable criticism. Now, in an era without meaningful stationarity, this thinking isn't an option. Going forward, we to need to plan infrastructure around flexibility—testing future scenarios during the design process and then developing a design that is adaptable mid-stream. Every solution should be developed on a forward-looking, flexible, case-by-case basis.

Future Ready is WSP's broad and adaptable forecasting framework for evaluating projects and programs, ranging from highways to stormwater management systems to wetland restoration, designed for our era of uncertainty and dynamic change. The framework is divided into four megatrend categories: climate, society, technology, and resources. Within each category are multiple subtrends, like flooding, urbanization, connected vehicles, and water scarcity, with insights and analysis on each. Viewing projects and programs through these four lenses ensures that a plan or design incorporates a range of innovation, goals, political realities, and human needs from the very beginning, creating an integrative, stronger understanding of the future.

Future Ready Megatrend 1: Climate

The climate lens focuses on how a project, infrastructure, or community will hold up against heat waves, drought, flooding, extreme weather, sea level rise, as well as other major climatic trends.

Of course, not every megatrend will be relevant for every project, so the climate lens is adapted to local needs and challenges. For example, Portland, Maine, sits on one of the fastest-warming bodies of salt water on earth, driving an expected sea level rise of 10–17 inches (25–43 cm) between 2000 and 2030. Future projects need to be designed around the likelihood of increasing sunny-day flooding in the city's center. Meanwhile, Portland, Oregon—which sits at the same latitude as its East Coast namesake—faces a different climate future that needs different solutions. Deadly triple-digit heat waves and drought have already become a regular feature of summers there, increasing demand for air conditioning, public cooling centers, water fountains—as well as multiple days of dangerous air quality due to wildfires. In other words, the two Portlands not only need different solutions from each other, but they may need different solutions from what worked in the same city just a few decades ago.

Future Ready Megatrend 2: Society

The society lens refers to human interactions with our built environment and each other. How we move around our cities, design our neighborhoods, and plan our infrastructure in the future should be informed by trends like growing diversity, aging, urbanization, and a changing workforce.

For example, cities with aging populations need to account for a larger number of people with health, vision, and mobility challenges. Cities in Japan, the country with the oldest population in the world, have installed sidewalks that melt snow and all-weather walkways to reduce weather-related injuries.[16,17]

In a future in which, say, 50% of work is done remotely, urban transportation systems might plan around more moderate rush hours. Mid-size cities and towns with more affordable housing and lower costs of living might expect an influx of remote workers from larger job-rich urban areas.

The society lens also integrates awareness of historic inequalities in infrastructure from the beginning of the planning process. In the United States, many roads, highways, airports, and waste facilities were built and developed in a way that degraded the health and well-being of minority and low-income areas. Knowingly or not, this infrastructure exacerbated economic inequality and diminished quality of life, including limiting access to healthcare, cool spaces, healthy food, public transportation, and job centers. Incorporating social equity issues and early community engagement into planning can avoid outcomes that literally divide and further disadvantage already-overburdened communities. Underappreciating or misunderstanding local concerns can undermine or degrade efforts to build infrastructure that improves sustainability and resilience.

Future Ready Megatrend 3: Technology

The technology lens tracks beneficial innovations in infrastructure like nanomaterials, multimodal transport, phase change materials, or virtual reality. Understanding today's cutting-edge materials and processes is essential to developing the best, most Future Ready solutions. However, because technological development is so rapid, new innovations that are not realistic options or don't even exist now could be incorporated into the design of programs with long-term goals.

A common interim deadline for net zero targets, 2030, is rapidly approaching, but, inevitably, so are technologies that will upturn markets and make previously unviable tools realistic, if not superior, options. Between 2008 and 2016, lithium-ion battery costs dropped from $1,236 per kilowatt hour to $271 per kilowatt hour, or 220%. Lithium-ion may very well prove to be a transition chemistry for batteries—they have environmental issues that still need to be solved and resource scarcity could lead their prices to rise again. Nonetheless, their improved performance has dramatically and quickly improved the prospects for decarbonizing personal mobility. Electric vehicles have reached cost parity with internal combustion engines in terms of total cost of ownership in many countries, including the United States. The dramatic change in EV viability over a few years is just one example of why any long-term design, program or plan needs to consider options that aren't yet available.

Future Ready Megatrend 4: Resources

Finally, the resources lens tracks areas like materials and energy with a focus on how we can produce what we need in ways that encourage the development of no-waste circular economies, decarbonization, and sustainable water management.

For example, on-demand manufacturing can reduce or eliminate the need to maintain large amounts of stock. Biomaterials or reusable modular units will change end-of-life buildings from waste to assets. The increased efficiency and lower costs of solar panels and battery storage will encourage the development of micro-grids decoupled from the centralized energy systems.

At the same time, the growing need for battery storage to support EV as well as utility infrastructure will require significant consumption of precious metals such as cobalt and lithium as well as create capacity constraints on supply chains. Additional concern over the associated embodied carbon of these resources' extraction has driven searches for alternatives. Among these novel approaches is exploring lithium extraction from Salton Sea in southern California—the 600°F (315.6°C) brine bubbling in the desert is one of the world's richest sources of lithium.

There is also continued innovation in battery chemistry, and greater understanding that there doesn't need to be a one-size-fits-all solution. For example, iron flow batteries, which are relatively low cost and have much lower negative environmental impact than lithium-ion and most other comparable batteries, are gaining traction at utility-scale energy storage. The relatively short term that they can hold charge—8 to 12 hours—is not an issue as the batteries are storing renewable power overnight, when usage is low, while minimizing the need for carbon-intense diesel plants.

Future Ready in Action

Researching and tracking these megatrends is critical to develop an adaptable Future Ready planning process, but they are ultimately only important in terms of how they manifest themselves in a specific, local case. Once the relevant megatrends are identified, they are leveraged in a scenario planning that integrates the key inputs of climate, society, technology, and resources to create coherent visions of the future. The following is a relatively simple example of what Future Ready might look like in action.

The town of Sleepy Hollow, New York, has faced challenges from multiple long-term megatrends. Several decades ago, it took an economic hit when a local General Motors (GM) assembly plant was shuttered, taking away manufacturing jobs and leaving behind a vacant, sealed, brownfield area. In 2012, it was damaged by Superstorm Sandy's high winds. The town, which sits on the eastern shore of a tidal portion of the Hudson River, faces ongoing climate change threats including flooding and sea level rise. Like many other cities in the United States, Sleepy Hollow also has to contend with challenges, including population growth, lack of housing, lonelier and sedentary lifestyles, and obesity.

The Sleepy Hollow Local Development Corporation (SHLDC) worked with WSP and other partners to design Future Ready solutions that integrated sustainability and resilience while proving community benefits. Comprehensive hydrologic, hydraulic, and coastal analysis of the project area determined that future flooding could inundate the nearby Metro North railway tracks as well as threaten the local Department of Public Works (DPW) headquarters. Green infrastructure was designed to improve storm water treatment and increase flood resistance. To promote resilience in extreme scenarios, the greenspace and porous parking lot were also designed to flood in order to protect critical facilities like the DPW building. The area around the GM assembly plant was converted into a civic focal point featuring athletic fields, an amphitheater, walking trails, and a skate park—providing community building space and exercise opportunities. Development of condominiums and apartments will provide additional housing for citizens in the growing area, as well as serving as a hub for economic development that reclaims the area's historic waterfront.

Rethinking Everything

In addition to rethinking obstacles to a just, sustainable, and resilient transition—like perverse economic incentives and overvaluing capital costs—designing for a dynamic future means reconsidering our current practices as well as searching different places for better solutions. Contemporary engineering practices created the cultural, architectural, and technological marvels that have made the modern world possible. However, there was a high cost to many of these achievements— including the unprecedented build-up of greenhouse gases in the atmosphere that are fueling climate change. Reevaluating design processes that have been largely sidelined in contemporary engineering can suggest novel solutions.

Take, for example, non-Western or indigenous building technologies. Chinese traditional houses feature roofs angled to let in more sun during winter than summer, courtyards with sophisticated air circulation, and water catchment and runoff areas. These traditional practices have helped inspire "new" trends in sustainable and resilient design like daylighting, passive heating and cooling, and zero-carbon water management. Although some of these techniques would have to be modified for changing local climatic conditions, new inspiration can be found in the past millennia of human innovation in infrastructure that utilized unique materials, techniques, and technologies.

Americans are also not fully utilizing the modern processes and technologies in use outside of the United States. China, Japan, and multiple European countries, among others, have a lot of innovation to share, from smarter urban design to low-carbon cooling systems, but the U.S.'s continued usage of inches, pounds, and other nonmetric units hampers this technology transfer. Officially, only three countries in the world don't use the metric system: Liberia, Myanmar, and the United States. So, if a new innovation is developed in Japan, it can relatively quickly be adopted in Europe—or virtually anywhere else in the world—as both regions use the metric system. However, retooling is required to enter the U.S. market, significantly delaying some innovative technologies' entry.

The long use life of buildings in Europe and many other regions versus shorter lifespans in the United States, suggests rethinking their full value. Buildings should be thought of as valuable assets with large amounts of embodied carbon (a concept addressed in greater detail later in the book), not disposable products.

In some cases, the most valuable rethinking of infrastructure overlaps with rethinking societal expectations. For example, heating and cooling buildings are major sources of GHG emissions, both from natural gas or oil furnaces as well as the fossil fuels used to create electricity for heating and air conditioning. However, the amount of GHG emitted is largely determined by how much heating or cooling occupants use, decisions which vary dramatically around the world. In tropical Singapore, for example, higher indoor temperatures or humidity—even in office buildings—is more acceptable than in Europe or the United States. In other regions, including warmer parts of the United States and the Middle East, "over air conditioning" often brings interior temperatures far below outdoor temperatures throughout the year. There is no doubt that air conditioning—or other lower-emission cooling systems—will be important resiliency measures in a hotter world. However, determining internal temperatures based on factors like health and productivity instead of cultural expectations will ultimately create a more sustainable and resilient infrastructure.

Avoiding False Choices

The mission of the authors and their colleagues in this fight is guided by the conviction that delimiting innovation and accepting either/or choices betrays a dangerous lack of imagination. Rethinking everything about how we have built for centuries, and even where we should build, means rejecting the supposedly immutable trade-offs that still plague all sorts of planning and design decisions.

For example, new infrastructure doesn't have to result in detrimental environmental impact. Incorporating nature-positive infrastructure, such as using public spaces for stormwater management, biodiversity, and flood and heat resilience, can have win/win/win effects. Even the hard infrastructure projects most associated with environmental costs can have very high sustainability ratings. A recent expansion project at New York's LaGuardia Airport, for which WSP provided a range of environmental and engineering services, received an ENVISION Platinum rating from the Institute for Sustainable Infrastructure for its high levels of sustainability, resilience, and community engagement.

We don't have to build back in the same location or not at all, and we shouldn't passively accept the logic of other either/or decisions. We don't have to pick between resilience and sustainability, or economic growth and biodiversity, or lower costs and lower carbon, or more jobs and a just, sustainable economy. We can choose from, and need, all of the above to meet the challenge of climate change in a just, sustainable, and resilient way.

Part I of this book covers "The What" by detailing some of the types of risks, challenges, infrastructure solutions, and other opportunities developed and implemented across the United States and around the world. Ranging across the built environment, transportation, energy, water, and waste management sectors, as well as taking a deep dive into New York City's ongoing transformation, the chapters are not exhaustive on any one topic. Instead, they include examples of how a wide variety of specific risks and challenges are being assessed and mitigated using innovative planning, sustainable, resilient, and innovative techniques, cutting-edge technologies, and the Future Ready framework. Part II is "The How," a practical guide that explores and explains some of the primary frameworks, strategies, target setting, and individual solutions for organizations to start, evaluate, or accelerate their own sustainability journeys.

Since WSP partners with a large number of organizations in the private sector as well as the public sector, the book shares our expertise broadly. After all, building a sustainable and resilient world that is ready to meet the present and future challenges of climate change requires the combined efforts of large corporations, mid-sized businesses, rapidly expanding startups, megacities, counties, and towns. While some of the specific challenges and solutions will be more relevant to certain organizations than others, we intend for the whole book to be engaging, informative, and inspiring for all readers.

This is a critical, but exciting, time for anyone working in the infrastructure sector. The green transition to a more sustainable, resilient world is a massive opportunity, but it is not optional. The proliferation of ESG disclosures and investment strategies, net zero targets, and climate action plans show us what we need to do. The emergence of climate risk has heightened awareness of why we need to do it. Our challenge is to figure out how to pick the right things to do, as well as how to do those things right. The next decade or two will be a major inflection point for the Earth, driven by both risk and virtually endless opportunities.

Notes

1. https://www.ipcc.ch/2022/02/28/pr-wgii-ar6/.
2. https://news.un.org/en/story/2022/02/1112852.
3. https://www.munichre.com/en/risks/natural-disasters-losses-are-trending-upwards/floods-and-flash-floods-underestimated-natural-hazards.html.
4. https://news.bloombergtax.com/financial-accounting/sec-pushes-tesla-to-reveal-how-regulatory-credits-boost-profits.
5. https://www.gobyinc.com/2022-another-historic-year-for-esg/.
6. https://www.bloomberg.com/professional/blog/esg-assets-may-hit-53-trillion-by-2025-a-third-of-global-aum/.
7. https://www.natlawreview.com/article/emerging-eu-esg-requirements-transatlantic-implications-multinational-companies.
8. https://www.natlawreview.com/article/emerging-eu-esg-requirements-transatlantic-implications-multinational-companies.
9. https://ukcop26.org/cop26-goals/.
10. https://climate.ec.europa.eu/eu-action/funding-climate-action/supporting-climate-action-through-eu-budget_en.
11. https://www.cnbc.com/2021/11/15/biden-signs-infrastructure-bill-how-it-fights-climate-change.html.
12. https://www.npr.org/2022/10/06/1127083845/hurricane-ian-florida-property-insurance.
13. https://www.fema.gov/sites/default/files/2020-07/fema_mitsaves-factsheet_2018.pdf.
14. https://www.theguardian.com/us-news/2021/dec/25/what-the-numbers-tells-us-about-a-catastrophic-year-of-wildfires?CMP=Share_AndroidApp_Other.

15. https://www.wired.co.uk/article/antarctic-walking-research-lab
16. ps://www.statista.com/statistics/264729/countries-with-the-largest-percentage-of-total-population-.
17. https://globalcoalitiononaging.com/wp-content/uploads/2018/06/AgingUrbanization_115.pdf.

PART

I

Touring a Dynamic World

2

On the Street

IN THE MIDDLE of the 1800s, Los Angeles (L.A.) was a small town of fewer than 8,000 residents situated near a meandering river that emptied into the Pacific Ocean. The area had been home to small communities of humans for millennia—the native Tongva and Chumash were followed by a Spanish colonial outpost that was passed on to Mexico after its independence—but it had always been sparsely populated. Then, in 1850, California became the 30th state of the United States, and L.A.'s population exploded in the space of a few generations. In 1890, L.A. first entered the U.S. Census Bureau's list of 100 biggest cities, at number 57, with a little over 50,000 people. By 1920, 576,000 people lived there, making it the 10th biggest city in the country and the largest on the West Coast. Over the next 10 years, the population more than doubled to 1.2 million, and L.A. rose to number 5, just behind Detroit, Philadelphia, Chicago, and New York City.

While L.A.'s rapid population growth was singular in U.S. history, its trajectory has been followed by urban areas around the world over the past two centuries. In fact, the recent population boom of some cities completely outpaces that of L.A. One example is Shenzhen, which was a rice-growing village in southern China's Pearl River Delta region until relatively recently. In 1980, Shenzhen was designated China's first Special Economic Zone (SEZ) and began four decades of

33

breakneck growth. Today, it is one of China's wealthiest and largest cities, with a population of roughly 12 million.

However, the rapid growth of both L.A. and Shenzhen also had dire consequences. For a time, each of the cities was well known for its choking air pollution, mountains of garbage, and raw sewage running into rivers and oceans. Following decades of ecological devastation, though, both L.A. and Shenzhen became environmental pioneers in their respective countries and greened their transportation, wastewater, electricity generation, and solid waste management systems. But even after cleaning up these visible blights, some of the most environmentally damaging parts of the cities' massive infrastructures remained—hidden in plain sight. Today, the buildings in L.A., Shenzhen—and around the world—contribute nearly 50% of total global greenhouse gas emissions when the full impact of their construction, operation, and disposal is included.

Construction has other detrimental and unsustainable impacts as well. The sector gobbles up about half of the roughly 100 billion tons of raw material extracted from the earth every year. It produces approximately a third of the world's solid waste, material that comes from both end-of-life disposal and inefficient construction processes. Buildings are also responsible for 33% of water consumption.

Despite buildings absorbing all these resources, they are still not meeting some basic needs. For example, there are over half a million unhoused people in the United States, including tens of thousands in L.A.[1] While there is no official international definition of "homelessness," in 2020, the U.N. estimated that there were 1.6 billion people living in "inadequate housing."[2] By 2050, the world's population is estimated to grow by another 2 billion people, increasing already insufficient demand on housing.

In short, there is absolutely no way we can meet even the most modest climate, sustainability, or equity goals without a huge change in how we construct and operate our buildings. While there is more energy and commitment to a green transition in the building sector than we've ever seen, the sector still isn't moving nearly quickly enough. According to the World Green Building Council, every building on Earth must be "net zero carbon" by 2050 to keep global warming below 3.6°F (15.8°C). Today, fewer than 1% of buildings meet those targets.

The Climate Bites Back

The construction industry has long been regarded as a laggard in adopting new technologies and processes. That assessment is not entirely accurate, though. On the margins of the industry there is, in fact, plenty of innovation in construction processes, materials, and technologies that can begin to drive down the sector's GHG emissions. The challenge is mainstreaming these innovations and deploying them at scale. Though this transformation isn't happening nearly as rapidly as necessary, some new processes and technologies are becoming more common. As in the financial sector, this decarbonization of the building sector is in large part being driven by our changing perceptions of climate risk. A combination of consumer demands, government subsidies, corporate sustainability commitments, broad adoption of sustainability frameworks, and new regulatory requirements will continue to accelerate these positive trends.

The growing awareness of the physical risk posed by climate change has also changed how developers and owners think about the relationship between their assets and environmental damage. When widely used sustainability rating systems like the Leadership in Energy and Environmental Design (LEED) were being developed back in the 1990s, the primary focus was on reducing the damage a building *caused to* the environment. Today, building owners, management, and tenants increasingly find that their buildings are being *damaged by* the environment, like extreme weather, flooding, and other climate megatrends. In 2022, for example, natural catastrophes like hurricanes, winter storms, wildfires, and flooding resulted in nearly $165 billion in damage and affected roughly 1 in 10 homes in the United States. When the environment is materially impacting their buildings—high winds ripping off cladding or extreme drought causing foundations to sink—building for a changing climate becomes that much more personal, urgent, and financially relevant for millions of people.

The damage suffered by some buildings even suggests that our engineering guidelines and standards are quickly becoming obsolete. For example, the investigation into the June 2021 collapse of a high-rise apartment building in Surfside, Florida, cites climate change as one of the leading contributory causes for the disaster, which killed 98 people.

Even without a final determination in the collapse of the Champlain Towers, a few facts are already established. 1) In 2018, an engineer found extensive cracking and crumbling of the columns, beams, and walls in the basement parking lot. 2) Saltwater is corrosive to reinforced concrete, the material used to provide structural support. 3) Champlain Towers was a beachfront apartment complex that sat on reclaimed wetlands on a narrow strip of land north of Miami Beach. 4) Sea levels in the area have risen at least 6 inches (15 cm) since 1980, when the building opened. 5) Residents had repeatedly complained about standing water in the building's basement. 6) A maintenance technician who worked at Champlain Towers in the 1990s claimed that, during very high tides, up to 2 feet (.6 m) of water would seep through the building's foundations.

It is likely that multiple factors played a role in the collapse. Even without a final determination, though, it also seems likely that engineers would not design the same building today that they did 40 years ago. At the very least, they would need to build better drainage systems and use more waterproof support structures. The bigger question to ask may be if it's possible to construct a truly Future Ready 12-story apartment building on low-lying oceanfront property in South Florida. Put another way, there are two considerations with new infrastructure projects or programs. It's not enough to ask if a project or program is being built right, but if it is the right program or project to pursue in the particular instance or location in the first place.

In May 2021, a different incident suggested another expansion of the risks associated with climate change. SEG Plaza, a nearly 980-foot (300-m) building in Shenzhen's rapidly growing skyline began wobbling, sending panicked pedestrians fleeing. A preliminary investigation found the incident was likely a result of three factors: 1) wind, 2) subway lines under the building, and 3) the stretching of steel caused by rising temperatures.

According to officials, there's no evidence that the steel was structurally compromised or that the wobbling was outside of acceptable parameters. But whatever role temperature played in the wobbling, the Shenzhen incident is another high-profile reminder of a more basic systemic issue. Architects and engineers typically design buildings to operate based on local climatic conditions. But these local climatic conditions will increasingly depart from their previous norms, becoming more variable and volatile. The more the climate changes, the more important it is to rethink and adapt our materials, processes, and targets to build in resilience and sustainability. If we exclusively rely on the same backward-looking guidelines and standards, we'll be designing buildings for yesterday's climate, instead of a dynamic future.

The rest of the chapter looks at some of the many environmental, engineering, sustainability, and resilience solutions needed to decarbonize the built environment. Rethinking how to build the interior spaces where we spend 90% of our lives is a huge challenge. We've been fortunate to work on these solutions collaboratively with public and private clients, as well as together with a variety of consultant partners. While many organizations are doing great work, we are primarily featuring projects in which WSP was a leader or prominent member of a team because they are the best examples of how we want to rethink, design, and construct Future Ready buildings.

Certifiable Transformations

In the late 1980s and into the 1990s, the growing awareness around the impact of buildings on the natural world led groups of architects, engineers, designers, and others to develop systems to rate building's environmental performance. At the time, there were no standardized, universal languages to discuss the qualities of buildings beyond categories like location, capital costs, or square footage. These systems were an invitation to reimagine what buildings were—and could be.

The first of these was launched in 1990, when the U.K.-based Building Research Establishment released its first version of the Building Research Establishment Environmental Assessment Method (BREEAM) standards. Eight years later, the U.S. Green Building Council (USGBC) launched its LEED standards. It took a while for either system to get past the early adopter phase. By 2003, LEED's then-five-year-old version 1.0 rating system for new construction had only certified 10 buildings, all in the United States. What's more, all but one of those buildings was either government-owned, an educational institute, or an environmental group headquarters—fairly niche markets. After a few more years of steady but slow growth, interest in LEED certification began to pick up. Now, its certified buildings include nearly 100,000 projects in 167 different countries, with most of them in the United States. BREEAM has likewise experienced rapid growth, with around 540,000 certified buildings globally.

LEED and BREEAM share a lot in common. Both are internationally recognized programs that indicate a building's level of environmental responsibility. Each offers a range of certifications for different structural types and projects, including new commercial construction, interior fit-outs, homes, as well as certifications for whole neighborhoods or communities. Both systems evaluate similar categories, like water efficiency, nontoxic construction materials, or indoor air quality. BREEAM offers certification at four levels: Good, Very Good, Excellent, and Outstanding. LEED certification is point-based, which translates to either Certified, Silver, Gold, or Platinum status.

The assessment process and geographic distribution of their certified buildings are the most notable distinctions between the ratings systems. For LEED certification, design teams collect evidence and send it to the USGBC for third-party assessment. BREEAM, in contrast, sends licensed assessors who collect building information and report it to BREEAM's parent company. The U.K.-based BREEAM is dominant in its home country, where it was developed to integrate with national building codes. LEED has more of a universal framework, but has been adopted as a sustainability standard by the U.S. federal government, in addition to multiple states and municipalities.

Between them, LEED and BREEAM are the globally dominant rating systems for green buildings, but they are not the only way to rate the environmental impact of buildings. In 2006, the Seattle-based International Living Future Institute (ILFI) unveiled the Living Building Challenge (LBC), an inspirational vision encompassing all aspects of a building's design, construction, and operation. The criteria for achieving certification, which involves meeting requirements in seven different categories or "petals," were more stringent than that of LEED or BREEAM. At times, the LBC's approach has been criticized for being too inflexible, but proponents describe it as more than a rating system—something more akin to a philosophy and advocacy platform.

In some cases, ILFI's guidelines read like motivational suggestions when compared to LEED's report-card–like checklist. For example, "Access to Nature" is one of 20 imperatives on ILFI's newest version, 4.0. Of course, nature provides all sorts of benefits to people who work or live in a building, but the LBC offers no specific metrics on how to achieve this goal, except evaluating "the benefits of daylight, fresh air and access to nature" for residents after 6–12 months of occupancy.

ILFI does offer technical support to every LBC participant, but becoming certified requires such a high level of dedication that its initial growth was limited. Between 2006 and 2010, there were only about 50 LBC projects, with fewer than a third achieving certification. While the LBC may never scale up to the size of LEED or BREEAM, perhaps its role is intended to be different. The world needs groups and ratings systems that are always pushing the envelope, shining a light on the parts of the built ecology that are very hard to make truly sustainable.

Over the past few years, LEED and BREEAM certification systems have also been exploring ways to capture the bold net zero goals first pushed by the Living Building Challenge, as well as integrating the attributes needed to see adoption at scale. For example, USGBC has recently launched its LEED Zero Certification, and the development of LEED v5 being initiated in 2023. Both are learning from the bold visions of Living Building Challenge and Well Certification to drive high performance design that deliver both healthy environments and very light environmental footprints. Proving actual performance, rather than theoretical design performance, is a similar emphasis. Most importantly, however, is that they also integrate the flexibility that has made LEED scalable globally. Whether a LEED or ILFI-certified building is, by itself, higher performing is arguably less important in the short term than building momentum and the total carbon reduction that can be achieved when delivered at the global scale that both LEED and BREAM have achieved.

In recent years, these visions have been validated. A growing number of companies, governments, and developers have recognized that the advantages of pursuing the highest level of certification from LBC, LEED, or BREEAM go far beyond responsible environmental stewardship or reputational gains. Meeting the demands of any of these programs creates assets that foresee the challenges of climate change over the course of their design lives. The buildings also meet the threats of climate risk—retaining value over the long term; playing an important role in net zero or climate action plans; responding to the ESG and carbon disclosure interests of investors; and anticipating emerging innovations, standards, and requirements.

A Watershed Event

The Watershed sits just north of downtown Seattle among the collection of cafes, quirky public art, and tech startups that mark the Fremont neighborhood, the self-declared "Center of the Universe." After it became one of just a few dozen large commercial buildings to receive ILFI's petal certification, the Watershed can back up the area's grandiose claim, at least in the field of cutting-edge green design.

Seattle already has very progressive requirements for energy efficiency and water usage, but the Watershed building goes significantly further. WSP was part of the team that designed the building, which uses 25% less energy than required by codes and found alternatives for about 70% of the originally specified lighting fixtures. On the exterior, bioretention planters treat not only onsite stormwater but runoff from an adjacent bridge. The ILFI certification also required a particularly high level of scrutiny into the building materials, eliminating any of the toxic materials still used in the construction industry.

Meeting demanding environmental standards isn't limited to reducing energy usage or cleaning up local water. It combines environmental stewardship and sustainability with Future Ready-informed climate resilience. For example, Seattle has long been known for its mild, wet climate. Although a global megatrend is extreme temperatures, it wasn't until 2021 that most people realized how devastating that heat could be for the Seattle area. In late June, record temperatures scorched the Pacific Northwest for days, killing over 110 people in Washington and becoming the deadliest weather-related event in the state's history.

To build resilience and keep occupants healthy while minimizing carbon emissions, the Watershed building keeps itself cooler in several innovative ways. One of these is electromagnetic glazing, which detects sunshine and uses electrical current to darken the tint—lowering cooling load as well as avoiding the glare of sunshine for occupants. It didn't take long for the new cooling measures to be needed. Over six days in July and August 2022, the Pacific Northwest experienced another heatwave that set records in Seattle and is believed to have killed at least 20 people in Oregon and Washington.

Putting Net Zero on the Menu

Resisting heat and humidity have long been important criteria for buildings constructed in the Orlando, Florida, area, but the primary solution is often air conditioning. A radically redesigned McDonald's restaurant at Walt Disney World pursued ILFI's Zero Carbon certification by integrating several innovative and nature-based solutions to cooling. Slatted jalousie windows on two walls automatically open to support natural ventilation, while rooftop-mounted exhaust fans draw outside air through the building, a lower-energy solution than running the air conditioning during spring, early summer, and fall. Other features like daylighting—strategically using and directing sunlight to minimize the use of artificial lighting—were combined with sensors that selectively turn off light zones based on daylight and occupancy levels. Sunlight was also used to power the restaurant—the photovoltaic array installed on the V-shaped roof was designed based on the projected energy consumption of the building.

The ambition of this design shows how LEED, BREEAM, and other certification standards for buildings have changed the way we talk and think about buildings. Champions like the International Living Future Institute help us visualize what buildings need to look like 30 years from now. Along the way, these ratings systems have also set the stage for policy and early market development.

Among the most important results of these experiments is data showing that buildings with sustainability ratings perform better for investors. According to one analysis, LEED-certified buildings delivered between 2010 and 2020 were consistently more profitable than noncertified spaces in terms of rent (11% higher in last five years) and had reduced vacancy. During the most recent three years, 2018 through 2020, LEED-certified buildings also had a 21.4% higher average sales price than noncertified buildings.

In short, the resiliency and sustainability of LEED buildings may cost incrementally more upfront, but they are better investments over the building's full life cycle. Put another way, thinking of a building as an asset instead of a disposable commodity makes financial sense in the long term. To accelerate the decarbonization of our building sector, developers and owners must insist that building for the future means investing in sustainability and resilience from the beginning.

Phase Shifts in Cooling

WSP works throughout the construction life cycle, including consulting, architecture, designing, engineering, financing, and implementing construction, monitoring performance, and end-of-life. One critical service line, known as Mechanical, Engineering, and Plumbing (MEP), involves designing what are essentially the guts of the building—electrical, plumbing, and Heating, Ventilation, and Air Conditioning (HVAC). Rethinking the design of these systems is essential to increase water efficiency and reduce power consumption, among other factors. They are, for example, among the services we provided on the ILFI-certified Watershed building as well as the McDonald's net zero restaurant. The systems that make up MEP are fundamental to safe, functional, and comfortable working or living environments. But they can also include high-tech innovations.

Take thermal storage, for example. The concept of saving energy for future use isn't new. The passive house design that grew in popularity during the 1970s uses heavy, dark materials like concrete or water tanks painted black to absorb sunlight during the day and release it at night, evening out temperature differences. Passive house design is a relatively simple way to reduce heating bills at night while using natural ventilation to disperse heat during daylight hours. However, the water tanks or concrete walls inside still heat up considerably over the course of the day, making the process less-than-ideal for certain spaces, like many office buildings. Engineered phase change materials, on the other hand, use a property of thermodynamics to add a fascinating new wrinkle to thermal storage.

Phase change occurs naturally all the time, like when a solid (ice) turns into a liquid (water), or when that liquid turns into a gas (steam). What we can't see is how energy-intensive this process becomes while phase change is occurring. When we heat water in a pot on the stove, it appears to steadily heat up from warm to hot to boiling. However, that steady rise is not mirrored by the energy consumption needed to get from boiling, or 212°F (100°C), to steam. The amount of energy needed to heat water all way from 32°F (0°C) to 212°F (100°C) is just a fifth of what is needed for the final jump from water to steam.

The most bizarre element of this whole process is that this enormous energy expenditure at the moment of phase change effectively disappears. Instead of massive amounts of heat being released, it is stored away as latent energy that is not released until the phase change happens in reverse—when the steam cools back to water. This property, sequestering away huge amounts of heat energy, is very useful for cooling a building with materials that go through phase change at comfortable office temperatures.

Today, the most common phase change materials are paraffin wax, salts, and water with additives—although concrete admixtures are continuing to evolve. These materials are then embedded in office spaces like drywall. As the room heats up to the phase change temperature threshold—maybe 68°F (20°C)—the materials in the drywall begin absorbing the large amounts of heat energy produced by occupants, electronics, or lighting. Unlike the concrete walls in a passive house design, this energy is effectively sequestered as latent heat until the phase change material cools down, usually at night or when the building is not in operation. Because the heat is absorbed with none of the mechanical activity associated with air conditioning, phase change materials also lower energy usage, noise, and maintenance.

Phase change technology could even be integrated with traditional concrete walls, like those used in a passive house design. The ability to integrate phase change capabilities within concrete structures will potentially increase the range of passive house applications. This is particularly useful because passive house applications were commonly used in areas of Northern Europe that previously needed heating much more than cooling. Phase change materials can adapt the technology to the changing environmental conditions—like increasing European heat waves and long-term rises in temperatures. Phase change material is inherently customizable to both the function of the building and environmental conditions—both internal and external. In some ways it is the convergence of smart technology and material science.

One project where WSP utilized phase change technology was in Federal Center South, an office building just south of downtown Seattle that was designed to meet rigorous goals. Among other energy reduction measures in the MEP, Federal Center South made use of thermal storage tanks with phase change materials that husband cooling energy for future use. Together, these high-performance features helped Federal Center South exceed its goals—the building achieved

LEED Platinum instead of the targeted Gold—and excel in the top 1% of office buildings in the country in terms of energy performance.

Electrifying Everything

The performance standards for Federal Center South were set by the U.S. Army Corps of Engineers (USACE). In addition to a LEED rating, USACE set another goal for energy performance using a metric called Energy Use Intensity (EUI). An EUI score is derived by dividing the amount of energy consumed in a year by its square footage.

Not surprisingly, the EUI of buildings varies greatly depending on their size and use. At the lowest end of the spectrum are massive drinking water treatment utilities, with EUI scores averaging just below 6. The next category, warehouses, usually score around 50, while most buildings—schools, offices, housing, malls—fall in a range between 100 and 300. At the top end are spaces, like grocery stores and restaurants, that constantly use refrigeration, cooking, heating, and lighting. Out of that category, fast food restaurants have the largest EUI scores, averaging around 880—one more reason why an expansion of McDonald's prototype restaurant with very low energy usage is much needed.

The Federal Center South building met its target of 20.3, one-sixth of median office building performance. But just as importantly, it achieved those goals with a combination of innovative but commercially available and scalable technologies. Innovation in energy efficiency will continue to be critical, but we also already have plenty of technology that can significantly decarbonize the building sector if deployed at scale. One of the simplest, but most widespread, barriers to sustainability measures is thinking that we are still waiting for some new technology. As much as possible, we can and must begin to use the best solutions we have now, not in 5 or 10 years.

Much of the energy consumed in the built environment, whether by the lighting, air conditioning or simply powering our laptops and office equipment, is electricity. This simple fact has two major implications. First, not only are we able to prioritize energy efficient design solutions, but also increase the long-term carbon benefit as a result of grid decarbonization. Second, transitioning as much, if not all, of our core building energy consumption to electricity is a critical strategy.

Historically, the two areas where energy reduction has proven the most challenging in terms of technology and cost has been heating—of indoor air and hot water—and cooking. In recent years, however, technology has evolved significantly. Outside of some specialist situations, technically robust solutions are now available. Electric kitchen equipment can provide chefs with the level of control that they need. Likewise, heat pump technology is at a point where buildings can achieve the carbon savings associated with the fuel switch from natural gas to electricity while providing a cost-effective solution when considered over the life of the project. In fact, heat pump technology designed originally for buildings has become a critical part of the heating system of electric vehicles, taking advantage of the same refrigeration cycle to heat the passenger cabin, while minimizing the burden on a battery's capacity and range.

Heat pumps reduce greenhouse gas emissions in two ways. First, they replace heating systems that burn natural gas or another fossil fuel. Second, they are more efficient than other electrical heaters. Many countries offer incentives for homeowners and businesses to install heat pumps. In the United States, the 2022 Inflation Reduction Act created large incentives for homeowners to make energy-efficiency upgrades, with a particular focus on heat pumps.

Project Drawdown is an initiative that estimates how much greenhouse gas emissions could be reduced simply by deploying market-ready solutions globally. A large-scale rollout of heat pumps globally would have large upfront costs—Project Drawdown estimates between $76 billion to $118 billion—but provides an impressive return on investment of $1 trillion to $2.4 trillion in savings. These life cycle savings would pay for the higher upfront cost many times over while reducing or sequestering 4.04 to 9.05 gigatons of CO_2 equivalent between 2020 and 2050.

For all their advantages, though, heat pumps are not a magic bullet. Although they are likely to play a major role in a low carbon future, not all properties will be able to use the same heating solutions. As evidenced by the constraints on heat pump availability as a result of the Ukraine war, there is also a need for more resilient supply chains, affordable heat pumps, and quicker and easier installations to make switching attractive. Time is not on our side to achieve the net zero targets—more and swifter action on installation capacity and ease of installation is needed. It's imperative that we don't let a "perfect later" get in the way of "good now."

Some parts of the US are accelerating this transition much faster than others. In California, for example, the drive to electrify building systems is rapidly growing far beyond installing heat pumps. Over 50 cities and municipalities, including San Francisco, have passed ordinances that either ban gas hookups in new construction or otherwise encourage fully electrifying buildings. These regulations and laws are an important example of a changing regulatory landscape as well as local governments' role in reducing GHG emissions and accelerating the decarbonization of the building sector.

As with other interventions into markets, any regulations need to be well designed, engaging all stakeholders. In worse-case scenarios, the additional paperwork needed to qualify for rebates may become a barrier for contractors doing the installation—unintentionally creating a perverse incentive to *not* install heat pumps. Likewise, if large incentives drive the growth in the market, an end to the rebates could create a huge cliff that can actually damage the performance of participating vendors of installers.

Just as importantly, rethinking how we heat and cool our buildings often requires a degree of education. The contractors who install, operate and maintain heat pumps are likely to have a lot more experience with traditional gas boilers or heating systems, which may make them less likely to recommend the heat pumps to consumers. Educating contractors on the benefits of electric boilers or furnaces is particularly important because people often make their decision about what to buy in an emergency—after the contractor tells them their gas-powered unit needs to be replaced. If the contractor is aware of the advantages of heat pumps and associated rebates, and offers them as a standard replacement option, there's a much greater chance consumers will take advantage of the incentives.

As with any major transition, the biggest constraint is not the technology itself, but our tendency to fall back on tried and tested approaches, even if they are carbon intense. In some cases, for example, people push back on reducing light levels in offices because they have become accustomed to excessively bright environments. Adopting a slower transition in light levels over time has proven successful in achieving not only the energy efficiency benefits, but also the well-being benefits of transitioning to light levels that are more aligned to the needs of our circadian rhythms.

Ultimately, energy efficiency is harder to both comprehend and deploy than a single measure like a solar field or wind farm. We need to consider it as flexible bundle of measures that each make an incremental saving, but together can have substantial impact. Often these are not exciting or sexy—simply changing a lamp can be part of effective bigger strategy. Likewise, the ability to enhance the energy efficiency of buildings is not limited to new construction or undertaking a significant renovation. Just like getting your car serviced, implementing a robust commissioning process can make sure that our existing buildings are working in line with their initial design—which can often achieve a 10% savings.

Around the World

Since the autumn of 2016, a series of two intricate superstructures shaped like crowns have risen from a porch-inspired base on the National Mall, just a few hundred yards from the Washington Monument. The National Museum of African American History and Culture (NMAAHC) is not only one of the Smithsonian's most popular museums, but also showcases several innovations in building performance design.

For example, the building's primary architectural concept was derived from African art and architecture. The crown shapes—referred to as the corona—on the roof and upper façade naturally improve energy efficiency by forming a sun-sheltering canopy. The perforated panel system in the corona also channels cooling breezes from a water feature below, while also allowing natural light into the gallery spaces and controlling solar heat gain. Both of these strategies have been used for centuries across Africa to keep occupants comfortable, which is hardly surprising as the need to keep its occupants safe and comfortable has always been a core function of the built environment.

Unfortunately, with the advancements in air conditioning in the 1950s, building architects and engineers got lazy, becoming overly reliant on mechanical cooling and brute force to maintain comfort. As our value structure, and design goals evolve to being more focused on carbon, design teams are reconsidering strategies from before the age of mechanical air conditioning as part of the decarbonization strategy.

The museum's energy performance was also enhanced by occupancy sensors for daylight harvesting, demand-controlled ventilation, a rainwater and groundwater storage and reuse system, and a 384-panel photovoltaic array capable of producing 102,562 kilowatt-hours (kWh) of electricity annually. As a result, the NMAAHC scored a 92 EUI, better than most buildings, most other museums, and all the other Smithsonian structures.

What is notable about the McDonald's, Watershed, Federal Center South, and the NMAAHC is that they combined technology like sensors and phase change technology with ideas borrowed from traditional African architecture as well as relatively simple natural solutions. Rethinking how to heat, cool, and light our buildings includes recognizing and seeking out solutions from previously untapped or overlooked sources.

A Spring Training Facility for the Whole Year

Indigenous groups, for example, have long been more aware of and prioritized the need to care for the natural world around them than modern construction practices However, as mainstream building processes become more sustainable, they are beginning to harmonize with these often-undervalued worldviews.

The Salt River-Maricopa Indian Community is located to the east of Phoenix, in the Arizona desert. When the community planned to build two Major League Baseball spring training complexes on 140 acres (56.6 hectares) of tribal resort land known as Talking Stick, environmental stewardship was critical to the project. WSP was an integral part of a team that designed Salt River Fields at Talking Stick, a stadium used by both the Colorado Rockies and Arizona Diamondbacks. It is referred to as the "Versailles of spring training facilities" by various baseball insiders. Salt River Fields is not only the first Major League Baseball spring training facility to achieve LEED Gold certification, but is also the first of its kind to be built on Native American tribal land.

Just as important to the Salt River-Maricopa Indian Community was the need to protect local plant and animal life. To do so, the site includes more than 85 mature trees and cacti that were preserved prior to construction and relocated throughout the new facility. An additional 2,400 native trees were also planted to provide shade for visitors, providing food for the pig-like javelinas and chuckwallas—a member of the iguana family—and a habitat for other indigenous animal species.

Another unique challenge of the site was accommodating a high number of visitors for only a small portion of the year. Providing surface parking was unavoidable, but that didn't mean that it all had to be a paved, impermeable parking lot that would essentially kill off a potentially large habitat. Instead, the hardscape was nearly halved by replacing it with native grass fields.

Like many natural solutions, the unpaved green space also provides benefits for the local community. In addition to reducing stormwater runoff, replacing asphalt with grass mitigates the heat island effect that is especially pervasive in this part of the country. Spring training runs for less than a month so, for the other 11 months of the year, the parking lots are playing fields for the community.

Sporting Sustainability

There is a special relationship between a community and its sports team. From the Los Angeles Dodgers in baseball to Manchester United in English football, this connection is a global phenomenon. The recent docuseries *Welcome to Wrexham*, which followed the fortunes of a fifth-tier Welsh football team, portrayed how this bond is something that is not limited to the large global teams, and that, in some ways, the connection can be stronger with the smaller regional teams.

For this reason, sports teams have a perhaps surprising responsibility to be leaders in our decarbonized transition and resilient future. Beyond simply being a refuge in the event of a major climatic event—as was most memorably witnessed in places like New Orleans' Caesars Superdome—new venues can also play an important role in the education of our communities. They are unique public spaces where municipal leaders, designers, engineers, and the private sector can demonstrate that sustainable, low-carbon solutions don't have to compromise the entertainment experience within the built environment.

Despite this responsibility, venues have historically been designed using brute force strategies, like air conditioning, that didn't hold sustainability, occupant comfort, or well-being as key design goals. In the last five years, this has begun changing with the Mercedes-Benz stadium, home of the NFL's Atlanta Falcons, and the NBA's Sacramento Kings' Golden 1 Center. Opening within months of each other, the stadiums were breakthroughs in sustainable venue design, becoming the first LEED Platinum-certified stadium and arena in the world, respectively.

What has been most exciting in the six years since their openings are the impact that these venues have had in their community leadership. In Sacramento, the Fan First Connected comfort strategy combines the first displacement ventilation system in a U.S. professional venue with 100-foot-wide (30.5-m) by 40-foot-tall (12.2-m) hangar doors to provide unprecedented air quality, energy efficiency, and operational control. This has led to a significant increase in the number and variety of events, and a reputation as one of the best venues in the country.

With the sustainability ceiling now shattered, the once unachievable LEED Platinum is now seen as a minimum requirement of those venues that want to provide leadership within their league and community. Most recently, the Intuit Dome in Inglewood, California—the new home of the NBA's L.A. Clippers—is being developed as a 100% carbon-free facility.

People First

Rethinking our buildings also means relocating people to the center of design decisions, increasing occupant health, well-being, happiness, and productivity. In any indoor environment, the lighting, air flow, and temperature make up the physical reality of where people live or work. Organizations routinely vow to create work environments that are, alternately, "positive" or "creative" and "successful," but these goals have to start with the physical environment. Take, for example, the Salesforce Tower, which is located in the city's SoMa (South-of-Market) district, the tallest building in San Francisco, and was awarded LEED Platinum certification. The design teams took pains to maintain and improve employee health and wellness on all levels of the 61-floor structure.

Many of these wellness efforts started with clean air. During the energy crisis of the 1970s, buildings began to be designed with airtightness as a goal in order to reduce heating costs. Unfortunately, striving to eliminate outdoor air can also result in less healthy indoor air quality, including increased risk from viruses. Post-pandemic, effective air filtration has become even more important to occupants as they return to work with heightened concerns over airborne illnesses. In a 2022 poll, an overwhelming majority—89%—of office workers agreed that the quality of air they breathe directly impacts their well-being and health.

More recently, scientific evidence indicated that the air within homes and offices can be more polluted than outdoor air—even in large, industrialized cities. Spaces may have eliminated mold or mildew and sent smokers outside, but just about every surface in an office—carpets, wallboard, cabinets, sofas, desks—could be releasing a toxic mixture of formaldehyde, volatile organic compounds (VOCs), and other chemicals that have been linked to a variety of illnesses and, in some cases, cancer. Efforts to greatly reduce or even eliminate these products and airborne compounds from workspaces, houses, and hospitals are all part of bigger push toward focusing on health and wellness.

Salesforce Tower's advanced HVAC system uses a low-energy under-floor air distribution to provide improved indoor air quality and increase energy efficiency by leveraging the thermal buoyancy of the air to keep people comfortable, draw contaminants out of the occupied zone, and avoid conditioning the area far above people's heads. The system improves indoor air quality by drawing the contaminants out of the occupied zone faster, and more effectively, than a traditional mixed air system that simply circulates the air—and the contaminants—within the space. The system also improves ventilation efficiency, distributing fresh air and lowering the noise floor—all of which improve worker productivity.

Quantifying the impact of air quality, thermal, visual, and acoustic comfort inside buildings is growing as a research field—made possible in part by the increasing amount of data created and analyzed by our smarter buildings. This is critical to the deployment of energy efficiency and other well-being focused strategies as demonstrating a single percentage increase in occupant productivity as a secondary benefit can transform the payback business case of an energy efficiency from years to months.

A converged network approach that integrated VOIP/WAN/LAN information technology with building management also improves the workspace by allowing occupants to adjust the temperature at their workstations to suit their individual needs. Humans are finely tuned to changes in temperature. Numerous experiments have demonstrated that adjustment within a narrow temperature range of 67–75°F (19–24°C) has measurable impacts on how people work and interact. In one test, participants completed complex tasks more easily and accurately at lower temperatures, but were more comfortable and collaborative at the warmer end of the range. Sixty percent said that having more control over their office's temperature would also increase their productivity.

Another solution at Salesforce Tower is over employees' heads—the 13-foot (4-m) ceilings. Experiments have documented how the height of a ceiling changes how people think. In one experiment, university students were individually shown to four small offices, each with a laptop on a desk and asked to rate their current body state and complete several word games. The only difference was that two of the rooms had 10-foot (3-m) ceilings, the other half had 8-foot (2.4-m) drop ceilings installed. The results were consistent across several experiments: high ceilings seemed to put test participants in a mindset of freedom, creativity, and abstraction, whereas the lower ceilings prompted more confined thinking.

Employees will feel less sense of restriction because the building systems are installed in the raised floor. Additionally, the office space is flexible and can change over time by easily reconfiguring power, data, and air systems. Combined with 10-foot (3-m) windows, which let in ample natural light around the building, Salesforce Tower offers the most sought-after perks by employees, some of whom are perhaps reluctant to return to workplaces. But in addition to the multiple benefits of looking after employees, there are also benefits for people far outside the building. For example, sourcing greener building materials encourages less polluting production around the world. The cooling and heating systems resulted in substantial energy savings, reducing GHG emissions.

One more perk just outside the building is a 5.4-acre (2.2-hectare) green space on top of an adjacent transit center that is accessible to the public via elevators and a glass cube. The long park, about 70 feet (21.3 m) above the sidewalk below, features drought-resistant palms, ferns, succulents as well as about 600 trees, a wetland watered by recycled gray water runoff, benches, and playgrounds—a living oasis surrounded by glass skyscrapers. The park is public, although Salesforce helped fund it by buying the naming rights.

The high performance, innovative, and lower energy usage of the prototype McDonald's, The Watershed, Federal Building South, the NMAAHC, and Salesforce Tower are exciting indications of the willingness of a wide range of organizations to rethink outdated design and construction practices. Enthusiasm for embedding sustainability and resilience in the built environment has increasingly grown over just the past 5–10 years. However, rethinking a building's systems and performance is only part of the challenge. A deep decarbonization of the built environment begins well before an asset is occupied.

The Other Carbon

In the 1870s, an English engineer named Ernest Ransome moved to San Francisco and began experimenting with techniques to build a stronger concrete for buildings. At the time, concrete was not considered a safe material for large buildings. While its load-bearing capacity—the amount of weight it could support—was high, concrete is very brittle. The material's low tensile strength and ductility leave it vulnerable to cracking and structural failure as a result of horizontal forces like wind. Ransome was not the first person to experiment with pouring concrete to set over top of a steel grid as a method of increasing concrete's tensile strength. European inventors had been developing various techniques since at least the 1700s. However, Ransome improved many of the existing techniques, and, in a stroke of either fortunate coincidence or genius, twisted the reinforcing steel bars, increasing their bond with the concrete. Over the next few decades, reinforced concrete established itself as one of the premier building materials for a wide range of buildings. Today it is used for everything from gas stations to Dubai's 2,717-foot (828-m) Burj Khalifa.

Concrete is relatively cheap, strong, and adaptable to different climates and projects. Its primary ingredients—sand, gravel, limestone, and water—are also abundant and nontoxic. Today, concrete is the highest consumed product on earth after water. It is so widely used that, in the United States, annual concrete production is roughly equivalent to two tons for every American. However, concrete also produces a tremendous amount of GHG emissions. Every pound of concrete produces nearly an equivalent amount—.93 pounds (.42 kilos)—in carbon dioxide emissions. In fact, the global concrete industry accounts for roughly 8% of the world's total carbon emissions. If it were a country, the industry would emit more carbon than all but China and the United States.

The carbon intensity of concrete is the result of two processes in its manufacture. Concrete is basically cement with aggregates like sand and rocks added. Cement is made by heating limestone to temperatures around 2,550°F (1,400°C), almost always by burning fossil fuel. While there are electric cement kilns that could be run on renewable energy, that would only eliminate roughly 40% of the GHG emissions from the production process. The other 60% is largely the result of the carbon dioxide that is cooked out of the limestone as it is heated. In other words, the largest part of concrete's massive carbon emissions is inherent in the chemistry of its manufacturing process.

The carbon emissions of building materials like concrete and steel, as well as other construction-related activities like supply chain or equipment operation, have come under increased scrutiny over the past decade. The whole building sector accounts for roughly 50% of annual global greenhouse gas emissions, but building materials and construction alone represent 10% of global emissions. So, while past efforts to decarbonize buildings focused primarily on reducing energy usage by the occupants—what's known as operational carbon—there is now a similar focus on the emissions that occur before a building is even occupied, often known as embodied carbon.

One of the reasons for focusing on embodied carbon now, even though it is a smaller percentage of the building sector's total greenhouse gas emissions, is that embodied carbon is not spread out over the decades of the building's life, as is the case with operational carbon. Once a building is constructed, embodied carbon cannot be reduced retroactively by future technologies. Through retrofits or equipment upgrades, it is possible to reduce annual operational carbon down to zero during a building's lifetime.

The urgency of reducing embodied carbon has prompted a rethinking of the building materials we use. Some cement blends release less carbon during kiln processing, while others soak in additional carbon dioxide while it sets (all cement soaks in some carbon dioxide while drying). Some builders use different processes that require less cement for construction. Electrifying the concrete supply chain—from mining to transporting raw materials to fueling the massive kilns—is another option. At least one company, Norway's Norcem, has an operational electric kiln.

Regulatory changes are also making the environmental impacts of building materials more transparent. Beginning this year, producers that bid on U.S. federal projects will need to produce environmental product declarations (EPD). An EPD requires producers to disclose data on seven impact areas, including global warming potential, ozone depletion, smog, and environmental damage to the earth. This new requirement should inspire additional investment in and awareness of existing and future innovations in lower-carbon concrete.

These technologies and processes are critical because, despite the undeniable cost of concrete's massive GHG emissions, the material will continue to remain essential to construction practices for the foreseeable future. There are, of course, existing alternatives to concrete as a structural material. Steel is very strong, widely used, and more recyclable than concrete, but the iron and other ore mining and processing of steel also creates enormous amounts of carbon emissions. The production of another widely used material, brick, also requires energy-intense kilns. However, cleaning up the emissions of concrete, steel, and brick are not the only way to accelerate the decarbonization of the built environment.

Mass Movement

If we think outside of the past 100 years or so—before concrete and steel became dominant materials—we can find many other construction materials. In fact, people continue to build structures out of locally available materials like packed straw, palm fronds, cob, sod, animal hides, adobe, and stones. But among the most successful answers to lowering embodied carbon in structural materials for buildings is a new take on one of the world's oldest construction materials. Wood has been used for millennia to build a wide variety of structures, including neolithic plank houses, Māori *wharenui*, Japan's Hōryū-ji temple, and North American log cabins. Of course, wood is still used to frame out many one- or two-story buildings around the world. In recent years, though, a new twist on the traditional building material is providing a lower-carbon alternative to steel and concrete.

Mass timber is engineered out of thick, compressed wood layers that are fire resistant and strong enough to replace concrete and steel as structural load-bearing materials in many cases. Mass timber retains wood's ability to sequester carbon, be recycled, and promote wellness. With modern techniques it can also be used to build 12- to 18-story buildings. In some cases and places, mass timber has become a cost-viable alternative to traditional steel and reinforced concrete construction.

In response, building codes that once limited timber buildings to 85 feet (25.9 m) maximum—about 5 to 6 stories—now allow up to 18 stories, or 270 feet (8.3 m). WSP staff in the United States and around the globe are engaging with building developers, other firms in the building trades, industry groups and building officials to spread knowledge and advance best practices for mass timber construction. One of the biggest questions: how viable is mass timber at scale?

A 2021 study of mass timber construction in Vancouver, British Columbia, suggested that broader adoption of mass timber was possible, but the material's benefits wouldn't be maximized if it was considered an interchangeable green alternative to reinforced concrete. In terms of cost competitiveness, designs developed for concrete don't translate to mass timber. Instead, playing to mass timber's strengths involves broadening building codes. Although some local codes are already changing, most generally assume concrete and steel as the primary structural building materials for tall buildings. For mass timber to scale up, insurers and regulators need to be educated about mass timber's fire and structural safety performance. Building codes and insurance policies need to evolve, creating a new classification for mass timber buildings.

One area where mass timber definitively outperforms concrete is the off-site fabrication of building units—walls, floors, bathrooms, whole apartments—in a manufacturing facility. The units are then transported to a building site where they are assembled or installed. Compared to concrete or steel, mass timber's relative lightness gives it an edge. Prefabricating, transporting, and installing loses many of its advantages if done with heavy concrete or steel units.

Combining mass timber with modular design brings other sustainability benefits. Because materials are bought at scale and a large part of the project is constructed in one place, waste can be drastically reduced. Tighter construction tolerances and more control over material sourcing can also lead to significant improvements in energy efficiency and indoor air quality.

Unfortunately, expanding modular building would disrupt much of the traditional construction industry, including supply chains, designers, architects, and skilled labor. However, because on-site assembly puts more emphasis on skilled designers and less emphasis on skilled labor, it can provide opportunities to upskill local mass timber construction practices to transition the workforce.

Reuse Everything

The ultimate rethink on how to build something differently and more sustainably is *not* to build it—or at least not build anything new. Since there is not enough existing built space to accommodate the earth's estimated population in 2050, adaptive reuse of materials can provide some answers. In 2011, after Christchurch, New Zealand, was devastated by an earthquake, some of the first rebuilt commercial spaces in the city popped up in shipping containers. The spaces were functional and cheap enough that some are still in use today. Adapted versions of these containers can also be used as housing following natural disasters or even as a temporary housing shelter.

Because they are functional, quirky, and relatively cheap, shipping containers are also reused outside of disaster areas. In London, containers are used in a chain of pop-up retail centers. With interior redesigns, the spaces offer prominent locations for chefs who have moved up from food stalls but can't yet afford a full brick-and-mortar restaurant. London was not the first city to create large retail space out of used materials. Shipping containers are also widely used for retail and hospitality in South Africa. For decades, Bishkek, Kyrgyzstan, has also hosted a massive market called Dordoi, which is full of Chinese goods that are flooding into central Asia. Though Bishkek is landlocked, the mall is made almost entirely of shipping containers.

Historic buildings also provide alternatives to new construction. Although they often don't comply with modern energy efficiency codes, reusing an existing building avoids the GHG emissions associated with building a new one. Many can be upgraded without ruining their heritage qualities, although it can take some creative thinking.

WSP is currently working on a project to significantly improve the energy efficiency of Copenhagen City Hall in Denmark, the headquarters of Copenhagen City Council for the past 120 years. The installation of a new heating and ventilation system makes full use of the building's original infrastructure—including original brick ventilation ducts, roof pipes, and basement corridors—combined with a state-of-the-art building management system, leading to energy savings of up to 80%. The upgrade to the building will make an important contribution to Copenhagen's ambitious goals for greenhouse gas reduction, and maintains the building's status as an important, usable space.

The city hall is nearly 120 years old but, as an historic landmark, it is more likely to be viewed as a valuable asset as opposed to a limited life product. Preserving the best of the past is certainly important to creating a rich, sustainable, and resilient future. However, getting to that future also means evaluating the assets we are designing and constructing today through the same long-term, holistic lens. This means moving beyond the dominance of capital costs to consider the cost-effectiveness of a project over its entire life. Frequently, sustainable and resilient designs create more long-term value, while also reducing GHG emissions throughout their lifespan, from construction, to operation, to end-of-life. Reuse and preservation can also be valuable in helping us rethink what we will build tomorrow.

Saving the Stump

In the early 2000s, the City of London's booming economy fired up the imaginations of developers and architects to design and build iconic buildings with nicknames like the Walkie Talkie, the Scalpel, the Shard, and the Cheese Grater that collectively remade the city's skyline between 2012 and 2018. It takes about ten years to build a skyscraper, which means that somewhere between inception of these landmarks in the early to mid-2000s and their unveiling over the following decade, the financial and real estate sectors went into a deep recession.

In this environment, some of the ambitious buildings dreamed up in the pre-financial collapse didn't make it through the build phase. One such building was the Pinnacle, a 945-foot (288-m) skyscraper-as-art-project in which no single pane of glass was the same. Construction was halted in 2009, at which point the Pinnacle was just a three-story basement and nine floors of concrete core and piles known locally as "the Stump."

The collapse of the Pinnacle project was a testament to the dangers of designing for an era that would end just a few years later. Building sustainably doesn't just mean improving energy efficiency or reducing the GHG emissions of new construction or planning for climate change, but designing for a wide range of potential disruptions, including stressors like economic or political shifts, cyberterrorism, or pandemics. The original Pinnacle project was simply not adaptable to changing conditions. As a result, a lot of GHGs were emitted for an unfinished building.

However, the project was salvaged with a more flexible design that accommodated a variety of potential futures much more successfully. In 2020, when a 62-story building known as 22 Bishopsgate was opened on the same site, it also faced multiple challenges that were unforeseen in the design stage. The most unpredictable was the COVID-19 pandemic, which pushed remote work into the foreground and made office space seem much more expendable to some businesses. Fortunately, the redesign of the building had veered away from a "maximize rentable space" mindset in favor of a people-centric design. Sometimes described as a village, the building featured restaurants, viewing galleries, gyms, and wellness centers. More importantly, 22 Bishopsgate was also built for a future in which reducing embodied carbon is a critical part of reducing the excessive greenhouse gas emissions in the building sector.

The Pinnacle's stump in London provided an opportunity for an innovative approach to reducing embodied carbon. Instead of excavating the building's foundations and starting again, WSP engineers led a team that successfully reused 100% of the existing foundations and 50% of the basement.

Redesigning any building on top of the beginning of another's core is complicated enough. The unique spiral shape of the original Pinnacle's core meant WSP had to push the limits of structural engineering—with mega-transfer girders, inclined columns with high-strength steel cable ties, triple-story A-frames, partial demolition of the existing basement, and partial top-down construction with 20 stories of the core built before the foundations were completed. As a result, WSP was able to reduce the embodied carbon and construction emissions of the foundations by 70%.

The innovative design for the core, in turn, reduced requirements for structural reinforcement. All the floors were built with concrete that was 30% lighter than the standard mix. The size of the beam-to-column connections was reduced by 40%. Each of these design elements further reduce embodied carbon.

However, the design phase is also the best time to reduce future operational carbon emissions as well. Electrical, security, and fire systems, the elevator, and the building management system were integrated to reduce energy consumption. Automated systems architecture allowed operations teams to see where the building was under-utilized, enabling them to reduce energy use for, say, heating, cooling, or lighting. This smart feature also provides an educational opportunity: tenants who see energy consumption displayed on a series of dashboards may adopt more sustainable behaviors.

Data Dilemma

The world's largest data center sits on a desert road, Nevada 439, outside Reno and just a few brown, rocky hills from Tesla's Gigafactory. Only one building of Switch's Citadel Campus had been completed in 2022, but it will eventually occupy 7.3 million square feet (678,190 sqm) and use 650 megawatts of power. The company sources all its power from solar and wind farms around Nevada, positioning it far ahead of many other players in a rapidly growing and electricity-hungry sector.

The expansion of the world's data is virtually impossible to conceive. In 2020, for example, the average human created 1.7 MB of data per second—as if everyone on earth snapped a digital photo every second forever. The total amount of digital data ever produced is now measured in zettabytes—that's 21 zeros. As a result, data centers consumed 100 terawatt-hours of electricity in 2021, or 1% of the world's total. Unfortunately, most of these buildings don't run on

100% renewable energy like Switch's Citadel Campus. As a result, cloud computing now has a greater carbon footprint than the airline industry.

There are efficiencies in this surging amount of data. Bytes have replaced countless sheets of paper. A joint WSP Microsoft initiative quantified the further benefits of cloud computing. Using life cycle assessment and GHG emissions accounting, the study found that the Microsoft Cloud is up to 93% more energy-efficient and can result in 98% lower carbon emissions than traditional enterprise data centers.

However, the current expansion of energy-gobbling data centers is unsustainable. As a result, big tech companies have made large investments to try and reduce their carbon emissions. Amazon, Google, and Microsoft have become among the leading corporate purchasers of renewable energy. But beyond simply purchasing renewable energy, some tech companies are now implementing real time alignment of renewable energy generation and consumption—in lieu of writing a retrospective check. Not only is this more credible, but arguably a more purposeful carbon reduction measure rather than just offsetting.

Many companies have also dramatically reduced how much energy they use to cool the physical data centers. Initially, servers were cooled down like people in an office building, by blowing cold air into the room. However, just as sustainable office buildings have begun rethinking traditional AC systems, data centers are using a variety of methods to cool the tightly packed—and much more heat intense—servers. In cooler climates, companies aim to use "free cooling"—simply pulling outside air across equipment, a process that uses comparatively little electricity. In dry, hot environments like Nevada, evaporative cooling—blowing wet air across servers—captures heat while using less energy than compressors and, somewhat unexpectedly, less water than traditional cooling systems. Other lower-power cooling methods include running cooled water in tubes along the back of a server rack or even fully immersing the servers into nonconductive fluids that carry away the heat.

However, servers are impacted by more than just temperature—moisture or airborne particulates can impact and even destroy equipment. In order to safely maximize the usage of alternate cooling methods, WSP used machine learning to understand how the temperature and environmental profile of the air in data centers affects reliability and performance of equipment. Expanding the range of outdoor air conditions that are acceptable for free cooling—rather than water cooling—by just one or two degrees can result in eye-opening net savings in operational carbon and water usage. By looking at real data, taking a holistic approach, and challenging the conventional wisdom of how IT equipment should be operated, WSP's team determined that making a small tweak to allowable environmental conditions could save 95% of cooling water and likely improve the reliability of the equipment.

While the operational expectations of zero downtime often constrain the tech industry's ability to meet these goals, the industry has continued to evolve. The American Society of Heating, Refrigerating and Air-Conditioning Engineers (ASHRAE) has since updated the acceptable design conditions to enable greater use of free cooling and evaporative cooling techniques that has resulted in PUEs (Power Use Intensity) dropping significantly over the last five years to less than 1.5 in average, and as low as 1.2 in optimal locations.

There is, however, a growing concern that the transition to low-energy cooling techniques that take advantage of local conditions may quickly become less effective—precisely as a result of climate change. As the atmosphere in many of the historically optimal geographies for data centers becomes warmer and more humid, the facilities and computing power they support are at increased risk. The use of innovative hybrid solutions such as thermosyphon-based cooling systems—a kind of passive heat exchange using fluids—can provide near equivalent cooling performance while reducing water consumption and providing increased mitigation of the climate risk to compute capacity.

Another WSP project examined the life cycle of a technology with the possibility of radically slashing both the operational and embodied carbon of data centers. Instead of storing data on hard drives, the data is etched into glass using a laser. Another technique encoded the data into artificial DNA. By replacing the four proteins found in DNA with ones and zeros, the data was much more tightly packed than on a hard drive in a data center. Recent research suggests that if every movie ever made was encoded in DNA, it could be stored in the volume of a sugar cube. Aside from potentially radically reducing the amount of real estate needed, DNA storage uses a lot less energy than traditional methods. Disk drives are constantly spinning, and thus, constantly using power and creating heat. DNA doesn't use mechanical motion, so it eliminates all the heat and energy use associated with mechanical motion.

Even in a future where data centers are running on fully renewable power, their high energy usage will still be contributing a substantial amount of GHGs into the atmosphere. Not only are the demands for data centers growing at a breathtaking rate, many are new, single-story construction built outside of urban areas. As such, they will not only contribute high upfront embodied carbon costs, but disrupt local ecosystems by adding impermeable surfaces, traffic, and noise to previously virgin land.

As a result, tech companies are already looking for alternative real estate. In 2018, for example, Microsoft stuck a functioning data center in a 40-foot pill-shaped tube and sunk it off the coast of Scotland for a 2-year-long proof of concept test. The test was considered successful, but there may be a more immediate, and dryer, solution: repurposing existing big box retail shells that are increasingly becoming derelict across the US and in other highly developed countries. While likely unable to support the same data density of a traditional hyperscale data center, repurposing large commercial spaces offers advantages in terms of speed to market, simplified integration within existing communities, and embodied carbon reduction benefits.

Designing the Right Buildings

There are innumerable available solutions for lowering the enormous amount of greenhouse gases emitted by the construction, operation, and the end-of-life phase of buildings. Project Drawdown lists alternative cement, building automation systems, retrofitting, heat pumps, insulation, light-emitting diode (LED) lighting, net zero buildings as some of the off-the-shelf solutions ready for massively scaled roll out.[3] Doing so would reduce or sequester dozens of gigatons of carbon dioxide equivalent over the next three decades. (By comparison, human industrial activity and fossil fuel usage resulted in roughly 34 gigatons of carbon dioxide equivalent in 2020.)[4] Those solutions would also create another benefit—trillions of dollars in lifetime net operation savings.

Continuing to develop or adopt additional solutions also requires rethinking our traditional approach. For example, import and seek out new processes and technologies from international, indigenous, and nature-based sources. Introduce alternate materials like mass timber or processes like modular construction. Sometimes, don't build anything new at all, but renovate, reuse, or repurpose. Always build for resilience, sustainability, and equity by designing Future Ready assets.

Although climate risk is now driving rapid change in the financial sector, the urgency to embrace new solutions has been more muted in many parts of the construction industry. Beyond broadening our range of technologies, we desperately need to rethink how we value our assets. The capital costs for integrating sustainability and resilience into projects and programs are often marginally more expensive. However, when developers, real estate companies, landlords, tenants, and other stakeholders look at buildings' cost effectiveness over their full life cycle, many will fully embrace the long-term savings and value of investing in Future Ready assets. This sort of rethinking of the whole sector is critical to meeting our various governmental, corporate, and other organizational climate goals.

Notes

1. https://spectrumnews1.com/ca/la-west/homelessness/2022/09/08/ tktk-people-are-homeless-in-la--according-to-new-lahsa-count.
2. https://news.un.org/en/story/2017/10/567552.
3. https://drawdown.org/solutions.
4. https://ourworldindata.org/co2-emissions.

3

On the Move

IN 1800, A person living in New York City would have needed two days to travel to Philadelphia. By 1830, commercial trains and improved roads meant you could travel more than twice the distance—to Washington, D.C.—in the same period of time. Twenty-seven years after that, two days took you to Chicago, and, by 1930, all the way to Denver.[1] Now, you can get from New York to Singapore, or just about anywhere else on Earth, in under two days. This revolution in personal mobility has expanded trade, globalized populations, and completely changed the way we think about our planet. It's easier to imagine a world with no skyscrapers than a world with no bicycles, trains, cars, or planes—not to mention the consumer goods that travel the world on massive supply chains.

As with any transformation that rearranges the planet, it's impossible to list all the positive implications of this transportation revolution, simply because they are now an essential part of the human experience around the world. There is, however, one glaring negative. The transportation sector is the second largest source of GHG emissions—27% of total GHG emissions in the United States and a similarly significant amount in other countries.

As with other infrastructure sectors, all of those planet-warming emissions that transportation has released into the atmosphere are now creating a self-destructive feedback loop. The mobility revolution has necessitated a rapidly expanding infrastructure. Today, train

65

stations, stop signs, bridges, highways, cargo docks, airports, and subway entrances aren't just commonplace, but iconic urban and regional symbols. They also provide a huge target for the climate-change–related extreme weather that regularly wreaks havoc on the transportation infrastructure—eroding roads, washing out bridges, and flooding subway tunnels.

Though all types of infrastructure are impacted by climate-related extreme weather, damage to the transportation sector may be the most expensive and critical. According to the Organisation of Economic Co-operation and Development's (OECD) modeling for a major flood in Paris, up to 85% of business losses would be caused by damage to transportation and electrical systems, as opposed to the physical damage of the flood itself. What's more, the damage to transportation infrastructure in the aftermath of a major storm makes it more difficult for first responders to reach people trapped in flooding, hurricanes, wildfires, or other events. While these transportation assets are built to withstand storms that are expected to hit once or twice a century, climate change has made predicting future risk a more uncertain science.

This cycle of burgeoning GHG emissions and increased infrastructure risk is one of the primary reasons we need to rethink transportation. We can't keep designing for the past if we want a resilient infrastructure. Keeping people and goods on the move is a non-negotiable part of our hyper-mobile society and globalized supply chains. But sustainability, in the form of rapidly decarbonizing the sector, is also essential to the future of transportation—and intimately linked to resilience. If we don't reduce the transportation sector's significant GHG emissions, the seas will keep rising, the Earth's surface temperatures will keep going up, record-setting floods will be more frequent, and the resilience of our transportation sector will repeatedly be overwhelmed. Decarbonizing transportation is an even more urgent goal as the world's population rises exponentially.

Rethinking transportation doesn't stop at embedding resilience and embracing sustainability, though. We need to ask ourselves what we want and need from transportation in the future. Should we prioritize throughput—moving people and goods quickly? Or should we first focus on ensuring reliable, resilient transport for people and goods? Transportation has always deeply interconnected with equity, should future designs and programs double down on providing reliable service to everyone, particularly those in historically underserved communities? Is reducing air pollution to improving community health the top priority? Does urgent decarbonization trump all other issues? Or can we design a transportation system that accomplishes all five goals simultaneously?

This chapter looks at the challenges of rethinking and redesigning transportation in the era of climate change, as well as urbanization, rapid population growth, and technological change While the technology to take the transportation sector all the way to net zero doesn't yet exist, we can successfully address many challenges with a range of solutions, from technical innovations to urban design to reimaging the functionality of the most difficult segments to decarbonize. If we want to stay on the move in the future, we need to do it much better.

EVolution

Automobiles—including cars, sports utility vehicles (SUVs), and trucks—are at the core of the American transportation system. Roughly 92% of households own at least one car. Over three in four commuters get to work in their own vehicles. There are roughly 4 million miles (6,437,376 km) of public roads in the United States, versus just 140,000 miles (225,308 km) in the rail network.[2,3] Cities have been designed and redesigned around the prerogatives of interstates. But personal vehicles also have innumerable negative consequences. They emit air pollution that negatively impacts our cardiovascular, respiratory, reproductive, or immune systems—and make us more depressed.[4,5] In the United States, automobiles are responsible for more than half of the transportation sector's total emissions and 15.4% of the country's total GHG emissions— more than concrete, steel, and all the other embodied carbon in the building sector.[6]

However, there is a relatively simple, road-tested solution to decarbonizing this segment of transportation. Electric vehicles (EVs), as well as hydrogen fuel cell vehicles, can rapidly reduce transportation's GHG emissions. In fact, if the 2 million American owners of EVs powered their vehicles with renewable energy—using off-the-shelf and relatively affordable technology—they could move around without emitting any exhaust or GHGs without substantially altering their current lifestyles. Of course, most EV owners today charge their vehicles using conventional power grids, most of which source a significant percentage of the electricity from fossil fuel. Even so, studies show that driving EVs powered by power grids in the United States significantly reduces GHG emissions versus traditional gas- and diesel-powered vehicles. A study by the International Energy Agency (IEA) showed that, over a 20-year lifespan, a mid-sized battery EV would emit less than half the carbon emissions of a comparable internal combustion vehicle.

Like high-efficiency heat pumps and LED lighting in the property and real estate sector, EVs are a market-ready decarbonization strategy. As is true across multiple infrastructure segments, we have solutions, but they need to be rolled out at a much larger scale. Even at current high rates of growth, EVs are only projected to comprise roughly 40% of vehicles on the roads by 2050.[7] To hit net zero by 2050, however, 100% of vehicles would need to be EVs. Because it takes roughly 15 years for a fleet to turn over—to be replaced by newer vehicles—sales of internal combustion engine (ICE) vehicles would have to end by 2035 at the latest. To meet this goal, the European Union voted to make sales of ICE vehicles illegal from 2035 and beyond. As of 2021, automakers, including Ford, Mercedes-Benz, General Motors, and Volvo, as well as the U.S. states of California, New York, and Washington have made a slightly less ambitious pledge—phasing out ICE cars and trucks by 2040.[8] However, the best way to ensure that these pledges are kept—as well as decarbonizing transportation by 2050—is accelerating the adoption rate of consumers and organizations.

There are several common explanations of low adoption EV rates in the United States. The first is "range anxiety"—concerns around how far an EV can be driven before needing to be charged, as well as the related issue of an insufficient charging infrastructure. However, rapidly improving technology has already dramatically increased the range of EVs in the past 5 to 10 years. In 2022, the top-selling EV, the Tesla Model Y SUV, had a range of 330 miles (531 km), while the more affordable Nissan Leaf got 226 miles (363 km) in total range—both of which are well beyond the 35 miles (56 km) an American driver averages in a day.[9,10] In order to reduce range anxiety, the United States and other countries have also invested large amounts of money into building a more comprehensive charging infrastructure. The 2021 U.S. bipartisan infrastructure law allocates $7.5 billion to build

500,000 EV charging stations around the country by 2030, which would be more than the country's current 145,000 gas stations.[11,12]

Another major sticking point for consumer adoption of EVs is higher upfront costs. EVs are generally more expensive than comparable gas- or diesel-powered vehicles, although that difference is consistently narrowing. As with more sustainable, efficient, and resilient buildings, the total costs of EV ownership are a case study of the significant value, and even savings, found in sustainable assets when evaluated over their full life cycle. EVs have fewer parts to service than internal combustion cars—no spark plugs, timing belts, or motor oil—meaning they cost about 50% less to maintain. Fuel costs are also significantly lower, at around 60% of comparable internal combustion vehicles. Studies that compare total cost of ownership for EVs versus internal combustion vehicles either found a near parity or significant cost savings—between $5,000 and $10,000 over the life of an EV. This combination of decarbonization and low total cost of ownership has encouraged many large corporations to transition their fleets to EVs, including Amazon, FedEx, PepsiCo, and Waste Management.

In 2022, the combination of technological advances, consumer acceptance, incentives, and erratic gas prices translated to a rapid increase of EV purchases in the United States. However, EVs still only have just over 5% of the total U.S. automobile market—not nearly the kind of wide-scale adoption necessary to rapidly decarbonize transportation.[13] How can we rethink EV adoption?

As we also saw with evaluating the risks associated with hurricanes or climate change, human personal experience tends to trump expertise. And, as a still relatively new technology, there are plenty of misconceptions that can be cleared up when consumers drive or ride in an EV.[14] For example, many drivers are concerned that EVs have sluggish acceleration when, in fact, electric drivetrains are far more responsive than ICEs. Many drivers are similarly concerned about lengthier charging times versus gas station stops, although most charging is done either overnight or while the driver is doing something else, like shopping. A study commissioned by Ford noted other common misconceptions. For example, 42% of Americans believed that fully electric vehicles still use some gas or diesel as fuel (they don't).[15] The study also found that a similar number of British drivers were uncertain whether fully electric vehicles could be driven through a car wash (they can).[16]

A large number of consumers are more likely to buy EVs when they understand their personal savings on fuel and maintenance—not because experts told them they need to urgently reduce in GHG emissions. As of 2022, American consumers can qualify for up to a $7,500 tax credit for purchase of some new EVs, which may be combined with state incentives. The combination of these incentives as well as improvements in EV technology and infrastructure will no doubt continue to encourage EV adoption. But we may also be able to accelerate adoption by learning something from looking abroad at the world's biggest success story.[17,18]

Chasing Norway

The adoption rate of EVs in Norway can only be described as stunning. Between 2011 and 2021, the share of new EV sales in the country went from 1% to 60%. In 2021, the second largest category of new car sales was hybrids, at 27%, with diesel and gasoline-powered cars fighting for the scraps.[19] What was the secret to the nation's runaway success?

Norway's demographics, a small country with a relatively wealthy population, are favorable to high adoption rate. However, the country also has cold winters, which reduce battery life and vehicle range, and long driving distances between cities. Surprisingly, Norway offers none of the generous incentives and rebates common in other European countries. France, Germany, and Italy offer cash rebates averaging around €10,000 ($11,000)—yet they have not achieved anything like Norway's success.

The nation's unique approach to rethinking EV adoption may have roots in a rolling protest carried out in 1995 by an environmentalist named Frederic Hauge and the lead singer of synth-pop group A-ha, Morten Harket. The high-profile couple drove around Oslo in an Italian EV, refusing to pay parking tickets or tolls until their car was impounded and auctioned to pay their bills. Twenty-five years later, Norway's EV adoption plan looks a bit more like a protest than a bureaucratic rebate scheme. Many of the biggest official incentives for EV drivers are very similar to the protest—free parking and passage on ferries, ignoring tolls, and driving in the bus lane. Norway also offers no tax on new EV sales and an extensive public charging network.

Norway's program may not be replicable in its entirety in other countries, but the nation's stratospheric rates of adoption points to an achievable, more sustainable future—at least for the United States and other wealthy nations. In brief, we could have an interconnected, hyper-mobile world that emits far fewer emissions simply through wide-scale adoption of EVs.

The nation's success also suggests that rethinking the traditional approach to adoption could be effective. For example, rebate programs could be combined with sustained community engagement efforts to educate drivers on the benefits of EV. Consumer feedback could likewise help governments design better programs. While financial incentives will continue to be a primary driver in purchase decisions, additional personal but non-economic factors will likely lead to more rapid adoption. Younger demographics are most likely to want to buy EVs, but not just because of lower costs of ownership or environmental concerns. In one poll, Generation Z—a cohort born roughly between 1997 and 2012—reported their primary interest in buying EVs was because they are "cool."[20] This generation has grown up at a time of rapid development and mainstreaming of EV technology, as well as an increasing price parity. These developments set the stage for many younger drivers to develop a preference for EVs that goes beyond number crunching, which would be a major boon to wide-scale adoption of the single biggest strategy for decarbonizing transportation.

Rating Resilience

While EVs can provide one solution for meeting net zero goals in the transportation sector, we will also have to ensure that the roads EVs and other vehicles drive on are resilient enough to last through to 2050 and beyond. This is increasingly challenging as the impacts of climate change call into question historic assumptions about how to build resilient, safe, and cost-effective transportation infrastructure.

In just one example, historic flooding sent torrents of water through Yellowstone National Park in mid-June 2022. As tourists fled, bridges and roads were completely wiped out. The park had to be closed for much of the summer tourist season while the roads were rebuilt. Later that summer, Yellowstone's superintendent, Cam Sholly, pondered the difficulty of predicting climate risk in an uncertain world, telling the

New York Times that the flood was a "thousand-year event, whatever that means these days."

What it means, at least in part, is that we need to rethink resiliency. Resilient infrastructure is critical while we decarbonize the vehicles using the roads and bridges and tunnels. However, we can't just rebuild the same roads. Sometimes roads shouldn't be rebuilt—the future climate risk is too high. But roads that are built and rebuilt must be designed for a less certain future.

Utilizing a rating system called ENVISION is one way to ensure that transportation infrastructure incorporates sustainability and resilience into its design from the beginning. Developed by the Institute for Sustainable Infrastructure (ISI) and the Zofnass Program for Sustainable Infrastructure, ENVISION mirrors other rating systems like LEED and BREEAM in multiple ways.[21] For example, it provides design criteria and a measurement framework to rate a project's usage of energy, materials, and water. Certification also guarantees a certain degree of sustainability, resilience, lower ecological footprint, and positive community impact. Unlike LEED and BREEAM, however, ENVISION is generally focused on aspects of the built environment that are not inhabited—often transportation infrastructure like roads, bridges, railways, and airports.

ENVISION designs also go beyond sustainability and resilience concerns. The system engages communities in project design as well as requiring the mitigation of negative impacts of construction, like noise, water contamination, and safety. Finally, ENVISION encourages teams to develop other community benefits into infrastructure designs, such as bike paths or pedestrian pathways.

Much like Future Ready, ENVISION requires that projects rethink designing for the future. Critical infrastructure is often built to last 75–100 years, but the more variable and extreme impacts of climate change are changing what it means to accurately predict local climates and conditions that far into the future. Several megatrends can limit transportation infrastructure's lifespan, including damage from snowfall, flooding, hurricanes, landslides, as well as denser highway traffic. ENVISION builds in a requirement that projects evaluate their vulnerabilities in a dynamic future in order to improve climate resilience.

LEED, BREEAM, the LBC, and other rating frameworks all share the ultimate goal of ENVISION's new standards: to be transformative within the infrastructure sector. There are two main components to reconfiguring how we approach transportation infrastructure. The first is designing the right project or program in the right place, particularly prioritizing sustainability, resilience, equity, and cost effectiveness when considering the full life cycle, and creating additional benefits for communities.

We've discussed all these factors previously. The trick, as we've seen, is not knowing what we need to do—like building for sustainability, resilience, and equity—but implementing these goals. ENVISION's second element is designed to deliver these results by doing the right projects and programs the right way. This includes:

- Engaging early and regularly with stakeholders to drive community co-benefits and equity.
- Considering other program or projects that are co-located produces gains in resilience, equity, cost-effectiveness, and other benefits, depending on what the other program is.
- Ensuring the current drivers for the project will remain in the future is essential for guaranteeing sustainability and resilience.
- Leveraging an integrated approach through the program's life, from design onward, maximizes the capacities of full-service companies like WSP and results in better designed, smarter programs that are able to deliver the right project—sustainable, resilient, equitable, cost-effective, with multiple benefits.
- Analyzing and being aware of emerging innovations, standards, and requirements—Future Ready megatrends in technology and society—produces a project or program that won't need to be completely changed.
- Considering other Future Ready megatrends in climate, society, and resources drives resilience and sustainability by establishing useful guidelines for everything from structural materials to site location.
- Advancing a right program, right way approach can, in itself, foster organizational and individual change.

WSP has been very active in ENVISION's development, application, and expansion over the last decade because of its potential for getting owners, investors, and builders to rethink how we design and build infrastructure. In 2021, Tom spoke before a U.S. congressional committee to advocate for the expanded use of ENVISION, including adoption by the federal government where it is applicable, to guarantee that the right projects are being done, and being done right, when it comes to sustainable and resilient infrastructure.

Self-Assessing Threats

For many Departments of Transportation (DOTs), reassessing their threat environment began with the September 11, 2001, terrorist attacks. With the transportation networks of the United States, United Kingdom, Spain, and other nations in the crosshairs, DOTs began a variety of initiatives to evaluate their unforeseen risks. Since then, extreme weather events like Hurricane Katrina and Superstorm Sandy, as well societal disruptions like the COVID pandemic, have compelled transportation agencies to continually evolve their understanding of resilience.

As part of the National Cooperative Highway Research Program (NCHRP), WSP was the primary author on a publicly available guidebook of practical, effective methods for measuring risk reduction and increasing broadly defined resilience. The guide, published by the National Academies, was developed specifically to support state and local DOTs as they develop, organize, and launch their resilience plans at the enterprise level. At the core of the guide is an understanding that resilience not only has many different features but is also constantly evolving. WSP's ultimate goal is to mainstream resilience concepts into DOT and agency decision-making.

The guide is primarily a self-assessment tool for transportation officials to evaluate the current status of their agency's ability to improve resilience. The scope of the tool is broad, covering natural and human-caused threats to transportation systems and services. In fact, it is based on a resiliency framework called Framework for Enhancing Agency Resiliency to Natural and Anthropogenic Hazards and Threats (FEAR-NAHT).

At a practical level, the guide consists of 10 steps toward mainstreaming resilience into transportation. The user scores its agency's successes for each step on a scale from 1 to 3. At the end of each step, managers can evaluate the total score to both assess the agency's current transportation resilience as well as identify actions to enhance their capabilities.

The first eight steps largely cover organization, communication, risk assessment, and developing responses. Step 1 is an assessment of what and how effective the agency's current practices are. Step 2 establishes organizational structures, relationships, and protocols. Step 3 offers communication plans that will make the case for climate resilience. Step 4 explains how to implement early wins by identifying resilience strategies and actions that can be implemented quickly and relatively cheaply.

The following three steps zero in on systems-level vulnerability and risk. Step 5 covers the evaluation of the types of hazards and threats likely facing the transportation system. Step 6 delves into fully understanding the likely impacts of these hazards and threats. And Step 7 explores how to determine vulnerabilities and risks in order to prioritize next steps.

With Step 8, the guide turns to a multifaceted process of identifying actions that will improve resilience in both system operations—enhancing emergency response and operations and maintenance—and capital improvements, like assessing exposed assets and integrating the data into asset management. Finally, Step 9 is implementation, followed by monitoring and managing the performance of new resilience measures in Step 10.

The program has been adopted by multiple DOTs. In order to further support mainstreaming resilience into transportation, WSP has also developed and teaches a related training program for the Federal Highway Administration (FHA) and state DOTs nationally. At the core of these programs is embedding resilience by recognizing the dynamic vulnerabilities and risks of transportation infrastructure in a changed future.

Aloha State Resilience

Across various infrastructure segments, climate megatrends are useful for identifying many of the resilience risks faced by companies as well as government agencies like DOTs. In transportation, for example, rising temperatures can soften the bitumen used to seal roads as well as expanding portland cement to the point of rupture, creating ruts, potholes, and even complete road surface failure. More extreme storms eat away coastal roads. Heavier rain and faster wind cause more landslides as well as trees and powerlines falling across streets. More extended and frequent droughts bring worsening wildfires that cut off access and egress routes. At a state or regional level, though, every transportation agency faces its own unique risks.

Hawai'i, for example, has a mild climate, but its highways are flanked by water and crisscross rugged volcanic island terrain. The climate megatrends most relevant to its transportation infrastructure are sea level rise, coastal erosion, wildfires, intensifying storms, and more frequent landslides and rockfalls from heavy precipitation.

To proactively address these hazards, the Hawaii Department of Transportation (HDOT) partnered with WSP to develop the Hawaii Highways Climate Adaption Action Plan. WSP compiled a georeferenced inventory of HDOT's 971 miles (1,562 km) of highway and other assets that are exposed to climate risk to better understand present and future vulnerabilities of the existing infrastructure. This peer-reviewed research included partnerships with local and technical experts from across the country, including HDOT, the University of Hawai'i at Mānoa, the University at Albany, the United States Geological Survey, and the FHA. The resulting report includes the most up-to-date data and literature resources available for Hawai'i and establishes a baseline that can be used as the foundation for a climate and disaster risk assessment and prioritizing future actions.

Going forward, the action plan serves several important functions. In addition to defining the extent and timeframe of changing conditions, it suggests changes to policies and practices to better incorporate resilience thinking into decision-making and infrastructure investment. The action plan specifically prioritizes recommendations in a multiyear implementation plan to take necessary projects from planning to construction in the most impactful sequence.

This same risk assessment and resilience approach that is being applied to roads and bridges can be used across the transportation spectrum—including shipping, aviation, rail, and urban transit. Building climate adaptation and resilience into all these segments—which are critical to our community lifelines and our entire physical supply chain—is essential.

Induced Demand

Assessing risks to transportation infrastructure as well as developing and implementing solutions is essential to provide the thousands of miles of roads and highways that are a baseline assumption of U.S. supply chains and personal mobility. Today, the average American driver uses those roads to drive about 13,000 miles (roughly 21,000 km) a year—a number that, pandemics aside, keeps rising. Americans are also spending a growing amount of time in traffic—an average of 54 hours a year in 2019, which translated to an estimated $166 billion in lost productivity and 3.3 billion gallons of fuel effectively wasted.[22,23]

The traditional way to relieve highway traffic congestion has been adding new highway lanes or constructing additional roads. But as far back as the 1960s, when some states were just getting their first interstates, there has been a debate over whether adding more lanes actually results in a sustained lack of congestion. An economist named Anthony Downs introduced the idea of induced demand, which holds that increasing supply—that is, building more capacity on crowded roads—ultimately won't reduce congestion. Rather perversely, it will instead draw in more commuters until the roadway is congested again.

The work of other urban planners and researchers has supported this theory. One study looked at travel times on the massive Katy Freeway outside of Houston, Texas. In 2008, commuting times on the highway temporarily dropped after it was expanded to 26 lanes.[24] A later study found that times have since risen dramatically. Between 2011 and 2014, for example, the morning commute time increased by 30% and the evening drive time rose by 55%, significantly outpacing the population growth of Houston. Other studies have suggested that, while adding more lanes to congested areas doesn't aggravate the situation, it may only improve it slightly.

Perhaps, instead of making traditional infrastructure bigger—which is expensive; expands the square footage of impermeable, heat-retaining, climate-vulnerable roadways; and may displace residents and businesses—we should make it smarter. Instead of size, we could focus on nimble scale and speed. Instead of providing people with more asphalt, we could provide transportation that is responsive to users' changing needs and real-time conditions.

Intelligent Traffic

Daisy Mountain Drive, a six-lane road bordered by wispy desert bushes and cacti, runs through Anthem, Arizona, a small, residential community just north of Phoenix. Several years ago, it became the test bed for what many experts think will be the future of vehicular personal mobility. The SMARTDrive program is a collaboration among the University of Arizona, the Maricopa County Department of Transportation (MCDOT), and the Arizona Department of Transportation (ADOT). Its goals include reducing crashes, improving pedestrian safety, and allowing truck traffic to move more quickly.[25]

The test track was outfitted with Dedicated Short-Range Communications (DSRC) radios mounted on streetlights. DSRC refers to wireless, short-range communication channels that the Federal Communications Commission (FCC) has dedicated to automotive use. The radio antennae provide communication between specially outfitted Maricopa County vehicles and traffic signal control systems for a real-world test of an intelligent drive system.

County vehicles tested the system during daytime, when most residents were at school or work. A screen inside the vehicle displayed the route and flashed colored symbols for potential hazards that had been staged along the road—an accident, a construction zone, an approaching emergency vehicle. At most intersections, the traffic control system recognized the vehicle and changed the light to green as it approached. When it approached the intersection with a fire truck, however, the display noted that the emergency vehicle would get priority and the light turned red. The U.S. Department of Transportation, which has been studying connected intelligent traffic technology for over two decades, estimates that connected vehicle (CV) technology—which essentially allows vehicles to share and receive data with other vehicles or the infrastructure itself—could reduce unimpaired crashes by 80%.

When the technology was expanded—with advanced traffic controllers, a fiber communication backbone, and integrated signal timing—to several corridors in the Phoenix metropolitan area, data showed a 27% reduction in travel time, even as average daily traffic roughly doubled and the county and its infrastructure continued to grow rapidly.

More recently, Maricopa County Department of Transportation brought WSP in to document the progress SMARTDrive has made to date and lead a concept development exercise to identify possible "Phase 2" opportunities, research national best practices, and conduct a workshop to gather input from partners and stakeholders. The results were two high-level illustrative documents that Maricopa County Department of Transportation can use in garnering ongoing support, new partnerships, and next-generation operational deployments, as well as new and innovative pilot demonstrations. In another part of the United States, WSP is leading a feasibility study for a startup called Cavnue that was selected by the Michigan Department of Transportation to develop the world's most advanced roadway. Appropriately, this segment of I-94 will link Ann Arbor, the home of the University of Michigan, and Detroit, the birthplace of American car manufacturing.

The corridor's design physically resembles a high-occupancy vehicle (HOV) lane separated from the main traffic lane. However, entry into the lane doesn't require multiple drivers, but the ability to share traffic data in real time. Using a communications infrastructure installed by the road, these CVs share a constant flow of driving conditions. Operators—whether robot or human—can use this information to safely travel closer together, and thus more efficiently than non-CVs.

So far, Cavnue has received support from the Ford Motor Company, the City of Detroit, the state of Michigan, and an industry advisory committee that, among others, includes General Motors, Argo AI, Arrival, BMW, Daimler, Honda, Hyundai, Motional, Toyota, and TuSimple. Being on the forefront of real-world CV technological development allows WSP to better analyze and understand technological megatrends that will be relevant to designing the future of resilient and sustainable transportation infrastructure around the world.

Completing the Circle

Across all segments of infrastructure, we know that the right program or project will be sustainable, resilient, equitable, cost-effective, and ideally provide multiple benefits. However, there may be more than one right way to achieve these results. For example, rapidly transitioning to EVs or hydrogen fuel cell vehicles is one way to build a more sustainable transportation sector with fewer GHG emissions.

However, even if GHG emissions and air pollution could be reduced or eliminated by clean cars and trucks, getting around in personal vehicles might still be bad for our health. Longer driving times are linked to higher odds for smoking, poor sleep, obesity, and worse mental health.[26] Multiple studies have linked heavy traffic to road rage and drive-by shootings.[27] The construction of highways has also had negative societal impacts, displacing city residents and sometimes exacerbating racial segregation.[28]

Maintaining a cleaner, smarter version of the current personal vehicle-centric transportation model has advantages—for one, it is the decarbonization strategy that is least disruptive to current transportation options—but it also follows a linear trajectory of limitless expansion. Given the continuing population boom, most of it in already-crowded urban centers, expanding capacity to meet the demands of hundreds of millions of new drivers is unsustainable. To rethink transportation, we need options beyond decarbonizing automobiles.

Instead of this one-way ticket to mega-freeways, mass transit offers a circular approach. Beginning in the 19th century, subways, trolleys, and streetcars provided an efficient way to move large numbers of people around urban areas, usually on a loop or repeated route. The systems were also scalable; when demand increased, more carriages were added without expanding the footprint of the tracks. Although the ridership capacity of mass transit systems is limited, they typically make much better use of urban space than traditional roadways.

Mass transit has also always been deeply enmeshed with equity issues. One of the foundational moments of the modern civil rights movement in the United States was the boycott of segregated seating on buses in Montgomery, Alabama. Today, public transit is essential for lower-income people who don't own cars to go shopping, get to work, visit friends and family, and other personal mobility activities. Public access to transportation will continue to play a pivotal role in creating a just and equitable future.

Today, some mass transit options are being combined with the high-tech efficiencies of smarter mobility like autonomous vehicles (AVs) and CV technologies. This solution provides an interesting hybrid approach to transit systems, while also bridging a digital divide. AVs and CV cars and trucks will initially be available as newer, higher-priced models, meaning lower-income people will be less likely to directly benefit from the technology or investment in the CV infrastructure. Public transit is one way that the advantages of these technologies can be shared more equitably.

In fact, when fully implemented, CV technology can revolutionize mass transit. In bus platooning, multiple CV buses travel much more closely together than would be safe for traditional vehicles. A company called Robotic Research estimated that running platooned buses through the Lincoln Tunnel between New Jersey and Manhattan would enable up to 180 extra buses a day, or additional service into New York City for 10,000 people. CV bus platooning is a massively scalable concept that could alleviate congestion and increase accessibility to rapid transit, especially in rapidly growing and dense cities like Manila, Mumbai, or Baghdad.

Off the Rails

Some cities in the United States are already leveraging these technologies to improve their mass transit options. In the late 1980s, Jacksonville, Florida, built a monorail transit system that eventually ran 2.5 miles (4 km) through the city's core and across the St. John's River. Today, the Jacksonville Transportation Authority (JTA) is rolling out a vision for a new, more responsive service for urban neighborhoods. The Ultimate Urban Circulator is a hybrid solution that integrates the existing, but aging, transit infrastructure with the city's streets. The monorail's existing guide beam was replaced with a smooth surface for the circulator—an electric AV bus—to cover the existing route on the elevated track. Additionally, new off-ramps from the track down to street level allow the circulator to cheaply expand transit into underserved areas. On the street level, the circulator drives in both dedicated transit lanes and in traffic.

With this new technology, the JTA can provide expanded service into surrounding urban neighborhoods—without disrupting their character by constructing expensive raised tracks and stations. Passengers can plan their trips, track the next service, and pay on an app. The vehicles are routed based on real-time demand, reducing wait times. When larger numbers of people are using the service, multiple vehicles can run close together in a platoon. For this project, WSP provided planning, technical support, and visualization services, including high-level graphics and animation used in funding and policy discussions.

During the COVID pandemic, when many public transit improvements were stalled and ridership plummeted, the JTA grabbed a unique opportunity to test its new AV capacity. With no driver on board, the autonomous vehicles were perfect for transporting samples from a drive-through COVID testing site to a Mayo Clinic–operated processing laboratory. Over the course of the trial, the AVs safely transported 30,000 COVID samples with no humans on board. The fully autonomous transport enabled the clinic to protect staff from exposure to the contagious virus and freed up much-needed time during the ongoing pandemic.

A similarly adaptable, low GHG-emissions transit system is being implemented halfway around the world from Jacksonville. Tainan is a rapidly growing city of over 1.8 million located on the west coast of Taiwan. Its population growth, in part due to the thriving semiconductor industry, has caused more congested road traffic during peak hours in the downtown. The city, which is one of the oldest in Taiwan, mixes skyscrapers and major arterial roads with neighborhoods of winding narrow lanes. However, existing public transportation, including bus and regional railway, can no longer suffice to quickly move people around the city. The city also places a premium on enhancing connectivity, environmental friendliness, and livability.[29]

So, when the Tainan City Government engaged WSP to develop a rapid-transit system, the solution had to address multiple megatrends, including urbanization, changing traffic patterns, and lower environmental impacts, while leveraging smarter and ubiquitous sensors and multimodal planning.

WSP's solution was an Advanced Rapid Transit (ART) system for urban passenger transport. The nimble system is based on a series of carriages—the number can be increased and decreased based on real-time numbers of passengers—that travel on "virtual tracks" along city streets. The ART system uses connected autonomous vehicle (CAV) technology—the carriages are equipped with sensors that enable it to automatically navigate its own route.

Other advantages of the system are its high energy efficiency, lower construction time and cost, the ability to adapt with mixed road traffic, better potential of technology localization, and fewer carbon dioxide emissions during the construction and operation phases. Traditional Ground Rapid Transit options usually involve larger structures and more supporting equipment.

As the master planner, WSP also helped the Tainan City Government execute a very rigorous environmental impact assessment (EIA), a report that will be essential to achieving the city's zero-carbon target. Not only will the ART system greatly enhance the city's connectivity, but it will also build the foundation that shapes its development for coming years. WSP is currently developing the master plan for Tainan's first advanced rapid transit line in the East District, now named the Blue Line.

Getting on the Bus

While expanding transit options provides multiple benefits to local communities—from raising property values to providing commuting options—the toxic emissions from internal combustion engines also have negative impacts on public health. Public transportation faced a Catch-22: by serving communities, they were also polluting them. However, the ongoing conversion to low emission and electric buses combines sustainability with equity and public health. Between 2018 and 2021, the number of zero emissions battery-electric buses on U.S. roads or on order has grown 112%.

Purchasing the buses, as well as installing charging infrastructure, carries a large capital cost, but the long-term rewards are huge. The operating and maintenance costs over the life cycle of the bus are significantly lower, the GHG emissions are potentially zero, and the health of residents will be improved. What's more, U.S. transit agencies can cover 80–85% of the purchase price of buses with federal funds. The 2021 $1-trillion infrastructure law has further increased U.S. funding for purchasing zero-emission buses and cleaning up urban areas.[30]

L.A. has one of the most aggressive approaches to creating a large zero-emission bus fleet. In 2017, the L.A. Metropolitan Transportation Authority (L.A. Metro) Board unanimously adopted a motion endorsing a comprehensive plan to transition the agency to a 100% zero-emission bus fleet by 2030.[31] WSP is working with L.A. Metro to create a masterplan with year-by-year schedule for this most ambitious undertaking in the electrification of public transit. It is the largest such commitment to a zero-emissions bus fleet in the United States, and, at 2,300 buses, one of the largest in the world.

Working on behalf of L.A. Metro, and in joint venture with STV, WSP is analyzing L.A. Metro's network of 165 bus and bus rapid transit routes and 12 maintenance facilities, making recommendations for the procurement of a new bus fleet, and identifying modifications at facilities necessary to support the fleet.

One of the key challenges in transitioning to electric buses is ensuring the new system has appropriate battery-charging capabilities. When the Massachusetts Bay Transportation Authority (MBTA) incrementally began transitioning to an electric fleet, transportation authorities initially found that the cold winters were unexpectedly decreasing the batteries' capacity to hold charge. This problem was exacerbated by the additional heating needs of a vehicle that, during winters, frequently operates in freezing temperatures. However, as electric batteries and other technological components have improved, the city has largely overcome those challenges.

L.A. initially ran up against a different problem. The city's electric buses are currently only capable of traveling 150–200 miles (240–322 km), a little shorter than some of the predecessor natural gas buses. As a result, L.A. Metro considered options such as layovers and getting additional buses that could cover the routes.

Two years after WSP delivered a master plan, L.A.'s first electrified bus route was completed—the Orange or G line. Each electric bus also includes public Wi-Fi and USB ports embedded in the seats. The battery charging and range issues were largely solved by rapid enroute chargers installed at three different stations—North Hollywood, Canoga, and Chatsworth—giving the buses all-day operating capability.

L.A. Metro hopes to completely replace its natural gas fleet with its "whisper-quiet" electric buses by 2030. In addition to being critical to the city's efforts at decarbonization, the new electric buses will also target equity goals like reducing disparities in access to job opportunities and improving medical care access and health outcomes due to cleaner air. For example, the Orange Line has 36 stops, of which 20 are directly located in or adjacent to lower income communities across North Hollywood, Valley Village, Van Nuys, Lake Balboa, Reseda, and Canoga Park.

Making Transportation Whole

Transport planners have long focused on optimizing ridership, or throughput, as the primary goal of mass transit. More recently, however, agencies across North America have begun approaching transportation in much broader terms—as a tool to accelerate equity, sustainability, multimodal transport, and public safety.

To help evaluate transportation in a holistic manner, WSP developed a tool for the city of Vancouver, British Columbia, to embed equity into the city's new transportation infrastructure. Designers for a rail line, for example, can evaluate where stops are located, the surrounding communities and their income levels, neighborhood walkability, and existing bus access. Though the unique factors are different for every city, the overall approach of the tools can be applied to any mode of transit. The city of Detroit has undertaken a similar project, mapping the pathways of low-income people around the city, recording the barriers they encounter, and using the data to determine where to invest in public transit.

Another city-wide transportation equity initiative in Detroit is called "Streets for People." The primary goal of the program is to make it easier and safer for people to move around Detroit without cars. A city-wide "slow streets" program includes placing barriers on selected streets, blocking one or more lanes of traffic, and opening up the space to bicyclists or pedestrians. Local traffic may still be able to access areas, but at reduced speed limits. Even if residents aren't encouraged to switch to bicycling for their primary mode of transport, they may be more likely to bike or scooter to a nearby metro station rather than commute by car. The goal of these programs is to provide people with healthier, lower-carbon mobility options, but also to create strong, thriving communities.

The New Jersey Department of Transportation (NJDOT) also took a holistic view of road planning in its award-winning Complete Streets Initiative. This approach shifted the focus of transportation projects from being concerned primarily about vehicle flow to a broader view of all current and potential users of a street. It was guided by the question of how the function of a street is influenced by surrounding land use, economic factors, and travel behavior.

For this project, the New Jersey Department of Transportation partnered with WSP to develop tools and methodologies to design "complete streets." Planners were given design tools to optimize every aspect of sidewalk and street design, from what kind of bicycle racks are best and how to orient them to the best soil mixture for bioswales to inserting parklets into sidewalks to narrowing lane widths to reduce vehicle speed.

Rethinking transportation in terms of assets that promote multiple benefits involves asking different questions like: What value is public transit providing? What mix of public transport is needed? Will expanding micromobility, biking, or e-scooters better serve the community than buses? Do land-use planners, economic planners, and transport planners need to talk to each other more often?

Put a Lid on It

Covering large expanses of highways in urban areas is another solution that can both reduce the historical equities associated with vehicles as well as provide multiple benefits in public health and economic opportunities. Interstate 5 runs up the entire West Coast of the United States from just north of Tijuana, Mexico, to just below Vancouver, British Columbia. In the 1960s, when downtown Seattle was bisected to make way for the interstate, construction displaced about 30,000 residents. The interstate's construction severely disrupted Seattle's street grid, making it more challenging to bike, walk—or even drive across the city. Overpasses exist, but they are loud, dirty, and inconvenient.

Though I-5 remains a critical artery for goods and services, it also continues to have negative community and health impacts that were largely unimagined 60 years ago—before modern environmental impact assessment laws and regulations were created. As with other such urban transportation projects, the highway bisects and separates the pre-existing community and produces greater heat island effects and near constant noise pollution into the surrounding areas, which are lower income than Seattle as a whole.

WSP provided a feasibility study for one solution, what's known as lidding, or covering parts of I-5 in a manner that had been successfully done previously in other cities with WSP support. Traffic flow under the lid was largely unaffected, while the city reclaimed area that could be used for housing, recreation, businesses, and cultural events, among other options. The study presented three different scenarios that considered factors, including varying levels of investment, the total amount of the freeway covered, and the density of development on the lidded area. However, each test case provided multiple benefits, which would be particularly valuable for the 40,000 Seattle residents who live within walking distance of the area.

Maximizing the lid space, for example, could support a large park of about 2 to nearly 10 acres (0.8–4 hectares), providing much-needed downtown greenspace.[32] Not only would this park provide access to nature, a recreation area, and lower the heat island effect, but the soil and plant life would also clean up a substantial amount of stormwater before it runs into the Puget Sound and other waterways.

Grounded by the Heat

On Tuesday, June 26, 1990, airline employees at Phoenix's Sky Harbor airport made an unusual announcement to waiting travelers. Dozens of flights were being cancelled because of the heat. With the temperature hitting a record 122°F (50°C) that day, the planes were grounded until things cooled off.[33]

In a sense, those flights were cancelled by physics. As a plane accelerates down a runway, it achieves lift by pushing air down, which in turn, pushes the wing up. However, at higher temperatures, the air expands, making it less dense and giving the wings fewer molecules to press against. At high enough temperatures, planes would only be able to get airborne by changing other factors, like lightening their payloads by unloading passengers and cargo or lengthening runways to provide more distance to reach a higher takeoff speed.[34]

Ultimately, it turned out that those planes could have taken off without extending runways or kicking off passengers. What really kept them grounded was a lack of data. Every plane has extensive information about the weather parameters in which it can be operated safely. The model of aircraft assigned to these flights simply didn't have performance data for 122-degree weather—no one had thought it was necessary—and so were kept out of the air due to uncertainty about whether they could be safely operated.

This extreme heat-related disruption of service at Phoenix Sky Harbor, the 8th busiest airport in the United States, has since reoccurred multiple times as average annual temperatures have continued to climb. Dozens of flights were cancelled again in 2013, 2016, and 2017. By that time, though, there was expanded heat performance data for aircraft—the manufacturer had determined that takeoffs in temperatures above 117.86°F (47.7°C) were unsafe.[35] After 2017's shutdown grounded 60 flights, though, the manufacturers and regulators looked again at the data and recalibrated it, clearing planes to fly at temperatures of up to 123.8°F (51°C). That recalibration explains why no flights were cancelled on, say, June 17, 2021, when the temperature hit 118°F (47.8°C).[36] But, for Phoenix, it's probably only a matter of time before the 123.8°F (51°C) mark is breached. The city already has over one hundred 100°F (37.8°C) and dozens of 110°F (43.3°C) degree days annually.[37] Eventually, more permanent changes to the fleets or airport operations in Phoenix may be necessary.

Phoenix has one of the hottest airports in the United States, but it is hardly the only airport threatened by climate change. Airports are frequently built on the flattest and most open areas adjacent to large cities, which also often border on oceans and harbors, making them particularly vulnerable to damage and delays from sea level rise. In response to climate risk, San Francisco International—built on a former cow pasture immediately adjacent to the rising San Francisco Bay—is encircling its entire airport complex in a 5-foot-high (1.5-m), 10-mile-long (3-m) wall. Other low-lying major U.S. airports include Oakland, Washington National, Boston Logan, all three major New York City airports, and those in several Gulf Coast cities, including Miami.

At a more systemic level, changes to the jet stream could impact the cost and time of transatlantic flights. Desertification and sandstorms near airports also sends sand into jet engines, where it melts and degrades performance and maintenance. A more exotic, but very real, problem is melting permafrost, which causes runways built on top of previously frozen earth to crack. From 2024 and beyond, Greenland's Kangerlussuaq airport will be closed to most commercial traffic, largely because of permafrost melt damage to the runway. So, what role can aviation play in reducing the GHG emissions that are driving extreme weather globally?

Flygskam

Compared to passenger vehicles, the airline industry produces a relatively small percentage of the world's GHG emissions—about 2.5%—but flying is still the most carbon intensive way to travel per passenger mile. What's more, aviation is expected to double to around 8.2 billion passengers per year by 2037.[38,39,40]

Awareness of aviation's carbon intensity was the primary motivator behind the 2018 *flygskam* (flight shame) movement in Sweden. Activists argued that, to fight climate change, people should opt for other forms of transportation. The movement is credited with reducing the number of domestic flights in Sweden by 9% in 2019.[41] The flight shaming movement was, effectively, another form of climate risk for airlines, joining the potential for carbon taxes, new regulations, and consumer expectations shift toward more low-carbon and zero-emissions performance. It also appears to have played a successful role in encouraging European countries to decarbonize aviation. Unlike the social pressure of flight shaming, however, these countries have simply made some shorter domestic flights illegal.

France, for example, has a nationwide ban on trips where a train journey of two-and-a-half hours or less is an alternative.[42] The banned itineraries include travel between Paris and Nantes, Bordeaux, and Lyon. Austrian Airlines has eliminated trips where a train journey of three hours or less is available, including Vienna to Salzburg. Lawmakers in Spain, Germany, and multiple Scandinavian countries are considering similar bans.[43] The idea is generally popular with Europeans, 62% of whom favor a ban on short-distance flights.[44] However, these measures are more practical in Europe because of the continent's well-developed rail network.

In the United States, where the train infrastructure is much less developed than Europe and several East Asian countries, the same poll reported less support for a ban on short-haul flights, although 60% of respondents did support a carbon tax on air travel.[45] That idea has long been embraced by some companies in the private sector. Among Microsoft's long-running commitments to reducing carbon emissions, the company has charged an internal fee on business air travel since 2012. In 2022, Microsoft redesigned and increased its carbon fee on business travel to $100 per metric ton of carbon dioxide equivalent in order to accelerate emissions reductions and better support the purchase of sustainable aviation fuel.[46]

Despite private and public sector efforts, aviation will be much harder to decarbonize. Because they are such a small piece of an expanding pie, the existing European bans on short-haul flights will have a limited overall impact on aviation's GHG emissions. From a technological standpoint, aviation also faces some steep challenges. Like most of the transportation sector, it is dependent on fossil fuels. However, there is not currently any market-ready equivalent to EVs or hydrogen fuel cell vehicles that can be plugged into the existing aviation model.

Into the Bunker

The maritime segment faces a similar climate dilemma. In the early 20th century, then First Lord of the Admiralty Winston Churchill ordered the British Navy to switch from coal to oil-burning ships. Burning petroleum instead of shoveling coal resulted in all kinds of tactical benefits. Ships could go farther, faster, and they could accelerate and decelerate more responsively. Because oil is more energy dense than coal, the fuel didn't take up as much space—marine fuel is still known as "bunker" from the days when coal was piled in massive rooms aboard ships. The decision was also, completely by coincidence, a small step toward the decarbonization of ship fuel: oil produces less carbon dioxide per unit of energy than coal. Today, oceangoing cargo vessels and ports handle about 80% of global trade by volume and 70% of global trade by value. Maritime shipping provides one of the least carbon-intense ways to transport cargo.[47,48]

Unfortunately, the fuel that 99% of shipping runs on is still far from clean.[49] Marine fuel has worse health and environmental impacts than just about any other fossil fuel, aside from coal. Bunker contains hundreds of times more sulfur than car diesel and produces a massive 15% of global nitrous oxide emissions. Any country with even moderate air quality standards would likely have banned the use of such a dirty fuel years ago on the basis of public health risks. But ships burn most of their fuel on the open seas—outside of the jurisdiction of national environmental agencies. As a result, the GHG emissions of the shipping industry—about 3% of the global total—are not counted in the national emissions of any country. In a perverse loophole, every country could meet its national GHG emissions reduction goals, even if shipping's emissions kept going up.

Despite the many nuanced differences between the two transportation segments, maritime faces many of the same climate change-related challenges as aviation. For starters, climate risk poses physical threats to land-based maritime infrastructure—sea level rise and high winds damage port equipment—as well as operations, with extreme weather like hurricanes and cyclones creating the need for additional cancellations or re-routing of itineraries. Maritime also faces similar transition risk, as corporate commitments, regulatory requirements, investor pressure, and partner and consumer demands are all driving companies to search for decarbonization solutions. Finally, both maritime and aviation are also almost completely dependent on fossil fuels and there are no off-the-shelf technological solutions that can drive steep decarbonization.

In short, despite their many differences, when it comes to managing climate risk, aviation and maritime both face the same macro-challenge: how to decarbonize when your business model is based on large vessels burning fossil fuels to travel long distances.[50] However, the segments may also be able to share solutions for their problems, including accelerating the development of new fuels and technologies, electrifying ground operations, and even rethinking the advantages of scale in favor of integrating some nimbler short-haul operations.

Multiple Pathways

WSP is working with American Airlines to address the challenges of lowering the carbon footprint of its operations. WSP's team looked at American's carbon emissions inventory, conducted an assessment, and helped report it to CDP (formerly the Carbon Disclosure Project). Since then, American has set a goal of net zero by 2050; it has an industry-leading CDP score; it has been included in the Dow Jones Sustainability North America Index for two consecutive years (2021 and 2022); and it is the first airline in North America to set a Science Based Targets initiative (SBTi) goal for greenhouse gas reduction by 2035.[51,52] WSP also helped American Airlines measure and report on climate risk as recommended by the nonprofit Task Force on

Climate-related Financial Disclosures (TCFD) to complete a qualitative analysis of its physical and transition risk and opportunities under multiple climate scenarios.

Although zero emissions airplane technology is still a long way from being viable and commercially available at scale, there are plenty of areas for airlines to increase efficiencies and focus decarbonization efforts. For example, American Airlines embarked on a historic fleet renovation effort in 2014, replacing older planes with newer, more efficient aircraft. Flight optimization software also provides more accurate information about weather and other conditions, so that flight crews can make better routing decisions, saving fuel and reducing emissions.[53]

Airlines can also lower the GHG emissions from their meal preparation and transport, their supply chain, electrify ground handling equipment, and plug into airport electricity to run the air conditioning and heat while sitting at the gate.

The early decarbonization of the shipping industry will also include electrifying its land-based support equipment. These measures are driven by public health concerns just as much as reducing GHG emissions, though. The health of surrounding communities is a major issue for local port authorities in the United States. Depending on prevailing winds, marine fuel sends large amounts of sulfur, nitrogen oxide, and particulate matter into nearby neighborhoods. This toxic combination aggravates asthma, causes chronic lung and heart disease, and premature death—impacts of which disproportionately fall on low-income, minority, and historically underserved communities.

Electrifying the gantry cranes, forklifts, trucks, and other equipment on port terminals reduces some of the air pollution. But attaching ships at berth to shore power—instead of idling their engines—while loading and unloading also lowers air pollution substantially. In the United States, the drive toward electrification has been led by L.A. and Long Beach, California, but it is spreading across to the East Coast of the United States now as well.

The Port of Miami is in the unique Biscayne Bay ecosystem, which includes two state aquatic preserves, a national park, and a national marine preserve, and is near both residential and commercial neighborhoods. The health of people and a diverse range of animals was threatened by toxic air pollution from the port. In response, a WSP team converted five cruise ship berths at the Port of Miami for ship-to-shore power. WSP coordinated efforts among the port, the shipping lines, local power company, and the companies that manufacture the power equipment installed both portside and onboard. Since then, the port has also replaced diesel cargo gantry cranes, uses biofuels in support vehicles, and introduced emissions-reduced electric control systems. The drive to decarbonize maritime will take longer than some other transportation sectors, but efforts to do so will also deliver immediate benefits, including cleaner air and reducing an inequitable health burden on lower-income communities.

Greening the Fleets

Ultimately, the biggest bucket in the decarbonization pathway for aviation and maritime is the challenge of replacing conventional fuels in a cost-competitive manner with adequate commercial availability.

Today, sustainable aviation fuel (SAF) from non-edible feedstocks can reduce life cycle carbon emissions by as much as 80%. When blended with conventional jet fuel at the ratios specified by international technical standards, SAF may be used in existing commercial aircraft without modifying engines. However, sustainably produced fuel isn't cost-competitive with traditional jet fuel yet, nor is there currently an adequate supply for scaled deployment.

Another GHG emissions-free alternative fuel, green hydrogen, has received recent attention as a replacement for both marine and jet fuels, although wide-scale adoption currently faces multiple challenges. For one, hydrogen is very low energy-density, meaning that it needs expanded storage capacity versus traditional fuel. These larger fuel tanks use up valuable shipping or passenger space, hurting the economics of hydrogen. Similarly, scaling up green hydrogen production to anything resembling what is needed to reduce GHG emissions in aviation or maritime will take sustained investment. Today, green hydrogen—the only truly GHG emissions-free hydrogen—comprises about .1% of total global hydrogen production.[54] Green hydrogen is also not cost-competitive with traditional fossil fuels yet.

Airlines are also looking at new forms of propulsion to reduce their long-term emissions over the long term. In October 2022, American Airlines announced direct investment in hydrogen propulsion, as well as innovative distribution that delivers hydrogen in capsules that can be quickly loaded on board.[55] Like SAF, hydrogen is a promising technology, but has a long way to go before it is commercially available at scale.

U.S.-based private sector investment in the technology is growing, in part, driven by the huge financial incentives—particularly tax credits—included in 2022's Inflation Reduction Act. Other companies, including Alaska Airlines, Delta, and Microsoft, have invested in the development of synthetic fuels using green hydrogen and carbon captured from the air that can eventually replace traditional jet fuel.[56] The arc of decarbonization will be longer in some segments, but there are still existing solutions that can be rapidly rolled out to accelerate a green transition.

Decarbonization Hubs

Hydrogen still has potential to play a role in decarbonization even if it never fully replaces marine or jet fuel. For example, it could transform the maritime industry by turning ports into hydrogen hubs. Some ports are, in fact, already designing and building the necessary infrastructure based on projections of a future global hydrogen market. Since Europe will most likely be a consumer of green hydrogen in that future, the Port of Rotterdam in Netherlands is developing infrastructure to import from around the globe, including Latin America, Middle East, North Africa, and Australia.[57] Ports in neighboring Belgium as well as Japan are making similar preparations. In the United States, several companies are investing in building export capacities, establishing a green hydrogen production pipeline and fuels hub at the port of Corpus Christi, Texas.[58]

Both import and export ports can take an integrated approach to this transformation and its decarbonization possibilities. Instead of electrifying port equipment, they could use hydrogen to power cranes and forklifts. The ports could also serve as refueling stations for local hydrogen-powered transport. Green hydrogen hubs could install power plants, providing power to homes and businesses or recharging electric vehicles. Heavy industry that uses hydrogen for energy-intense processes could co-locate at hydrogen hubs. Finally, these hydrogen hubs could serve as multimodal distribution centers, delivering hydrogen via rail, vehicle, or pipeline.

The current interest and investment in hydrogen is also being accelerated by geopolitics. The war in Ukraine has severely tested the resiliency of Europe's energy supply, prompting an urgent and growing exploration in the role that hydrogen will play in the continent's energy future. The targeted integration of hydrogen generation facilities, connected into the existing natural gas system, can repurpose existing infrastructure, expediting decarbonization and reducing the cost of deployment. Existing systems that use natural gas cannot be completely switched over to hydrogen overnight. Enabling technologies need to be adopted and installed. Dual fuel boilers, for example, are capable of providing heat using both electricity or a blend of natural and hydrogen gas. Because of the need to adopt and upgrade certain equipment, localized hydrogen microgrids may be a first step in adoption by servicing a limited number of end consumers with upgraded equipment.

The larger issue is that, in the race to decarbonize buildings, transportation, and other sectors, we need a "yes and" approach. While electrification should absolutely be at the core of our decarbonization approach, we have to recognize the capacity constraints in the utility infrastructure that will slow the process. Transforming the natural gas grid to a hydrogen grid can provide a robust alternative by providing low-carbon fuels to our communities. This hydrogen could then be used to power some vehicles or to fuel boilers when high temperature water or steam is required in buildings, like hospitals, where heat pumps may not be a strong option yet. Hydrogen and electrification can also be complementary. For example, onsite fuel cells could create zero carbon electricity to service electrified buildings.

A similar reinvention of airports is possible through electrification. Many airports have the space necessary to become clean energy hubs, including open areas to site solar panels or other renewables, as well as room for large stationary batteries. As on-demand services and autonomous vehicles reduce the need for large parking lots, more capacity will open up. Some parts of airports could be dedicated to additional renewable production or EV recharging centers. With its large storage capacity, airport energy hubs could also recharge at night when electricity is cheaper. When they produce excess electricity, airports will increase regional power resilience and generate additional revenue. Finally, efforts to electrify will result in cleaner air, improving respiratory and cardiovascular health, especially in communities near the airport. Electrification doesn't have to be a cost to be borne, but an opportunity with multiple benefits. A well-crafted solution toward electrification will create multiple benefits for the airports, passengers, community, and environment.

Straight Up

A major problem with electrical propulsion technology in both aviation and shipping is that conventional batteries cannot produce the same energy per unit of weight as the fossil fuel currently used. Both marine fuel and jet fuel produce far more energy for their weight, or specific energy, than the best electric batteries on the market. For example, EV batteries produce about 250-watt hours per kilogram, while jet fuel has a specific energy of around 12,000.[59] The practical result of this discrepancy is that you'd have to stack an enormous number of batteries in a plane in order to fly a long route in a conventional aircraft. The batteries would weigh down the plane, even after subtracting the roughly 22.5 tons of jet fuel in a fully loaded 737-800. An oceangoing cargo ship faces a similar challenge—a massive tower of batteries would be needed to make a transpacific crossing without recharging.

But if batteries aren't price-competitive—or even possible—as a replacement for jet or marine fuels, maybe we need to change the way we approach the industry model. What if we started with decarbonization as an imperative and then built a commercially viable aviation network around the solutions we need, as opposed to what we've inherited from the past?

For example, multiple startups have begun testing electric planes that aren't just retrofitted into existing aircraft bodies but designed around the batteries. These planes won't replace aircraft ferrying 400 people coast-to-coast any time soon, but they can fly shorter routes with fewer people with substantially lower GHG emissions. The short-haul market is quite large—just under half of all passengers in the United States fly routes shorter than 500 miles (804 km). It is also a market in which electric planes may have an advantage. Using large planes designed for long-haul flights for regional trips is very inefficient. Those aircraft are much more fuel efficient once they are cruising at altitude—takeoff uses about twice as much fuel per hour as cruising. So, on a short flight of an hour or two, the fuel costs are much higher on average. In fact, flying regionally is so inefficient that many airlines have severely limited or eliminated their routes. As a result, a whole network of smaller FAA-licensed airports is under-utilized.

Enter eVTOL (electric vertical takeoff and landing) planes. As their name suggests, the machines can take off without runways like helicopters, making them viable for landing in cities or other dense areas.[60] The designs for existing eVOTLs range from what resembles a small plane sitting on a circular frame with propellers attached, to a massive multi-rotor drone. At present, most models are targeted at replacing helicopters—eVOTL need less maintenance, are quieter, and potentially much safer. The technology is also promising enough that multiple manufacturers, including Boeing, Airbus, Rolls Royce, and Bell, as well as multiple airlines, have invested in or developed prototypes, most of which are in design or test flight stage. Among these carriers, American Airlines has invested in a company called Vertical Airspace that has pre-orders for 500 of its four-passenger eVTOLs, named the VX4.[61] The vehicle has a top speed of around 200 mph (320 kph) and a reported range of over 100 miles (160 km).

eVTOL aircraft have also gained interest from a company that has already disrupted personal mobility. Uber is working on its own vehicle, in part to upgrade multimodal services like New York's UberCopter that takes passengers directly from Manhattan to JFK airport.[62] Many investors see eVOTLs operating in urban areas as a natural use case for autonomous piloting and CV technology, eventually lowering costs and improving safety.

As the rapidly developing technology improves, eVOTLs could plug directly into the larger, existing aviation network. By using smaller regional airports as well as nontraditional sites—tops of buildings or even centrally located open areas like parking lots or playing fields— eVTOLs with capacities of up to 90 people could provide dispersed regional services of 500 miles (804 km) or less, while avoiding the congestion of large airports. On demand aviation would shake up the scaled, centralized network, but it could also make it more sustainable and resilient.

Rescaling Maritime

A similar starting point—thinking in terms of solution we need—can also produce some interesting ideas in how to integrate electric propulsion technology into maritime shipping.

Today's cargo ships are built to maximize scale, piling tens of thousands of containers on ever-bigger ships. But they are also very slow. Largely to reduce fuel costs, cargo ships use "slow steaming," traveling as speeds as low as 11 mph.[63] These modern boats average somewhere around the same speed as the mid-1800s clipper ships.

So, while electric ships can't currently—and may never—replace the massive, lumbering cargo ships that dominate the industry in scale, they can be nimbler and faster. Smaller electric ships that take routes with more stops in order to recharge their batteries are also more feasible technologically. They would have a smaller cargo capacity, but also service the smaller ports that can't accommodate the depth of the biggest cargo ships.

By adjusting their routes, electric container ships could potentially even bring goods on the long trip from Asia to the U.S. West Coast. And, because container ships are often very slow, electric ships with only slightly higher average speeds could theoretically travel from, say, Shanghai to Long Beach in roughly the same number of days.

A direct route between Shanghai to Long Beach is about 6,550 miles (10,541 km). An alternate route with shorter hops—say, Shanghai, Tokyo, Anchorage, Portland, Long Beach—covers roughly 8,150 miles (13,116 km). But, if the electric boat averaged 18 mph, just one mph faster than the container ship, it would cover the distance 17 hours faster. Of course, the electric ship also made three additional stops, so it wouldn't *arrive* at Long Beach 17 hours earlier. But, given how much time is often wasted at backed-up massive ports, the electric ship stopping at intervening smaller ports begins to look like a more viable alternative. In a bid to speed up the recharging process for electric ships, a startup called fleetzero has designed batteries the same size as shipping containers.[64] Ships could use the existing crane infrastructure to swap in pre-charged batteries while berthed.

Beyond eliminating marine fuel, electric ships' more frequent stops at smaller intervening ports may also have other environmental benefits. Today, commercial goods are offloaded from massive ships at large ports and then often trucked long distances to their end destination. However, cargo on an electric ship that made stops closer to the final destination would require less land transportation. Having a smaller, nimbler fleet that isn't reliant on mega-ports would also increase supply chain resiliency. In recent years, backlogs lasting weeks at major ports like L.A. and Long Beach created supply chain backlogs across the United States that led to product shortages and higher prices.

As electric cargo ships get faster and more efficient, the multiple benefits of electrifying maritime trade—better health, zero emissions, low carbon, and a more resilient supply chain—could start to make a lot of sense.

Moving Forward

Transportation is the second biggest emitter of GHG emissions, making net zero targets throughout the sector nonnegotiable. Without rapid decarbonization, the world will not meet any of the 2050 targets essential to avoiding the worst impacts of climate change. But building a more resilient infrastructure is also critical in the face of increasing climate risk and physical damage. We rely on passenger and freight vehicles, subways, trains, ships, planes, and other means of transporting people and goods safely and reliably around the world. Despite the challenges in meeting these interrelated goals, there are multiple, diverse solutions across segments, including EVs, CV and AV technology, electric buses, short-haul flight bans or fees, sustainable jet fuel, tools for assessing transportation system vulnerability, and frameworks for embedding resilience.

While pursuing decarbonization and resilience are the right projects, we also have to do them the right way. Decisions about how to rethink transportation to meet these goals should be informed by factors including early and consistent stakeholder input, evaluation of full life cycle costs, risk assessment, and future megatrends like urbanization, remote work, on-demand mobility, AI, demands for corporate responsibility, EV recharging infrastructure, and the future viability of alternative fuels including green hydrogen.

As much as any other segment of our infrastructure, transportation has always been deeply enmeshed with questions of equity. The designs for transportation programs and projects should be mindful of the historic harm done by previous infrastructure—like highways that physically segregated communities—as well as the potential for positively addressing these issues through expanded transportation opportunities. From lidding highways to complete streets, sustainable and resilient transportation programs and projects can provide a range of co-benefits, including public health, safer roads, and increased economic opportunities. Each individual solution within the broad and diverse transportation sector will vary widely based on different needs, schedules, capacities, technologies, and location. By rethinking what is possible, we can move beyond one-purpose solutions to integrate resilience, sustainability, equity, and multiple co-benefits into our transportation sector.

Notes

1. https://www.inverse.com/article/27562-m.
2. https://www.fhwa.dot.gov/policyinformation/pubs/hf/pl11028/chapter1.cfm.
3. https://www.infrastructurereportcard.org/wp-content/uploads/2017/01/Rail-Final.pdf.
4. https://www.epa.gov/mobile-source-pollution/research-health-effects-exposure-risk-mobile-source-pollution.
5. https://usa.streetsblog.org/2020/10/28/study-how-cars-are-making-us-all-depressed-even-if-we-dont-drive/.
6. https://www.epa.gov/greenvehicles/fast-facts-transportation-greenhouse-gas-emissions.
7. https://www.nytimes.com/interactive/2021/03/10/climate/electric-vehicle-fleet-turnover.html.
8. https://www.nytimes.com/2021/11/09/climate/cars-zero-emissions-cop26.html.
9. https://www.fueleconomy.gov/feg/PowerSearch.do?action=noform&path=1&year1=2022&year2=2022&make=Nissan&baseModel=Leaf&srchtyp=ymm&pageno=1&rowLimit=50.
10. https://www.kbb.com/car-advice/average-miles-driven-per-year/.

11. https://www.smithsonianmag.com/smart-news/biden-administration-allocates-900-million-for-electric-vehicle-chargers-180980776/.
12. https://www.api.org/oil-and-natural-gas/consumer-information/consumer-resources/service-station-faqs.
13. https://www.caranddriver.com/news/a39998609/electric-car-sales-usa/.
14. https://www.forbes.com/wheels/news/j-d-power-electric-vehicle-consideration-study/.
15. https://blinkcharging.com/fact-from-fiction-the-real-reason-why-consumers-dont-buy-electric-vehicles/?locale=en.
16. https://blinkcharging.com/fact-from-fiction-the-real-reason-why-consumers-dont-buy-electric-vehicles/?locale=en.
17. https://www.npr.org/2022/04/29/1095481101/usps-postal-service-gas-trucks-lawsuit https://www.engadget.com/usps-faces-lawsuits-over-gas-mail-delivery-trucks-163723456.html.
18. https://www.engadget.com/usps-faces-lawsuits-over-gas-mail-delivery-trucks-163723456.html.
19. https://electrek.co/2021/12/03/norway-again-shows-all-electric-car-future-closer-than-people-think/.
20. https://www.wardsauto.com/dealers/why-do-young-people-want-ev-because-they-re-cool.
21. https://www.linkedin.com/pulse/envision-certification-10-questions-claude-bourbeau/?trk=related_artice_ENVISION%20certification%20in%2010%20questions%20_article-card_title.
22. https://www.fhwa.dot.gov/ohim/onh00/bar8.htm.
23. https://www.census.gov/newsroom/press-releases/2021/one-way-travel-time-to-work-rises.html.
24. https://www.bloomberg.com/news/articles/2018-09-06/traffic-jam-blame-induced-demand.
25. https://www.wsp.com/en-US/projects/anthem-connected-vehicle-test-bed.
26. https://www.ncbi.nlm.nih.gov/pmc/articles/PMC4049576/.
27. https://www.sciencedirect.com/science/article/abs/pii/S0277953603005677.
28. https://www.sciencedirect.com/science/article/abs/pii/S0277953603005677.
29. https://www.wsp.com/en-GL/projects/tainan-advanced-rapid-transit-system-blue-line.
30. https://www.metro.net/about/l-a-metro-now-running-all-zero-emission-electric-buses-on-the-g-orange-line-in-the-san-fernando-valley/.

31. https://www.metro.net/about/l-a-metro-now-running-all-zero-emission-electric-buses-on-the-g-orange-line-in-the-san-fernando-valley/.
32. https://lidi5.org/feasibility-study/.
33. https://www.azcentral.com/story/news/local/arizona/2020/01/20/why-cant-planes-fly-when-its-too-hot-valley-101-podcast-finds-out/4454460002/.
34. https://interestingengineering.com/why-planes-cant-take-off-when-its-too-hot.
35. https://www.azcentral.com/story/news/local/arizona/2020/01/20/why-cant-planes-fly-when-its-too-hot-valley-101-podcast-finds-out/4454460002/.
36. https://www.azcentral.com/story/news/local/arizona/2020/01/20/why-cant-planes-fly-when-its-too-hot-valley-101-podcast-finds-out/4454460002/.
37. https://www.azcentral.com/story/news/local/arizona/2020/01/20/why-cant-planes-fly-when-its-too-hot-valley-101-podcast-finds-out/4454460002/.
38. https://www.wired.com/2015/11/commercial-airlines-might-get-all-the-emissions-efficiency-they-need-for-free/.
39. https://ourworldindata.org/travel-carbon-footprint.
40. https://ourworldindata.org/co2-emissions-from-aviation.
41. https://www.bbc.com/news/world-europe-51067440.
42. https://www.cntraveler.com/story/how-short-haul-flight-bans-are-transforming-european-travel.
43. https://www.cntraveler.com/story/how-short-haul-flight-bans-are-transforming-european-travel.
44. https://www.eib.org/en/surveys/2nd-climate-survey/climate-action-and-policy-solutions.htm.
45. https://www.eib.org/en/surveys/2nd-climate-survey/climate-action-and-policy-solutions.htm.
46. https://cloudblogs.microsoft.com/industry-blog/sustainability/2022/03/24/how-microsoft-is-using-an-internal-carbon-fee-to-reach-its-carbon-negative-goal/.
47. https://www.wsp.com/en-au/insights/hydrogen-in-maritime-opportunities-and-challenges.
48. https://www.wsp.com/en-us/insights/hydrogen-in-maritime-opportunities-and-challenges.
49. https://www.eea.europa.eu/publications/rail-and-waterborne-transport.

50. https://www.cnbc.com/2022/09/24/how-airlines-plan-to-end-one-billion-tons-of-carbon-emissions.html.

51. https://www.climateaction.org/news/american-airlines-announces-investment-in-hydrogen-projects.

52. https://www.climateaction.org/news/american-airlines-announces-investment-in-hydrogen-projects.

53. https://www.climateaction.org/news/american-airlines-announces-investment-in-hydrogen-projects.

54. https://www.iea.org/reports/the-future-of-hydrogen.

55. https://www.climateaction.org/news/american-airlines-announces-investment-in-hydrogen-projects.

56. https://www.cnbc.com/2022/09/24/how-airlines-plan-to-end-one-billion-tons-of-carbon-emissions.html.

57. https://energy-utilities.com/rotterdam-moves-on-plans-to-become-key-hydrogen-news117614.html.

58. https://www.offshore-energy.biz/port-of-corpus-christi-to-become-green-hydrogen-hub/.

59. https://www.businessinsider.com/electric-planes-future-of-aviation-problems-regulations-2020-3.

60. https://www.wsp.com/en-US/insights/electrification-of-airports-from-landside-to-airside.

61. https://www.smartcitiesdive.com/news/american-airlines-evtol-aircraft-vertical-aerospace/627713/.

62. https://www.uber.com/blog/new-york-city/uber-copter/.

63. https://www.statista.com/statistics/1268217/average-speed-of-ships-by-ship-type/.

64. https://www.fastcompany.com/90738126/this-startup-designed-an-electric-cargo-ship-to-cross-the-ocean.

4

Below the Surface

On June 15, 1849, former U.S. President James Polk died at his home from cholera, just three months after leaving the White House. Though he had been a well-off, healthy 53-year-old when he left the presidency, Polk's death from simple waterborne bacteria was not considered particularly unusual. Cholera spreads through feces-infected water and, at the time, much of the world—including most of the United States—had no modern infrastructure for providing clean drinking water. As a result, waves of infection regularly swept through every country on Earth in the 1800s, killing hundreds of thousands of people annually.

Today, Europe, North America, and other wealthier nations have comprehensive water and wastewater infrastructures, and, as a result, virtually no cases of cholera or any of the other deadly diseases caused by contaminated water. In fact, the modern ubiquity of water infrastructures and other basic sanitation measures in wealthier nations has meant their significant historic impact is often underestimated—or ignored altogether. Between 1860 and 2020, life expectancy in the United States doubled, with similar gains being made in rapidly developing European countries. Today, many people assume this amazing, historically unequaled expansion of human longevity to be most directly attributable to rapid advancements in medical practices. However, the single largest jump in life expectancy in the United States, an extra 22 years, coincided with the 60 years between 1880 and

1940—the same time when modern water infrastructures were built across the country. In the 80 years following 1940, life-saving medical advances such as chemotherapy, polio vaccines, and the widespread use of antibiotics were introduced. However, average life expectancy in the United States rose more slowly over this time than during the great expansion of water infrastructures and public sanitation. In other words, the modern water infrastructures now hidden underground were historically at least as important in expanding life expectancy as the drugs and medical technologies found in modern hospitals.

The importance of clean water is also tragically evident in countries that still have insufficient water infrastructures. Today, a stunning one in four people globally do not have regular access to clean drinking water. As a result, cholera and the other diseases caused by contaminated drinking water are still major public health threats, collectively killing over 480,000 people annually.[1] Providing access to clean water is not an insurmountable problem, though, if we invest the necessary time and money. Many organizations from the private, public, and nonprofit sectors are working to improve water treatment and access in some of the poorest, most water-stressed countries in the world, primarily in Sub-Saharan Africa. To date, these efforts have played a large role in raising the life expectancy in Africa by 10 years since 2001.[2,3]

Unfortunately, these efforts to create healthier communities around the world are now seriously threatened by climate change megatrends. Extreme temperatures, prolonged droughts, and increased flooding are creating new stressors on the planet's water infrastructures. In 2022, for example, historic flooding in Pakistan overwhelmed wastewater facilities, leading to hospitals and health clinics being swamped by patients—many of them children—infected with cholera and dysentery. A severe drought in the Horn of Africa has also dramatically driven up the price of clean drinking water in parts of Kenya, Ethiopia, and Somalia, from 50% to 400%, making it unaffordable to many people, who then have to drink and cook with sources of water that are often contaminated with deadly bacteria.

These same climate megatrends are also stressing the water infrastructure capacities of wealthy countries. Following Hurricane Ian in 2022, for example, rain overwhelmed the wastewater system in Brevard County, Florida, causing sewage to rush out of manhole covers on streets as well as 7.2-million gallons (27.2 million liters) of sewage to spill into a manatee sanctuary. That same summer, drought and heat-waves in the U.S. Southwest dropped water levels in the country's two largest reservoirs to record lows, prompting the federal government to reduce water allotments to states dependent on water from the reservoirs. Among those states, Arizona faces the largest cuts—a full 21% of its yearly allotment.

The risks from climate change megatrends also extend to other critical but largely hidden infrastructures—like power and solid waste management—that are essential for healthy, prosperous, and thriving communities. Wildfires can knock out power lines. Heavy rains block collection routes and can accelerate the deterioration of garbage bags. Extreme weather events like hurricanes stress waste management capacities with tons of single-use emergency equipment—tents, blankets, water bottles—as well as the debris washed from damaged roofs and buildings. The ongoing electrification of transportation, heating, and cooking will strain grid capacity, as will increased demand for air conditioning during heat waves. Replacing fossil-fuel-generated power with electricity from renewable sources like solar, wind, and green hydrogen requires rapid development of new energy infrastructures. Finally, population growth and urbanization will stress all of these infrastructures—water, wastewater, energy, and solid waste. As the destructive impacts of climate change accelerate, we urgently need new technologies, practices, and programs to create critical infrastructures that are smarter and more resilient, while also making them more sustainable.

Sponge Cities

Every year, following heavy rains, billions of gallons of sewage run out of municipal treatment facilities and into Boston Harbor, New York's East River, Seattle's Puget Sound, and other urban waterways around the world. In a worst-case scenario, wastewater might also back up locally, sending sewage into neighborhood streets or even houses. This filthy discharge is not the result of a system failure or engineering gaffe, though, but an occasional feature of the combined sewage systems used in most American cities. Combined sewage means that stormwater, raw sewage, and industrial waste ultimately end up in the same pipes to the same treatment plant. When heavy rains inundate the system, overflowing into water bodies is the safety valve.

When engineers designed these systems many decades ago, very few of them had much, if any, data in terms of the maximum amount of water their systems might be required to manage. Even if they did have such data, they would still build capacity around the historic assumptions of a 3- or 10-year rain event. However, climate change has made these basic assumptions more and more out-of-date. The combination of swelling populations and climate-related extreme flooding has made it more likely that wastewater systems designed one or two centuries ago will be overwhelmed more frequently.

Urban flooding is exacerbated by another aspect of intense urbanization—the largely impermeable ground surface found in cities. As more buildings go up, roads are laid, and green areas paved, the amount of hard surfaces increases. During large heavy rainfall, there is very little permeable ground to absorb it, so most water flows directly to the storm drain, increasing the danger of overwhelming a treatment facility.

To contend with this problem, the Chinese government endorsed a local and decentralized solution as part of its official wastewater policy. "Sponge cities" are a way of reimagining how the urban landscape deals with large amounts of rain. Instead of storm drains and miles of poured concrete pipes, roads or sidewalks are designed to act more like natural settings, built from permeable surfaces that allow water to seep into the ground. Instead of fast-flowing drains, sponge cities favor meandering streams.

According to one study, permeable surfaces are remarkably effective at reducing runoff. In a natural setting, about 50% of rainwater goes into the ground, 40% evaporates, and about 10% runs off into streams. In a densely built-up urban area—one with 75–100% impermeable surfaces like roofs, sidewalks, and streets—only about 15% of rainfall will make it into the ground and 30% evaporates, leaving 55% of the precipitation flowing into stormwater drains, rivers, or other bodies of water. By recreating a more natural dynamic, sponge cities can not only reduce the chances of flooding, but also store the water in the earth to be released in times of drought.

One of the architects and longtime advocates for the plan, Kongjian Yu, claims that even transitioning a small amount of impermeable urban surfaces to a sponge city–like program will have a significant impact. If just 1% of urban land is dedicated to water drainage, he claims, most flooding will be stopped. In the most extreme flooding imaginable, Yu estimates that allocating about 6% of land will mitigate the damage sufficiently.

Green Infrastructure

While the "sponge city" name is novel, many of its practice are thousands of years old. Prior to the installation of large, hardened water management systems, indigenous people around the world respected and adapted to the water's natural pathways. In Aotearoa New Zealand, official government policy is integrating traditional Māori water management practices with its existing modern sewage and waste treatment plants. Part of Māori philosophy holds that polluting water is forbidden, and that water must discharge first to land, where it can be naturally cleaned by plants and soil before reaching waterways. Another preference is for water not to run in a pipe, but open on the surface, a more flexible method that copes with higher flows more easily.[4]

Techniques similar to sponge cities or traditional Māori water management have been applied to modern environments in the United States. and Europe for decades, often under the names low impact development or green infrastructure. Typically, these strategies try to get rainfall into any of a variety of permeable surfaces as soon as possible. For example, green roofs—roofs designed to support soil and plants—can capture the water before it even gets to ground level. In addition to preventing runoff, green roofs create a cooling effect when the captured rain evaporates in drier, hotter weather.

When water flows off a traditional roof, it can instead be directed to a rain garden or other natural service, preventing it from rushing into municipal stormwater systems. Even replacing green lawns with other more permeable landscaping can reduce runoff. While superior to, say, asphalt, most lawns aren't particularly good at capturing water and often require chemical fertilizers or pesticides, which can end up polluting local water bodies. In urban areas without space for rain gardens, streetside bioswales slow and filter water with plants and soil. Even delaying rainfall's entrance to the centralized storm water system makes overflow events less likely, increasing the entire infrastructure's resilience.

Like other nature-based solutions (NbS), green infrastructure produces benefits beyond resilience and sustainability. For example, water that is filtered by ground-covering plants, native grasses, and the earth will be cleaner before it reaches lakes, rivers, oceans, or treatment plants. The urban heat island effect—the tendency of cities to be hotter than surrounding areas—is lessened. Pollinators get new habitats. Rain gardens and bioswales are also more attractive than storm drains, raising aesthetic and property values. Green roofs and bioswales also serve as small-scale carbon sinks, sucking GHGs out of the atmosphere.

Parking Lots and the First Flush

Green infrastructures aren't designed to replace centralized stormwater systems in urban areas. But a well-designed green infrastructure can add redundancy and resilience to a municipal stormwater system. Ultimately, this means local authorities, water management experts, land use planners, and developers working together toward the goal of reducing flooding.

Take parking lots, for example. New commercial and residential buildings are usually required to provide enough parking spaces to avoid traffic spillover into neighboring areas. Unfortunately, most parking lots are paved with asphalt or cement, which increases the square footage of impermeable surface far beyond that of a new building.

In many cases, however, parking lots rarely operate at full capacity. Perhaps reducing the size of the parking lot in order to plant rain gardens and reduce flood risk is a good trade-off. City planners could also require that a certain amount of the parking lot be made of a permeable surface, or that runoff is directed into bioswales. Municipalities can also accelerate a paradigm shift by requiring a certain amount of green infrastructure from any new development and provide funding or incentives for it.

San Diego was one of the first regions in Southern California to apply green infrastructure principles to its roads. With its dry, sunny climate, San Diego doesn't often suffer from flooding. When a heavy rainfall does come, though, the resulting runoff carries months of accumulated dust particles, automotive oil from streets, cigarette butts, wrappers, and bacteria into the ocean, a phenomenon known as first flush. In California, the rainfall in the beginning of a wet season contains up to 20 times the pollutant concentrations as rainfall at the end of the wet season.[5] San Diego's climate magnifies that first flush into a filthy deluge that keeps swimmers out of the ocean for days following initial rainfalls.

In order to limit runoff and improve water quality, San Diego County and WSP developed a Green Streets technical guide, standard drawings, and specifications to help planners and staff understand what is expected, permitted, and what can be approved for redevelopment or retrofitting of existing paved surfaces. Illustrations and text outlined technical details about, for example, bioswales, permeable pathways, graded shoulders, and the different uses for engineered, structural, and native soils. The first targeted project is a stretch of semi-rural roadway in the county, which will have a bike lane, drainage swales, and a 6-foot (1.8-m) wide graded parkway added as part of a larger improvement project. Rethinking urban design holistically can provide multiple benefits beyond water management, including increased access to nature, recreational opportunities, and aesthetic improvements.

Reclaiming an Urban Shoreline

Lincoln Park sits on the west side of Jersey City, in the middle of one of the most densely populated urban areas in the United States. It's bordered by bridges crossing the Hackensack River, trucking depots, and factories. When WSP first became involved in a project to restore tidal wetlands and create one of the few waterfront public access points to the Hackensack River, the area was filled with over 250,000 cubic yards (190.000 m³) of illegally dumped debris. Today, it is a large expanse of clean, restored wetlands, complete with walking trails and recreational areas.

In times before modern wetland protections, many people viewed marshes as unproductive land, or associated them with mosquitos and disease, all of which made it that much easier to justify draining and paving them over. Now, most people recognize and value wetlands as productive and sophisticated ecosystems, but the integrated technical skills used to restore them need to be as diverse as the wetlands.

The project to restore Lincoln Park began with coordination between Hudson County, New Jersey Department of Environmental Protection (NJDEP), and the U.S. Army Corps of Engineers. NJDEP received funding for restoring the marsh as an offset for other environmental damage. The plan was not just to create a tidal marsh, mud flats, and a network of flood channels, but also to connect Lincoln Park to the urban landscape—bringing nature to a largely paved environment. The restored marsh would provide multiple benefits, as a carbon sink, recreation area, natural habitat, and more resilient shoreline.

Not only do marshes support all sorts of wildlife, including serving as stopovers for migrating birds and breeding grounds for shellfish and fish, but they also come in different varieties. At lower elevations, where the land becomes more inundated with water for longer durations during tidal cycles, the makeup of vegetation is different from high marsh where the periods of inundation are shorter. Working with the client and stakeholders, engineers, biologists, and others had to decide what kind of marsh they wanted to rebuild. With so much input into the project, the design process was iterative.

For example, biologists and surveyors gathered bio-benchmark data from a healthy marsh, surveying where healthy target vegetation is growing. Then they could apply that data to model and design in the project's specific conditions. Marshes also need to have water move in and out in just one tidal cycle. Water resource engineers evaluated how big a channel was needed to move that much water—without making the marsh too exposed to the Hackensack River.

However, all this data was based on present conditions. Designers also had to consider what the marsh would look like in the future. For example, how much would sea level rise impact the habitat at the marshland? Water levels would clearly be rising, but the intent was to design a system that relies on the natural processes of the marsh to raise its level through accretion—possibly enough to avoid permanently inundating the marsh.

In addition to surveyors, biologists, water resource engineers, and other specialists, construction contractors had important roles to play. Before the project was over, roughly 300,000 cubic yards (230,000 m³) of clean sand dredge spoils from the Hudson River Estuary would need to be placed as the wetlands substrate to serve as a clean pallet for the restored habitat. This added a communication and education challenge. Often, construction contractors have more experience laying down asphalt than restoring wetlands. Maneuvering around mucky wetlands in a heavy truck is a completely different job.

Another restoration challenge was pollution. At one point, work hit a creosote hotspot. Geologists and environmental engineers had to sample the area and figure out how to manage its disposal without slowing down the rest of the production. The timeframe left little room for delays. While biologists had selected the vegetation and plants most appropriate for the environment, the flora could only be planted in certain seasons.

A pedestrian walkway was built on the upland meadows, providing recreation around the fringe of the wetland. This project required adapting other technical skills—geologists and geo-tech engineers are often more accustomed to putting in bridges for highways than a pathway.

In the end, this integrated approach and coordination between the county, state, local contractors, and WSP biologists, engineers, surveyors, and other experts resulted in the restoration of more than 42 acres (17 hectares) of tidal habitat, including high marsh, open water, and mud flats. To restore tidal flushing, over 4,000 linear feet (1,219 m) of new inter-tidal channels were carved into the restored marsh plain. Walking trails and interpretive signs were established along the perimeter of the marsh. In addition to removing polluted infill from the shorelines of the Hackensack River, the Lincoln Park Wetlands restored fish spawning habitat and supported an effort to establish more resilient coasts in the face of climate change.

The Lincoln Park Wetland Restoration Project also won a Coastal America Partnership Award, which recognizes outstanding projects that make a significant contribution toward the restoration and protection of the coastal environment of the United States.

A Storage Breakthrough

While nature-based solutions can be invaluable for increasing the resilience of stormwater systems and cleaning up polluted urban runoff, a climate-change–related resilience challenge in the beach town of Destin, Florida, was solved by reusing natural resources as well as more conventional engineering.

Destin is a tourist destination that sits on a barrier island in the Gulf of Mexico, just off the northern panhandle. Over the past 40 years, the gulf-facing side of the island has become tightly packed with condominiums, hotels, and motels. The population more than triples during the busy spring and summer tourist season, a population spike that puts a significant strain on local water resources.

For decades, Destin's drinking water came from drilling into an enormous aquifer over 400 feet (121 m) below the island, but growing demands eventually made that situation unsustainable.[6] Over-pumping the groundwater aquifer could lead to several serious negative impacts—beyond simply running out of water. First, over-pumping causes land subsidence, or sinking, effectively accelerating the sea level rise that already threatens Florida's coastal regions. Second, as the water level gets lower and the pumps work harder, the operation can suck salt water into the freshwater aquifer. The Florida aquifer system doesn't have an impermeable skin. It's carved out of limestone and bordered by ocean water. Salt water even flows hundreds of feet beneath the aquifer. Limestone is also very porous, so when enough suction is applied from pumping wells, the ocean water will flow through the aquifer's walls and contaminate the freshwater, eventually making it unsuitable for drinking or irrigation.

To avoid the over-pumping scenarios, Destin Water Users (DWU), the local utility, took several measures to make its water supply more resilient.[7] First, DWU capped the amount of water they were pumping from the immediate Destin area and began piping in more water from a well further inland. They also educated the residents and hospitality staff about how to reduce water usage. The measures have been successful enough that water usage has dropped even as the permanent population grew. With less water being pumped from nearby, the coastal wells are refilling, reducing the chance of subsidence

DWU's other big water-saving initiative was to use wastewater for irrigation purposes. The 7.5-square-mile (19.4 km^2) island has a state park and two golf courses, which require substantial water if the owners want to keep the links green. By switching its irrigation from freshwater to reclaimed wastewater, DWU could save large amounts of potable water for the residents, tourists, restaurants, and hotels that need it.

The wastewater reuse initiative was also successful, but it faced a seasonal problem. When wet weather returned, the golf courses and other parts of the island didn't need to be watered. As a result, DWU ended up with millions of gallons of reclaimed wastewater that it couldn't use. There was practically no undeveloped land for DWU to send the excess water and disposing of it into the ocean was not permitted for environmental reasons. Injecting the reclaimed wastewater into a deep well was feasible technically, but prohibitively expensive. There was, however, a fourth option, the one that DWU pursued.

Aquifer storage and recovery systems, known as ASR, allow users to store water in an aquifer for later use. During Destin's wet seasons, DWU could store excess reclaimed wastewater in shallow sand and gravel aquifer about 115–170 feet (35–51 m) below layers of quartz, sand, and clay.[8] Then, during drier weather, the water would be recovered for irrigation. Because it was considerably shallower than the aquifer, the ASR storage zone couldn't contaminate the drinking water supply. About 250 feet (26 m) of limestone, clay, and sand separated the wastewater storage from the drinking water aquifer.[9]

Storing excess water to reuse when it's needed was a sensible and elegant solution, but nothing like the Destin ASR project had ever been built before in Florida. As a result, it faced an uphill battle to be permitted. Even though the wastewater was not used for drinking, the low level of solids in the water meant the water had to meet the Florida Department of Environmental Protection treatment and disinfection standards because the water could end up being used as drinking water.[10] This additional level of scrutiny would have made the ASR project prohibitively expensive. However, WSP helped the Destin Water Users to get a variance from the state for its innovative storage program.

Like similar infrastructure projects, Destin's ASR system took years to complete, but WSP assisted DWU along the whole path, from the initial pilot testing system to the groundbreaking permitting process, along with construction, operational testing, and later, system expansion. Today, numerous other localities in Florida are using the system pioneered by DWU and WSP to make better use of the state's natural water resources.

As the Earth's atmosphere continues to heat up, the climate megatrends of drought and extreme precipitation events are projected to increase, increasing strain on our critical wastewater and drinking water infrastructures. However, rethinking these challenges by using nature-based solutions and innovative engineering can not only improve the resilience of our existing impermeable and centralized water infrastructures, but also provide immediate local benefits like additional green space, cleaner oceans and rivers, increased biodiversity, recreational opportunities, and access to nature.

The Future Is Electric

The electrification of everything—cars, water heaters, airports—has become one of the primary pathways toward decarbonization and meeting global net zero goals for companies, cities, nations, and other organizations. But electrification also yields public health and equity benefits. For example, burning fewer fossil fuels means cleaner air, which, in turn, reduces heart and lung conditions, asthma attacks, and even premature deaths. These improved health outcomes will disproportionately benefit marginalized communities, which are more likely to be located near major sources of dirty fossil fuel pollution like ports and highways. Mass electrification in the United States has also created millions of new jobs. In 2021, there were three million renewable energy positions in the United States.[11] Many of these jobs—installing solar panels, wind turbines, or electric heaters—can't be outsourced. Increasing production of electricity with renewable local or regional sources also improves nations' energy security and resilience by reducing dependency on international fossil fuel markets.

Due to technological advancement and heavy investment, electrification will continue to provide benefits into the future. From the moment it's purchased, the carbon footprint of a fossil fuel-powered water heater, furnace, or car is pretty much locked in. Anything powered by electricity, however, will continually reduce its GHG emissions as the energy grid decarbonizes. If a company or organization begins powering their electrical devices with photovoltaic panels or purchases of green energy, those devices become functionally net zero.

In short, electrification broadly meets all our criteria for the right program. It is sustainable, resilient, equitable, cost-effective over a life cycle, and has additional community benefits. As the infrastructure and storage needed to fully integrate renewable energy into power grids, it will have additional cost benefits as well. In 2020, the International Energy Agency called solar "the cheapest electricity in history."[12] Today, however, most countries' power grids are far from decarbonized—in 2020, only about 20% of electricity generation came from renewables like hydro, wind, solar, and biomass. The good news is that we have most of the technology we need to create a largely decarbonized power grid—it's more a matter of funding and installing that technology.

Land and Sea Power

Siting is one of the interesting challenges of scaling up production of renewables. Large solar and wind installations on land are often located in pristine or ecologically delicate areas, meaning they need to be designed without endangering habitats. WSP is investigating the expanding field of what's known as "agrivoltaics," ground-mounted panel placement on farms. Placing panels on fields where sheep graze keeps down maintenance costs because sheep provide low-carbon vegetation control. In return, the area can be planted with tailored seed mixes that are suitable for pollinators and sheep. The constant shade provided by solar panels can, in turn, be used to grow edible mushrooms. Additionally, condensation from the panels can provide drip irrigation for crops. Though there is potential for co-benefits at alternate sites for solar power generation, researchers are still studying possible potential negative impacts to the local ecosystem.

Water-based renewable production avoids these specific ecological concerns, but can run into other obstacles. Off-shore wind—turbines located in water—is expected to be one of the main sources of additional renewable energy. However, the United States is well behind other countries, including China, the United Kingdom, Germany, the Netherlands, and Denmark, in developing installed capacity. One project, slated to be the first large-scale offshore wind farm in the United States, was planned for development off the coast of Nantucket, Massachusetts, in 2001. However, the project, known as Vine Wind, ran into a variety of political and personal opposition as well as financial setbacks. In 2016, it was finally cancelled.[13]

Today, the United States' first utility-scale wind farm is finally rising out of the Atlantic, roughly 50 miles (80.5 km) from the proposed site of Vine Wind. Known as Vineyard Wind, after nearby Martha's Vineyard, Massachusetts, the project will capture the area's high wind speeds to generate around 800 megawatts of electricity, enough to power about 400,000 houses. The lower carbon emissions resulting from the project will be equivalent to removing 325,000 cars from the roads, making electricity both cleaner and cheaper in the area. WSP provided design of the turbine foundations as well as the permit compliance tracking and construction management for the offshore-to-onshore export cables.

Vineyard Wind also developed an agreement with three environmental groups—National Wildlife Federation, National Resources Defense Council, and Conservation Law Foundation—to protect the critically endangered North Atlantic right whales. Among other actions, Vineyard Wind will adjust its turbine construction around the whales' annual migratory schedule and invest $3 million to study and develop technologies that can help safeguard marine mammals.[14]

At least eight U.S. states are committed to buying over 20 GW of offshore power through 2035, creating an urgent need to scale up domestic capacity that includes the development of training programs.[15] Vineyard Wind can be a pioneering example of the right project to meet these needs, but also how to do it the right way.

Storing the Sun and Wind

Though the technology and adaption of renewables have improved rapidly, one of the biggest criticisms of renewables like solar and wind is still true. There is still a big demand for power when the sun isn't shining, and the wind isn't blowing. Any future powered by renewables will rely on large amounts of electricity storage to even out peaks and troughs in supply.

This isn't a new problem for renewables. Hydropower, by far the largest source of renewable energy in the United States and the world, sometimes has to balance out seasonal shifts in water availability, a situation exacerbated by heavy rain events, extreme temperatures, and droughts. One time-tested solution is pumped hydro, which uses excess electricity to pump water back up to a higher reservoir. When demand rises—or water levels are low—the water can be released to generate additional electricity.

As solar and wind production scale up, renewables will produce more energy than can be used immediately. Pumped hydro isn't a likely or efficient storage solution for this electricity. Likewise, lithium-ion batteries, which are used in EVs, are unlikely to be able to provide sufficient renewable storage capacity either. Meeting organizational net zero goals—decarbonizing the operations of cities or companies—will require much larger storage options.

One potential future solution for renewable energy storage sits beneath the flat farmland near Brazoria, Texas, just a few miles from the Gulf of Mexico. Thousands of feet underground are the massive, abandoned salt mines where Chevron Phillips once stored large amounts of hydrogen. The voluminous, out-of-the-way mines make perfect storage spaces because, in its gaseous state, hydrogen's energy per volume is many times less than fossil fuels, meaning it needs large spaces. Today, the increasing amounts of investment flowing to hydrogen storage is expected to expand the market from $13.8 billion in 2022 to over $119 billion in 2027.[16]

Ultimately, these storage facilities are intended to be filled with green hydrogen, the only totally GHG emissions-free version of hydrogen. While other types of hydrogen are made using fossil fuels, green hydrogen is produced by using a direct current—generated from renewable electricity—to break water down into oxygen and hydrogen. The hydrogen gas—light, odorless, tasteless, and very flammable—can be captured, stored, and later burned to drive turbines without creating any greenhouse gas emissions. Although some energy is lost in the electrolysis process, hydrogen gas can hold energy longer and more efficiently than lithium-ion batteries.

Of the U.S.-based hydrogen storage projects, none is bigger than the ACES Delta clean energy hub. Sitting 130 miles (209 km) south of Salt Lake City, Utah, the hydrogen storage facility will consist of two large salt domes with a combined holding capacity of 11,000 metric tons (12,125 U.S. tons). The storage facility is adjacent to a coal-fired power plant that is being transitioned to a hydrogen-capable natural gas plant. Beginning in 2025, the plant will begin production with a mixture of 70% natural gas and 30% green hydrogen that will incrementally transition to 100% green hydrogen by 2040. Owned by the L.A. Department of Water and Power (LADWP), the facility is a critical part of L.A.'s ambitious plans to run its city on 100% renewable electricity between 2035 and 2045. WSP is providing a variety of services for the ACES Delta project, including engineering, procuring, construction management, and assisting with environmental compliance and permitting.[17]

Sharing the Wealth

There are other utility-scale methods for evening out the natural ebbs and flows of wind and solar power generation. Island nations like Great Britain and Ireland connect their grids to each other—and with continental Europe—using High Voltage Direct Current (HVDC) networks. Connecting grids to multiple energy sources increases the resilience of the overall grid, but it can also expand the amount of renewables in national grids, helping organizations meet sustainability and decarbonization goals

Both Great Britain and Ireland produce large amounts of wind energy—in 2019, 21% and 37%, respectively. Like other wind-producing countries, however, they have to increase their reliance on fossil fuels when the wind goes slack. By sharing peak renewable production between countries, both can reduce their reliance on fossil fuels.

In a simplified example, a weather front blows across the islands from west to east, generating higher production in Ireland first. But Ireland is only about 170 miles (273 km) wide. When the front passes through, the country's turbines will no longer generate as much electricity. By then, however, the front will be moving across the United Kingdom, generating additional high wind energy. However, if Ireland and the United Kingdom could share their peak wind production across the roughly 450 miles (724 km) combined width of their countries, they will effectively be expanding their renewable supply and distribution networks—while avoiding the need to store excess energy.

Eirgrid, the Irish transmission system operator, is now building one of Western Europe's longest such interconnectors.[18] Stretching 360 miles (579 km), the HVDC system, known as the Celtic Interconnector, will run from Ireland to Brittany, linking the Irish electricity system to the broader European network. The project will be challenging not just because of the length of the cable, but also because it runs under French, Irish, and British territorial waters. Ultimately, the Celtic Interconnector will help cut energy prices, providing extra sources of supply resiliency, and another market for renewables. WSP is currently serving as technical advisors on the project.

Across the United States, a similar sharing scheme would cover over 2,000 miles (3,218 km), which could be extended to other renewables. For example, peak solar production is 11:00 a.m. to 4:00 p.m., but if electricity production was shared across the four U.S. time zones, that five hours of peak productivity could be expanded to eight.

Lessons in Resilience

Power grids in the United States—there is no true national grid—are relatively well developed, but as the country shifts toward more renewables, the current network will be increasingly stressed by additional demand from EVs, heat pumps, convection stoves, and water heaters. In February 2021, much of the United States, as well as parts of Mexico and Canada, got a naturally occurring stress test—a severe winter storm with record cold temperatures that killed around 250 people.[19] Texas's power infrastructure—including wind turbines, but, more importantly, natural gas facilities—experienced serious failures in the extreme weather and were unable to meet a spike in demand from electric heaters. For over two weeks, millions of Texans had to endure rolling blackouts and the resulting food and water shortages. However, the event did provide some hard lessons about how to better prepare for a future with both higher demands for electricity and historically unpredictable weather.

While most of the United States and Canada are interconnected by either the Eastern or Western Grid, Texas has run its own power grid for decades. The state grid is primarily an effort to avoid regulators—as long as electricity doesn't cross state lines, it can't be regulated by the federal government. In 2011, for example, Texas experienced serious power outages problems during a cold snap. Following the event, a federal agency made suggestions on how to winterize the equipment, but it had no enforcement authority. Most of Texas chose not to follow the federal suggestions. However, El Paso, which is connected to the Western Grid, invested in implementing the federal government's recommended changes. As a result, El Paso didn't suffer any of the blackouts during the severe weather of February 2021.

The costly and deadly impacts of the storm on the state power grid presented a classic example of the risks of underestimating life cycle costs in favor of lower capital costs. Texas saved money upfront by not following regulators' suggestions to make its equipment more resilient. But this emphasis on low cost over reliability was a major factor in the huge cost of the storm's damage, estimated at up to $300 billion.[20] This total cost to the state was just slightly less than the combined damage of the two most expensive hurricanes on U.S. history, Harvey and Katrina.[21] Some of these costs are, in turn, being passed on to residential customers of Texas' grid. Customers saw their rates rise significantly—some doubling—in the year following the storm. Taxpayers will also likely be paying about $10.5 billion to cover utility-related debt—gas and electricity—or as much as $921 for a single customer. Ratepayers in all-electric homes didn't have to pay the gas utility debt, though.

If put under enough stress, any power grid will experience similar failures. As climate, societal, and other megatrends accelerate the risks to our electricity infrastructure, we need to assess these threats and mitigate the possibility of catastrophic failure. We can develop more coherent policies toward strengthening the grid, including additional investment to make the grid more reliable. To disperse generation and reduce GHG emissions, we can also invest in allowing the grid to accept additional renewables.

Thinking Small

Some types of buildings in Texas were less likely to lose power during February 2021, including hospitals and other critical services like fire or police departments, as well as self-contained districts, like college campuses and business parks. This resilience was largely because they were on their own microgrid, which allowed them to detach from the failing larger grid with their own sources of backup power. Smart microgrids can enter what's known as "island mode" in which they operate independently from the central grid. This process can be automated by software that detaches when it detects a failure in the larger grid.

While they can be powered by any source electricity, microgrids are particularly compatible with developing sustainable, resilient renewable supplies. The software in smart microgrids can also manage the system to meet goals like efficiency, leveraging the lowest energy costs, or using the highest level of renewables. It could also analyze weather forecasts to make decisions about likely solar production capacity or future energy needs for heating. WSP designed a microgrid for Las Positas College in Livermore, California, that stores excess solar power by diverting it to batteries. During the hot and sun-drenched summer, the grid also uses excess power to make ice, which is used to cool buildings during the night. The smart microgrid also reduces peak power and balances energy loads to increase efficiency, saving the school roughly $100,000 annually.

If Texas had been made up of strategically deployed microgrids—not just for critical facilities, but apartment building or neighborhoods—it would likely not have experienced such widespread power failures, which could have saved lives, and reduced the strain on hospitals.

Organizations that power themselves off a clean, smart microgrid can make accomplishing sustainability goals much easier, especially for those companies located in states with a dirty energy mix heavily reliant on fossil fuels. Microgrids can also be designed to increase demand diversity. Linking, say, office and residential buildings, could smooth out peak energy use, which typically occurs during the day at an office and during evenings at home.

One of the smallest states in the United States, Vermont, has gone big with the microgrid concept. Green Mountain Power (GMP), which supplies power to 75% of the state, is moving away from scale—long transmission lines and big generators—in favor of a sustainable, resilient decentralized model.

GMP's energy mix is 100% carbon-free and 78% renewable, most of which is hydro.[22] However, as the utility grows its mix of solar, wind, and other more variable renewables, it needs to be able to meet peak power demands. To that end, part of GMP's decentralization program includes leasing large Tesla Powerwall battery backup systems to homeowners at a rebate. In exchange, homeowners agree to allow the utilities to draw on the stored energy when necessary to cover peak demand. GMP is effectively building resilience into their renewable grid with hundreds of storage sites dispersed in garages and basements across the state. But the system also builds resilience and other community benefits into the system. If snow brings a tree down onto a powerline during winter, for example, the lights will stay on in nearby communities as they draw from their own microgrid of Powerwalls.[23]

The electrification of everything is a huge, ongoing program that will provide many benefits in terms of sustainability, cost-effectiveness over a full life cycle, and public health. However, it requires a resilient electricity infrastructure that is capable of withstand the changing and more extreme impacts of climate change. Networks also need to integrate additional renewables. These transformations can be enabled, at least in part, by two seemingly contradictory approaches. One is to go big—like employing large-scale wind farms, increased power sharing internationally, and massive hydrogen storage facilities. The other is to pursue smaller decentralized projects—employing smart microgrids powered by renewables that provide resilience through redundancy and dispersion. Rethinking our electrical infrastructure will include evaluating and integrating the full range of solutions.

A Journey Begins

There doesn't seem to be anything profound about tossing a plastic drink bottle into a recycling bin, but it's the beginning of a long, multistop journey with a huge impact on the Earth. In fact, just the act of placing a recyclable item in the proper container is somewhat rare—70% of recyclables end up in landfills. After making it into a recycling bin, the bottle travels along with cardboard boxes and empty cans of pet food in a large, probably diesel, truck to a sorting facility. There, the water bottle is laid out on a conveyor belt with all the other items from the recycling bin. Magnets, blowers, and tumblers work alongside some humans to separate the various recyclable items from the rest of the material. About 50% of what goes into a recycling bin ends up in the landfill because it isn't recyclable. This rejection rate is so high because of poor education efforts on what is actually recyclable, a confusing labeling system on plastic, a lack of investment in infrastructure, changing guidelines in each city and state, and a mismatch between what we want to be recyclable and what actually is recyclable.

Ultimately, metal, glass, cardboard, paper, and the plastic water bottle—the most valuable materials—are sorted and separated. In the case of the bottle, the next steps are likely being crushed, baled, and shipped along with thousands of other water bottles to a specialized facility. Then the bottles undergo the final processing—a cleaning liquid melts the paper label and cap off, followed by shredding, washing, and drying. Finally, the bottle ends up as little plastic balls called nurdles that could theoretically be used to make another plastic bottle. However, most plastic bottles are made from virgin plastic, so the nurdles are more likely to end up in carpet, textiles, the lining of winter jackets or inside a stuffed animal. After they are either down-cycled or end up in landfill, a plastic bottle's component pieces will probably last for hundreds of years, outliving its consumers and any of the facilities it passes through.

Other post-consumer journeys are shorter—like everything that ends up in a landfill—or fraught with confusion. For example, despite their labeling, biodegradable and compostable food containers usually can't be recycled and normally aren't composted properly—they must be processed in high-temperature industrial facilities. While there have been some steps toward making recycling easier in the United States, the total percentage of recycling has stagnated at around 30% for years.

Ideally most products would be part of a circular economy that maintains their value for as long as possible instead of the linear trajectory of "make, take, use, and dispose." Like buildings, wetlands, or transportation infrastructure, consumer products should be viewed as valuable assets. But changing our approach to waste must start well before a water bottle gets tossed in a recycling bin. Ultimately, the most important end-of-life decisions are made by designers in the very earliest phase of the product's life. Apparel, for example, can incorporate used textiles or plastic into its materials. Food packaging can be made of materials that can easily be recycled. Cars can be designed to have fewer types of plastic, making recycling easier.

Waste is also an equity issue. Generally speaking, the wealthier the country, the more waste it produces. Many poorer countries end up importing that waste, especially plastic, which litters their beaches and roadsides, and rests in huge mounds on the outskirts of cities, transmitting diseases and causing respiratory issues. Megatrends like population growth and the rising spending power in developing countries—which gives more people the ability to buy more plastic goods—point toward the urgency of rethinking how we approach solid waste management.

Rethinking Waste

The first step toward reducing waste might be semantic—not calling used products waste, but assets, materials, or resources. Microsoft has several major sustainability goals, like being carbon negative and water positive for the entire company by 2030. Just as ambitious, though, is its pledge to achieve zero waste for its direct operations, products, and packaging by 2030. To accomplish this, the Microsoft Circular Centers are reframing "e-waste" as end-of-life assets.

The Microsoft Cloud has grown exponentially over the past few years. It is supported by millions of servers and other hardware spread across 140 countries. Each server has, on average, a lifespan of five years. To responsibly approach the end-of-life for this potential e-waste, Microsoft created Circular Centers, a dedicated space co-located within its data center facilities. The Circular Centers receive used hardware and servers from data centers, decommission, and disassemble it. Some components are harvested for spare parts, others are donated to local schools or end up in other consumer goods. The first Circular Center was launched in Amsterdam in 2020, the program has expanded to six Circular Centers in Europe, North America, and Asia. By 2025, Microsoft expects 90% of its servers and components within regional data centers will be recycled or reused.

Microsoft has also shifted toward design for repair on some of its consumer Surface devices. New Surface designs can be repaired by professionals or everyday consumers using Surface replaceable components, while following Microsoft instructions outlined within the Surface Services Guides found on Microsoft's Download Center. Products like the new Surface Laptop 5 can also be repaired using common computer repair tools. Combined, these new designs for repair features can help prevent devices from ending up in landfills. Microsoft Surface YouTube channel hosts videos of the disassembly of certain Surface Laptop products.

Lifting all Boats

The modern infrastructures designed to manage water, wastewater, power, and solid waste can be hard to see, but they are the foundation for building healthy and productive places to work, play, and thrive. However, they are under increasing stress from megatrends including population growth, urbanization, electrification, and multiple types of extreme weather. Embedding resilience and sustainability in these hidden infrastructures is essential for wealthier nations to maintain their standard of living. However, similar innovations should also be used to provide clean water, electricity, and reduce waste in the many countries of the world where modern infrastructures are either insufficient or don't exist.

While the hot, arid Middle East is home to the most severely water-stressed countries on Earth, Africa is home to a group of nations with the lowest levels of access to clean water.[24] The importance of sanitation and water infrastructure is driven home starkly by the challenges of the residents of Kibumba Island.[25] Kibumba is located in Lake Victoria, Tanzania, one of the biggest bodies of freshwater in the world. However, the water is polluted with viruses, bacteria, and schistosomiasis, which kill about 200,000 people a year. What's more, the local geology doesn't allow for drilling productive wells. As a result, residents of an island surrounded by fresh water get most of their drinking water in bottles that are shipped over on boats.[26] Once they are consumed on the island, the plastic water bottles become a waste problem—they are either thrown away, littering the land or lake, or incinerated, producing toxic fumes.

However, combining natural resources with adaptable technology provided solutions for all these issues. A photovoltaic microgrid was installed on the island to power a pump that passed water through filtration. The system provided multiple solutions—sustainable electricity, clean drinking water that reduces incidents of waterborne illnesses, and reduction of plastic bottle waste. Not only was a sustainable water source provided, but the water was estimated to produce water at lower cost than any other source. Rethinking how we design, deploy, and maintain these critical hidden infrastructures can provide immediate benefits around the world, as well as long-term sustainability and decarbonization.

Notes

1. Falk, J., Globisch, B., Angelmahr, M., Schade, W., Schenk-Mathes, H. "Drinking Water Supply in Rural Africa Based on a Mini-Grid Energy System—A Socio-Economic Case Study for Rural Development." *Sustainability* 2022, 14, 9458. https://doi.org/10.3390/ su14159458.
2. https://www.macrotrends.net/countries/AFR/africa/life-expectancy.
3. https://news.un.org/en/story/2022/08/1123972.

4. https://www.wsp.com/en-US/insights/water-new-zealand-applies-maori-philosophy-to-21st-century-challenges.
5. https://pubmed.ncbi.nlm.nih.gov/15491663/.
6. https://www.nwfdailynews.com/story/news/2018/12/22/where-does-your-household-water-come-from-how-is-it-treated/6567606007/.
7. https://www.wsp.com/en-NZ/insights/destin-water-aquifer-storage-and-recovery-system.
8. https://fwrj.com/techarticles/0218%20tech%203.pdf.
9. https://fwrj.com/techarticles/0218%20tech%203.pdf.
10. https://fwrj.com/techarticles/0218%20tech%203.pdf.
11. https://www.weforum.org/agenda/2022/07/renewable-energy-jobs-us/.
12. https://www.weforum.org/agenda/2022/07/renewable-energy-jobs-us/.
13. https://www.power-technology.com/analysis/vineyard-wind-delayed-project-reveals-bluster-in-uss-offshore-wind-ambitions/.
14. https://renews.biz/51138/vineyard-wind-commits-to-whale-protection/.
15. https://www.power-technology.com/analysis/vineyard-wind-delayed-project-reveals-bluster-in-uss-offshore-wind-ambitions/.
16. https://finance.yahoo.com/news/global-hydrogen-energy-storage-market-194500321.html.
17. https://www.wsp.com/en-au/news/2022/aces-green-hydrogen-underground-storage-project.
18. https://www.irishtimes.com/business/energy-and-resources/french-connection-eirgrid-looks-to-build-1bn-power-line-to-france-1.4621745.
19. https://www.texastribune.org/2022/01/02/texas-winter-storm-final-death-toll-246.
20. https://www.keranews.org/texas-news/2022-02-16/cost-of-last-years-winter-storm-could-reach-300-billion-new-report-says.
21. https://www.keranews.org/texas-news/2022-02-16/cost-of-last-years-winter-storm-could-reach-300-billion-new-report-says.
22. https://greenmountainpower.com/energy-mix/.
23. https://time.com/6082973/vermont-electric-grid/.
24. https://lifewater.org/blog/how-many-countries-dont-have-clean-water-top-10-list-and-facts/.
25. Falk, J., et al., "Mini-Grid Energy System."
26. Falk, J., et al., "Mini-Grid Energy System."

5

In the Big Apple

CITIES ARE GHG emissions hot beds. Urban areas account for a little over half the global population, but 75% of global GHG emissions.[1] Cities also face a disproportionate amount of climate risk and vulnerability. Their large, densely clustered populations make the potential human and economic toll of local climate disasters much higher. Extreme temperatures, drought, hurricanes, or storm surges that hit a city will, on average, displace, injure, or kill far more people while creating larger economic losses than a similar event in a less-populated area. But while cities play an outsized role in driving the climate crisis and have greater vulnerability to its impacts, many cities are also leaders in climate action—often going further than national governments in their climate commitments and programs.

Every part of the Earth faces climate risk. But, in many ways, the successes of our global and organizational sustainability journeys will be largely contingent on the actions of the people, companies, and governments packed into less than 3% of the Earth's surface.[2] What's more, the impact of cities will continue to increase. By 2050, cities are expected to be homes for nearly 7 in 10 people on Earth, further increasing their environmental toll, climate vulnerability, and environmental responsibility.[3] As a result, the paths taken by cities like London, Shanghai, Chicago, Lagos, and L.A. to build more resilient, sustainable, Future Ready communities are critically important for all of us. While this chapter specifically focuses on just one mega-city, New York, many other cities are facing and addressing similar challenges, solutions, and opportunities.

How the Subway Went Underground

In 1888, a powerful blizzard hit the U.S. Northeast. It left up to three-story snowbanks in Brooklyn, shut down the New York Stock Exchange, and paralyzed the rapidly growing city's infrastructure. Ice brought down electrical and telegraph lines. Elevated train service was literally frozen for days. In a few hours, the largest city in the United States was effectively cut off from the rest of the country. Local leaders promised quick action to make sure the same damage couldn't happen again, by promoting what we would call resilience today.

One of their first steps was requiring that utility wires be placed underground. At the time, Manhattan was blanketed by a thick mesh of wires belonging to multiple telegraph, electrical, police and fire departments, a stock ticker, and even burglar alarms.[4] In January 1889, newly sworn-in Mayor Hugh J. Grant publicly harangued the utilities for not undergrounding their wires quickly enough. In mid-April, he made good on a promise to chop down utility poles regardless of whether the wires had been removed, a decision that left some parts of Manhattan in darkness.[5] Though crude and possibly illegal, the city's swift undergrounding of the wires demonstrated how quickly certain types of resilience can be achieved when there are no perverse incentives blocking action.

The next step to safeguard the city's infrastructure was to get the trains in Manhattan underground, a move that became the origin of the city's subway system. (Boston had the first subway system in the United States, a project that was also driven by damage from the same winter storm.) One of WSP's founders, William Barclay Parsons, was responsible for the design and construction management support for the Interborough Rapid Transit lines, or IRT, New York's original subway line. By the early 20th century, utility lines and trains were weaving underneath the most densely populated part of the city, providing a vital service to the world above.

Over the following century, those investments in resiliency served New York City well, protecting important parts of its essential infrastructure from high winds, snow, and ice. Today, however, New York City is adapting to different, and more severe threats. The subway system, for example, was built for winter storms, not Hurricane Sandy's massive coastal storm surge. In fact, it was uniquely vulnerable to the deluge. Not only are many subways stations and tracks below sea level, but ocean water leaves behind a salty residue that inflicts corrosion-related damage for years after the waters recede.

By the time Hurricane Sandy had passed, every subway tunnel under the East River was filled with seawater—as were many subway stations, particularly in Lower Manhattan. For days, the only trains on the tracks were pump cars sucking water out of the network. Service between Manhattan and Brooklyn was disrupted for weeks while damage was repaired. Sandy-related damage cost the New York City Metro Transit Authority (MTA) roughly $5 billion.[6] The situation, and a very real possibility of a similar event in the not-too-distant future, was clearly untenable. As in 1888, it was time to radically rethink the resilience of the city's infrastructure.

Hold the Line

In 2015, WSP led a post-Sandy study for the New York City Transit Authority (NYCTA), a division of MTA that assessed and analyzed the overall resilience of the subway's systems and services. Since flooding is a global issue, the study explored what was being done abroad to understand how all major transit systems in the world deal with similar threats. The Tokyo Metro, for example, manages a huge network in a city that was built on a coastal plain surrounded by rivers. To build in resilience, the transit system is designed for 1,000-year events like tsunamis or typhoons that could flood underground concourses up to 33–49 feet (10–15 m).[7]

Because of sidewalk-level space limitations, Tokyo Metro had to design unobtrusive resilience measures. One initial line of defense for the subway is a simple aluminum water stop plate, installed by hand at the top of subway entrances to block floodwaters These plates, however, would only prevent a moderate flooding event from inundating the stations, so Tokyo Metro also designed metal-flood doors that seal shut. To avoid disrupting pedestrian traffic and concerns from nearby retail stores, Tokyo Metro had to develop a variety of custom-fit

solutions, including just about every type of door imaginable—
including bi-fold, swing, overhead, counter-pressure sliding, and
retractable shutters.

Inside the network, large doors are capable of closing across the
tracks where they pass above ground. One massive, thick, circular door
designed to prevent flooding inside the system resembles the front of a
bank vault. Tokyo Metro also installed anti-flooding mechanisms for
the street-level ventilation shafts that can withstand up to 6.5 feet
(2 m) of water pressure, although in the most flood-prone areas, the
mechanisms can withstand up to 19.5 feet (6 m) of water.

Metro Taipei, located in Taiwan, has addressed its frequent flooding issues—in 2001, a typhoon filled the subway system with 7.5 feet
(2.3 m) of water—with some lower-tech solutions.[8] For example, all
entrances to the metro are required to be raised above the surrounding
street level and at least 6 inches (15 cm) above a 100-year flood event,
a sort of permanent version of sandbagging. To prevent more extreme
flooding, entrances also need to have floodgates that reach 19.6 inches
(50 cm) above 200-year events.[9]

Designing flood resilience for the NYCTA started with understanding its vulnerabilities, which, in turn, meant gathering data outside of the subway system proper, including coastal defenses and the
likely inundation of surrounding streets. City-wide resilience measures
might include solid harbor-facing barriers, nature-based solutions
along coastlines or inland stormwater management measures. The vulnerabilities of these measures would, in turn, help determine NYCTA's
different risk levels from location to location, as well as the relative
impact of loss of service.

As in other cities, solutions to these vulnerabilities had to include
New York's specific, unique surroundings. Certain solutions, like rip-
ping up the subway system and rebuilding it to meet the new specifications of a changing climate, were not options. Even more modest
measures like rebuilding street-level subway entrances with protective
barriers might block pedestrian traffic or nearby retail and office space.
Resilience could also not be based on keeping the whole network dry
during events. (In fact, the subway is never really dry. Thirteen million
gallons—49 million liters—are pumped out of the system even on days
with no precipitation.)[10] Instead, the subway needed a nimbler flood
hazard mitigation and risk-based systems approach.

Like many other systems, NYCTA uses multiple types of barriers to stop flood water from entering the stations or flowing freely along tracks. One solution is a flexible, black fabric cover made from Kevlar and waterproof mesh.[11,12] These covers can be stored in a metal box at one end of street-level entrances and then rolled out, completely sealing an entrance in a few minutes. At least 70 of the covers, which can support up to 16 feet (4.9 m) of water, have been installed at the most vulnerable entrances.

The NYCTA has also installed passive automated shutters to prevent water entering from sidewalk-level ventilation shafts. When the ventilation shafts are covered, the subway won't have adequate ventilation, making it unsafe to use. By protecting the infrastructure, however, the subway can return to servicing riders more quickly.

When water breaks through the first two lines of defense and gets onto the tracks, rapidly inflatable tunnel plugs that act like massive airbags can block the inflow of flood water between stations.

In the past few years, New York's subway system has faced stress tests in the form of historic rain and flooding. In August 2021, for example, Hurricane Henri set a record for New York's heaviest rainfall in an hour, nearly 2 inches (5 cm) fell in Central Park. A few weeks later, the remnants of Hurricane Ida again brought very intense precipitation to Central Park and many other locations across the city. That summer was also New York's second wettest on record, providing a real-life test of resilience measures that had been deployed after Hurricane Sandy.

During the worst rain and coastal surge events, some layers of protection were overwhelmed. Streets were inundated and stairwells turned into rivers. The subway system itself experienced some flooding and disruptions to service, but nothing like the long-term paralysis caused by Hurricane Sandy. Train service was only disrupted in a few parts of the city and for much more limited periods of time, with faster returns to service and less long-term damage with freshwater rather than saltwater intrusion. The programs and projects that protect New York City's subway system will also continue to change and adapt—in a rapidly changing world, no solution is permanent.

Though these agile and ever-expanding set of technologies are primarily driven by resilience, protecting the transportation infrastructure always brings additional benefits. For example, subways are electric, so they create no on-site dirty emissions and produce fewer GHG emissions than just about any other form of transit, except walking or cycling. One analysis found that driving emitted three times as many GHGs as subways per passenger mile.[13] In addition to promoting sustainability, resilient subways provide local communities with reliable mobility options. This benefit is particularly important for lower-income people who don't have personal vehicles and can't easily afford private services like taxis.

On the Ocean's Edge

A picturesque collection of one and two-story houses with sandy yards, Breezy Point is a unique community located on a spit of land between the Atlantic Ocean and Jamaica Bay. Just 22 miles (35km) from Manhattan, the area resembles a vacation town found much farther away. Breezy Point started as a summer holiday spot for primarily Irish immigrants, some of whom stayed the summer in tents. Though houses have replaced tents over the years, the neighborhood has retained its Irish-America population; the area is sometimes known as the Irish Riviera. However, Breezy Point shared at least one problem with Manhattan—massive flooding. The area's infrastructure has improved over the years, but the neighborhood still has no centralized stormwater management. Parking lots and other flat, impervious surfaces were regularly inundated after summer thunderstorms, forcing residents to wade through ankle-deep water in grocery store parking lots.

In 2012, Hurricane Sandy hit Breezy Point hard. An enormous storm surge swept in from both sides of the thin spit of land. Some residents who were trapped by rising waters drowned in their homes. An electrical short caused by the surge also started a fire that spread to neighboring houses. The fire department was unable to respond immediately due to flooding. When they did arrive, over 100 houses had burned to the ground. By the time the storm passed, about 20% of the houses in Breezy Point had been destroyed by rainwater and more than half had sustained water damage.

Following the storm, then New York Governor Andrew Cuomo and the Dormitory Authority of the State of New York (DASNY), which manages properties and projects for the state of New York, funded measures across the state designed to improve resilience, including flood-proofing. To ensure strong community input and engagement, the governor's office also created a network of local organizations—including churches, community centers, synagogues, libraries, senior centers—to form the New York Rising Community Center Program. Breezy Point was selected for multiple projects, partnering with WSP on several prevention measures.

The highest percentage of deaths during Hurricane Sandy—as well as many other extreme weather events—occurred in and around homes. To reduce fatalities and damage, some resilience programs fund homeowner relocation and the wholesale removal of homes and other buildings in flood zones. Other programs raise buildings above flood levels. To be effective, though, designers first need to determine the base flooding elevations—the level to which floodwater is anticipated to rise during a 100-year storm event.

As part of an award-winning study, WSP developed home elevation and urban design guidelines. To encourage community input, WSP produced charts that simplified dense information about, say, complex and high uncertainty methods for calculating required elevation to avoid future flood damage. Technical drawings and 3D modeling tools also helped community members visualize how their choices of architectural standards would affect their community. Feedback from residents and organizations informed design guidelines, helping to retain the close-knit neighborhood's unique character while embedding resilience into the future of its housing.

In another Breezy Point flood resilience project, WSP developed master plans to improve stormwater management. Significant amounts of water pooled in parking lots and streets after heavy rains. Managing that water brought several challenges unique to Breezy Point, which is essentially a giant sandbar. The topography of the land—very flat—meant that water falling on impervious surfaces tended to collect in pools as opposed to draining off. The sand that covers most of Breezy Point soaks in water quickly, but it doesn't retain the rainfall like soils that absorb and then slowly release the moisture.

WSP developed several solutions for the terrain, the first of which was building dozens of bioswales around flood-prone parking lots, giving the water a place to pool and either evaporate or runoff more slowly while reducing nuisance flooding. The project also targeted three ballfields and their parking lots for flood mitigation, combining resilience and community benefits. Sustainable landscaping and pedestrian improvements were installed, and a sprinkler park was added near a playground.

The project also required an integrated approach, with a wide range of WSP technical experts playing roles. Environmental scientists tested the local soil for contamination before any construction began to see if it could be reused on-site or to be disposed of off-site. Water resource engineers did modeling and grading design. Geotechnical engineers calculated infiltration rates for the sprinkler park. Plumbing engineers designed piping for the sprinklers. Electrical engineers worked with local utilities to provide site lighting, including adding light poles. Biologists determined what native plants would thrive in Breezy Point's sandy soil to enhance biodiversity. Finally, cultural resources experts were involved in assessments and permitting associated with historical resource preservation.

In 2021, soon after construction was finished, the remnants of Hurricane Ida hit the New York area with diminished winds but very intense inland flooding. On Breezy Point, unlike some other parts of the city, the projects passed their cloudburst performance tests. The water went where it was supposed to go—and people had dry feet walking through parking lots to their cars. The parks held the water, reducing street runoff and pooling. Building resilient communities can take many different forms, from large sea walls to raising houses to dune protection to bioswales. Among other things, selecting the right program involves inclusive input, community engagement, and an understanding of local conditions as they exist today as well as how they will change in the future.

Oysters to the Rescue

The exposed south shore of Staten Island was another of the most hard-hit areas of New York during Hurricane Sandy. In addition to causing extensive property damage, the storm killed 24 people on the island. In water-front Tottenville, waves pulled houses right off their foundations—in one case killing two people. However, the extent of the damage also brought attention to the degraded and neglected state of the natural environment around Staten Island. Though some leaders proposed a conventional sea wall, there are potentially destructive environmental repercussions to cutting off natural waterways like the Hudson River. Moreover, sea walls are very expensive throughout their life cycles. Instead, a visionary alternative approach caught on, one that involved returning to New York's past.

By some accounts, New York City was once the oyster capital of the world. Some biologists estimate that New York Harbor contained half of the world's oysters at one point. Since then, a combination of over-harvesting, dredging for shipping channels, and pollution decimated what had been large stocks of mollusks the size of dinner plates. The loss of the oysters, which are also natural water filters, was a further blow to the area's water quality. The habitat loss for other animals was also expansive, as the nooks and crannies of oyster reefs shelter all sorts of aquatic species.

Oyster reefs have an additional, sometime overlooked benefit too. When intense storms like Sandy hit, the reefs absorb some of the wave energy that would otherwise directly hit the shoreline. Just like the roots of trees and other plants stabilize soil, oysters are hard, natural barriers that protect shorelines from erosion. Reefs also reduce the height and force of waves before they reach places like Staten Island. Of equal importance, oyster reefs can naturally rebuild when parts are broken loose during a major storm.

Following Superstorm Sandy, the federal Department of Housing and Urban Development (HUD) launched a project called "Rebuild by Design" to seek sustainability and resilience solutions. WSP was a key part of several Rebuild by Design projects, including an interdisciplinary team led by SCAPE Landscape Architecture that successfully proposed a nature-based solution for Staten Island called "Living Breakwaters." The program envisioned a necklace of offshore breakwaters that would reduce coastal erosion, revive ecologies, connect the community to the Staten Island shoreline—and breed oysters. One of the group's other members, the Billion Oyster Project, has restored 75 million oysters in New York Harbor to date.

The interdisciplinary group spent years on research, shore walks, oyster pilot programs, hydrodynamic modeling, and community planning meetings. WSP was specifically tasked with the in-water geotechnical engineering analysis and design of the living breakwaters, which included designing a large-scale model of the project in an Olympic-sized swimming pool. WSP also supported the community engagement effort, including the siting and design for the Water Hub, an on-land space for visiting groups, recreational activities, and educational programs.

Like other nature-based solutions, the Living Breakwaters programs seamlessly combined resiliency and sustainability, while providing additional community benefits like encouraging residents to reengage with their ecology, cleaning up water, and providing habitats that increase marine biodiversity in New York Harbor

Honoring a Vision

Shirley Chisholm, the first Black woman elected to Congress, represented Brooklyn's Bedford-Stuyvesant community from 1968 to 1983. She has since been honored with tributes, statues, and a U.S. stamp. But the creation of her namesake park in a once-neglected part of Brooklyn's shoreline has an even longer history.

What is now Shirley Chisholm State Park sits on Jamaica Bay, just a few miles west of JFK Airport. The area was designated as parkland soon after World War II, but in the following decades it instead became a dumping ground for solid waste such as demolition debris, and, later, municipal rubbish.[14] In a 1983 study, residents of the nearest buildings, a public housing development called Starrett City, showed above average levels of respiratory illnesses. Though tragic, the findings were relatively unsurprising given that toxins, including DDT, asbestos, acid, cyanide, and dichlorobenzene had been dumped in the landfill for years. After decades of municipal use and illegal dumping, the landfills were capped in the early 2000s.

Over a decade later, WSP supported the cleanup of the site in preparation for finally delivering the park promised in the middle of the previous century. This project again required integrating a wide range of capacities, including site investigation, environmental permitting, monitoring programs, and guaranteeing that the excavated soil was handled properly. The team also needed to create a design that ensured the landfill cap would be preserved and that the new park wouldn't encroach on existing wetlands.

During the project, more than 1.2 million cubic yards (917,000 m³) of clean soil—enough to fill nearly 100,000 dump trucks—were imported and placed on the capped landfill.[15] Then, 35,000 trees as well as other plants and native grasses were installed to enhance resilience as well as biodiversity. WSP also coordinated with a diverse group of regulatory agencies and key stakeholders to limit the permit requirements and accelerate completion of the complex project.

In July 2019, the first half of the park opened to the public, giving the community an opportunity to interact with a previously buried natural world. A bicycle library loaned free bikes for rides to picnicking sites and waterfront facilities. Other visitors walked the miles of trails that extend 140 feet (43m) up the side of a landfill—one of the highest points in New York City. Others brought fishing poles or just rolled up their pants and walked to the edge of the saltwater marsh, which houses a huge array of aquatic and terrestrial wildlife.

While the community benefit of natural access was the primary driver of the park's revitalization, flourishing coastal estuaries are also very effective carbon sinks, which play an important role in reducing GHG emissions.[16] Capping landfills, like the two in Shirley Chisholm State Park, also reduces the emission of planet-warming biogases like methane.

Rain Catchers

Excluding Antarctica and Greenland, just .45% of the world's surface is impervious to water.[17] However, a very high percentage of that water-resistant land is in mega-cities like New York City, exacerbating some of the worst impacts of climate megatrends. Instead of absorbing rain, impermeable surfaces like streets, sidewalks, and rooftops create high runoff volumes and velocities that drive erosion and overwhelm water management systems. The stormwater backed up into streets naturally flows downhill into basement apartments, subways, road underpasses, tunnels, and other subsurface infrastructure. There are few better examples of a systemic urban ecosystem collapse than the combination of heavy rainfall and impervious surfaces shutting down subway systems, blocking the access of emergency responders, and potentially sending sewage into nearby bodies of water.

Fortunately, there are number of simple and nature-based techniques to repair this ecosystem. Among them is New York City's rain barrel giveaway program. Attaching the barrels to a building's drainpipes delays the impact of rainfall on storm management. In drier weather, watering lawns or gardens with nonpotable water also reduces strain on water services.

Impervious surfaces are also a primary driver in creating urban heat islands, the tendency of population-dense areas to be hotter than surrounding areas. This effect isn't just limited to the hottest days in a year, but also drives a measurable climatic difference for cities. While average temperatures are rising around the world, the urban heat island effect means that cities heat up at a faster rate than surrounding regions. For example, in a scenario in which the temperature of the region of Argentina around Buenos Aires rises 2.2°F (1.2°C) between 2000 and 2100, Buenos Aires itself would heat up by an average of 4.3°F (2.°C).[18]

Buenos Aires is one of more pronounced examples, but the same dynamic holds for New York City versus surrounding greener areas, as well as Central Park. In a thermal scan, all of Manhattan shows up as yellow or red, except the long, well-defined rectangle of blue in the middle of the island.[19] Trees lower temperatures in Central Park even compared to immediately surrounding areas of Manhattan—even across the street from a park entrance. The trees also significantly reduce the level of particulate matter pollution inside the park while removing roughly one million pounds (450,000 kilos) of carbon dioxide every year.[20]

To mimic Central Park's nature-based adaptability, New York has launched thousands of multi-benefit green infrastructure projects that not only lower heat-island effects but mitigate flooding and enhance biodiversity. In 2022, the city also published a new rule regarding how stormwater is managed on new and redevelopment sites, with the goal of reducing runoff before it becomes unmanageable.

The first impervious surface that a significant amount of stormwater hits is not sidewalks or streets, but roofs. Preemptive water capture is a technique that building owners can use to reduce flooding locally—near their properties. It also benefits the larger city by reducing stress on stormwater systems and reducing the urban heat island effect. On top of New York City's largest convention facility, the Javits Center, is the largest water-capturing green roof in the city. As part of the team on the building's recent renovation, WSP upgraded the mechanical, electrical, and pumping systems to improve indoor air quality, reduce ambient noise, and save on energy consumption—improving the building's overall impact on its natural systems around it. The improvements included 100 rooftop air handling units installed on the completely new green roof.

There is, however, still plenty of room for green roofs to proliferate in New York. The Nature Conservancy estimates that out of a total of 40,000 acres (16,000 hectares), only 60 acres (24 hectares) of New York City's rooftop space is green. Installing soil mixes and plants on top of buildings isn't the best resilience solution in every case—due to engineering, regulatory, and other issues. However, the rooftop green infrastructure has other financial benefits over its life cycle. Several studies have found that buildings with green infrastructure have higher retention and rental rates. One study, which looked specifically at the Battery City Park neighborhood west of the financial district, found that rents in buildings with green roofs were 16% higher on average.[21]

Paying the Price

New York has a unique GHG emissions mix. Its per capita emissions are the lowest of any other U.S. city, largely due to the lifestyle differences of dense urban living. Heavily reliant on the biggest transit system in the United States, residents are more likely to walk or take mass transit than drive. As a result, only 21% of New York City's GHG emissions come from on-road transportation, significantly lower than the U.S. average.

Heating smaller houses or apartments also generally uses less energy than larger, free-standing houses. Nonetheless, as a percentage, buildings are far and away the biggest source of greenhouse gases, emitting 71% of New York City's total. Of that, 40–60% comes from building operations such as heating, hot water, steam generation, cooking, and other activities that often use natural gas or other fossil fuels.

In 2019, the city council passed the Climate Mobilization Act, also known as the Green New Deal. Broadly speaking, the act's goal is to reduce New York City's emissions 40% by 2030 and 80% by 2050.[22] It does so, in large part, by requiring certain energy efficiency upgrades on buildings larger than 25,000 square feet (2,322m^2), or two or more buildings that are on the same tax lot and have a combined square footage of over 50,000 square feet (4,644 m²). Its main tools to reduce energy use are the off-the-shelf but effective—energy efficient lighting, electric appliances, and retrofitting some buildings with better insulation. These are the sorts of solutions that need to be rolled out at scale rapidly in cities around the world.

The law also includes strong enforcement mechanisms. For example, owners of buildings that don't meet targets will be fined $268 per ton of carbon, a price that is more than twice even the top end of national carbon taxes.[23] New York's law also includes additional fines for not filing reports, exceeding limits, or making false statements. The Climate Mobilization Act also contains other requirements, including mandatory green roofs or solar photovoltaics on some buildings, but the dramatic reductions in greenhouse gas emissions from apartments, hotels, commercial space, and other large buildings are the most important.[24]

There are always built-in, long-term advantages to thinking in terms of life cycle costs. For example, buildings that achieve LEED certification retain their value longer and have lower vacancy rates. But the Climate Mobilization Act amplifies this reality for all stakeholders in the real estate market. For example, fines established by the law are calculated based on a building's carbon footprint.[25] However, buildings that were initially built to high energy efficiency standards will not be subject to most or all the fines—without making any further investments in energy efficiency upgrades.

Though the initial burden for compliance falls on owners or landlords, those expenses can be quickly passed on to tenants. As the act's provisions become increasingly strict through 2050, the issue of future compliance—or noncompliance—will become a critical factor in real estate transactions. For purely financial reasons, investors, sellers, purchasers, lenders, and other stakeholders will be forced to consider an asset's life cycle costs.

The law will also compel real estate business decisions to be seen through the matrix of climate risk, including the potential transition risk of all property assets. If the impacts of climate change accelerate or reduction goals are not being met, the Climate Mobilization Act may become stricter, or expand to the emissions of smaller properties. If the act is successful, it will likely serve as an example for other cities.

On the other hand, buildings that exceed energy efficiency standards may develop a new revenue stream—selling credits to noncompliant buildings.

The law will also grow the market for new buildings that meet high energy efficiency standards. Among the new green buildings that WSP worked on as structural engineer is Hudson Commons in Midtown Manhattan. The project presented unique challenges—the client envisioned an energy-efficient 17-story skyscraper on top of an existing 1960s-era building. Engineers were able to retrofit the existing columns, slabs, and foundation systems into the new design. In 2019, WSP won platinum honors from the American Council of Engineering Companies for their work on the building. Hudson Commons has also gained LEED Platinum, the highest level of certification for green construction principles.

Another sustainable new building, 15 Hudson Yards, is a 918-foot-tall (280 m) residential tower on the west side of Manhattan. WSP served as the engineer of record for the project, which also faced specific design challenges since it sits on top of several subway tunnels. In March 2019, the community, of which 15 Hudson Yards is an anchor building, was awarded the LEED Neighborhood Development Gold certification, making it the first neighborhood in Manhattan to receive the certification.

To continue to advance energy efficiency in New York and across the United States, WSP has also partnered with Northern European industry peers, who tend to use building heating and cooling equipment and designs that are much more thermally and energy efficient. For example, there are high-efficiency electric heat pump and geothermal heating and cooling measures used in Sweden that could be imported and employed in New York to meet the requirements of the Climate Mobilization Act. WSP is engaged in developing associated training and supply chain improvements to deploy these technologies at scale in New York and across the United States.

The Climate Mobilization Act is changing the landscape of New York's real estate market by making energy efficiency and GHG reduction central to business decision-making. But it also provides other community benefits, like lower utility bills due to better insulated buildings. Reducing the use of fossil fuels will also provide residents with cleaner air to breathe.

Regenerating the Past

In cities, derelict buildings or even whole neighborhoods can become disused and neglected for many years. This phenomenon creates a range of negative impacts, including increased crime and a loss of housing stock in cities that frequently already have insufficient levels of affordable housing and high levels of homelessness. These wasted buildings shine a light on the toll of noncircular economies in which potentially valuable assets—homes—are simply abandoned. In densely packed urban centers, there is no space for waste. Sustainable end-of-life options should be designed into buildings from the beginning, preferably by keeping buildings operational as long as possible.

After centuries of population growth, New York lost more residents than it gained between 1950 and 1980. Beginning in the 1980s, the influx of people and rising real estate values resulted in many formerly abandoned buildings, particularly in Brooklyn and the other outer boroughs, getting second lives. One of these rebirths occurred in the 11-acre (4.4-hectare) complex around the old Domino Sugar building.

Since the mid-1850s the Domino Sugar complex, located just across the East River from Lower Manhattan, has been a fixture of Brooklyn's skyline. At one point, it was the largest refinery run by the American Sugar Company, which controlled most of the sugar trade in the United States. After a long decline, the sweet-smelling operations were shuttered in 2004, leading to a rezoning and various redevelopment project proposals. WSP provided green building planning and environmental design, working with developer Two Trees on energy modeling and a LEED strategy for each of the five buildings in the complex. The design also included substantial input and coordination with the local community and city leadership.

In 2018, the six-acre (2.4 hectare) Domino Park opened. Stretching out along the waterfront, a public park features a sugar refinery-themed playground, a splash pad, access to the waterfront, and a view of Manhattan's skyline. Elements of the building's industrial past are also preserved in the park, including two 80-foot (24m) cranes.

The renovated Domino Sugar building and the other four new buildings are intermixed and multipurpose—office, commercial, residential—by design. With a quarter of the 2,800 rental units designated affordable, it also provides homes for a large cross-section of the community and helps alleviate the city's affordable housing shortage.

Renewing existing buildings will almost always result in lower GHG emissions from the construction process as compared to constructing new ones. Beyond sustainability gains, the new Domino Park also retained and reinforced the historic character of the community, while providing local recreational and exercise opportunities.

On New Year's Day 2021, an even more high-profile example of an historic renewal opened to enthusiastic crowds in midtown Manhattan. The *New York Times* praised the Moynihan Train Hall's aesthetic value as giving "the city the uplifting gateway it deserves."[26] However, the building is also a prime example of preserving and reusing existing structures. Moynihan is not a completely new build, but a reconfiguration of the historic James A. Farley Building that served as the main and largest post office for the borough of Manhattan. Now, instead of a place to send letters, the building serves as an entrance to the Amtrak rail and other public rail and transit lines.

These mass transit services were previously only accessible through the subterranean, crowded, and antiquated Penn Station, which has no natural lighting and less-than-optimal ventilation. The extra room in the new building—Moynihan increases Penn Station's concourse space by more than 50%—meets the needs of heavy passenger traffic. Moynihan Train Hall serves the busiest passenger transportation facility in the Western Hemisphere, used by more than 700,000 passengers per day—more than LaGuardia, JFK, and Newark International Airports combined.

The hall's soaring ceilings and skylights, reminiscent of the original Penn Station that was demolished in the 1960s, have been combined with public art, more attractive and comfortable waiting areas for trains, and modern wayfinding technology. The extra space and cleaner air also create a healthier travel experience, an addition welcomed by pandemic-weary New Yorkers.

As an adaptive reuse project, Moynihan Hall provided a unique environmental opportunity to improve energy efficiency and operations within an existing, landmarked building. Because the stone-clad post office was kept intact, construction-related GHG emissions were dramatically lower than constructing new building. The building envelope was also upgraded with double-pane windows, and insulated roof skylight glazing. Moynihan included other sustainability features throughout, including LED lights, low-flow plumbing, and advanced controls for mechanical, lighting, HVAC, and water to improve efficiency across each system.

The large main concourse space is also heated and cooled with a radiant, multizone system built into the floor slab. The innovative floor is what might be called a "smart slab"—it only heats the floor where visitors and passengers circulate, saving energy by not conditioning untraveled spaces. WSP administered the LEED certification and commissioning process, which resulted in Moynihan becoming the first building worldwide to receive a LEED for Transit certification.

WSP worked with eight different agencies and other stakeholders and a total of 28 subconsultants to help guide the project to successful completion. In 2022, Moynihan Train Station received a national recognition award for special projects from the American Council of Engineering Companies.

Shining Light

Rebuilding on the former site of the World Trade Center's twin towers, which were destroyed in the terrorist attacks of September 11, 2001, was one of the most closely watched construction projects in the United States for decades. The design of 1 World Trade Center, also known as the Freedom Tower, had major symbolic, almost spiritual, importance. WSP structural engineers knew the building had to declare the city's resilience in the face of tragedy and embrace sustainability.

The core of the Freedom Tower was constructed out of ultra-high-strength concrete using a continuous pouring operation, allowing column-free expanses. However, incorporating sustainability was part of the design from the beginning as well. Using industrial byproducts in the concrete mix as well as 95% recycled steel significantly cut the GHG emissions of the construction, contributing to 1 World Trade Center's LEED Gold certification. The Freedom Tower may have even helped restore faith in tall buildings. Following the 2001 collapse of the 110-story World Trade Center, no building over 55 stories was constructed in New York until the 2014 completion of the Freedom Tower.

Since then, there has been a flurry of newly constructed buildings between 59 and 98 stories.

Given its imposing height, 1 World Trade Center could be an excellent place for solar panels; however, the roof's soaring design left no place for them. In fact, New York is lagging on solar power installation compared to other large cities. Expanding solar in the city has been hampered by a combination of factors, including technical issues, policy, administrative and code challenges, and a lack of standardization and cohesion among various groups and the utilities. For example, fire departments require a certain amount of space for roof access, eating away at what is usable for panel placement. There are various interconnection requirements with utilities, as well as the need to assuage their concern that too much solar generation won't flood their grid on sunny days. These types of pre-construction "soft" costs—effectively everything but the cost of the hardware itself—are also those most easily impacted by leadership, coordination, policy decisions, and improvements to codes and administrative processing.

To speed the transition, a current WSP sustainability expert helped develop a streamlined, standardized solar zoning ordinance that is now used throughout New York State. This standardization paved the way for then-Mayor Bill DeBlasio to announce in September 2016 a new target of 1,000 MW of solar capacity by 2030.[27] The 2019 Climate Mobilization Act's requirement for rooftop solar panels will further accelerate the city's efforts to build a large solar canopy.

Technological Inspiration

Beginning in the 1990s, a tech hub known as Silicon Alley expanded in the Lower East Side of Manhattan. Although tech companies can be found throughout the five boroughs, a 22-story multi-use building called Zero Irving is providing a collaborative space for startups, premium office space, and community tech training. A new addition to the Lower East Side, Zero Irving's design also incorporates many of the flexible and integrated features that make commercial space adaptable and relevant in a post-pandemic world.

Among the building's hallmarks is multipurpose flexibility that brings together different groups. The bottom floor is a food hall open to the community and residents. To ensure a diverse and locally inclusive mix of businesses, vendors cannot be large chains or have additional locations near the building. The second through seventh floors house Civic Hall, a nonprofit that focuses on expanding tech industry training and employment opportunities for underserved communities.[28] The group has over 1,000 individual members, including government employees, academics, journalists, and artists. Civic Hall's lowest floor is an events space, which is available for community use as well as building tenants. Within Civic Hall, five floors will house a digital skills training center that offers free and low-cost jobs training in the digital economy. Zero Irving offers a unique resource to the many residents of nearby low-income housing buildings—a tech education that will help them find higher paying work in an increasingly digital economy. Beyond its jobs training mission, Civic Hall also serves as a central location for technology, thought, and entrepreneurship where community members and nonprofits build tools and solve public interest problems together.

The 8th through 14th floors are dedicated to step-up offices—centrally located but more affordable than premium space—to help developing local tech companies and serve as a local tech incubator. The building is topped off with several floors of premium office space, with tenants including Melio, a fintech company that provides a business-to-business payment commerce platform.

Taking inspiration from the mission of the building's tenants, technology is at the core of its systems. WSP designed a more efficient and compact HVAC system that circulates refrigerant rather blown air, reducing space requirements between floors, in walls, and on the rooftops. As a result, Zero Irving had more rentable space and was able to install a green rooftop patio. WSP was also able to increase efficiency by leading the building system design, smart building strategy, and sustainability initiatives that earned a LEED Gold certification. This included the use of computational techniques to map data such as when and where the building received the most sunlight and how that would impact heating and cooling loads.

Additionally, Zero Irving received a platinum certification from the international digital certification organization WiredScore. Launched in New York in 2013, WiredScore measures digital connectivity benchmarks to encourage developers and owners to improve their buildings' digital resilience. WiredScore Platinum represents the top marks for criteria, including the physical security of its digital infrastructure, cyberattack prevention, mobile coverage, and internet speed.

Zero Irving is a sustainably designed mixed-used building, but also an investment in a broader version of resilience. As important as robust traditional infrastructures are, resilient design also considers megatrends like on-demand transport, connected and autonomous vehicles, the internet of things, edge computing, and ubiquitous sensors when designing internet connectivity. Zero Irving's resilience also occurs at a societal level, including collaboration, mentoring, and job training that prepares people for work in an economy increasing driven by robotics, automated manufacturing, AI, and other technologies.

The Mission that Never Sleeps

Hurricane Sandy's direct hit on New York City kick-started countless programs and projects designed to create a more sustainable and resilient future. Many of these projects have provided multiple benefits—Shirley Chisholm State Park cleaned up a toxic landfill and provided a historically underserved part of the city with new access to nature. Moynihan Train Hall reused an existing building to alleviate crowding and provide a healthier, inspirational experience for commuters. The green roof of the Javits Center slows runoff during heavy rainfall, but also absorbs heat, reducing the urban heat island effect. Zero Irving encourages equity through local, affordable jobs training. In short, the past decade has not just been about repairing historic damage, but also about building a more Future Ready city.

In an era of new and ever-escalating climate-related challenges, however, there is no time to rest. The 2019 Climate Mobilization Act is dramatically increasing investment in and value of sustainability measures for large buildings. But local government, nonprofits, community groups, and other stakeholders must continue to push for programs that combine sustainability, resilience, equity, and cost-effectiveness over a full life cycle, and provide immediate community benefits.

However, meeting net zero targets and other sustainability goals needs private sector support and leadership. Recent analysis from some of the largest companies listed on the New York Stock Exchange (NYSE) indicates a growing and sustained enthusiasm for Environmental, Social, and Governance (ESG) factors in making investment decisions. In 2019, for example, Bank of America Merrill Lynch reported that "ESG is the best measure we've found for signaling future risk" and that "15 out of 17 (90%) bankruptcies in the S&P 500 between 2005 and 2015 were of companies with poor Environmental and Social scores five years prior to the bankruptcies."[29] In fact, not only was ESG becoming as important in analyzing companies as traditional purely financial metrics, but a full 70% of U.S. assets cannot be analyzed *without* ESG.[30]

In 2022, J.P. Morgan, the 10th largest company listed on the NYSE, issued a report that echoed this enthusiasm for ESG on financial grounds, including over $500 billion in investments flowing to ESG-integrated funds.[31] The report also defined climate resilience in purely financial investment terms as "the readiness of sustainable portfolios to withstand the transition to clean energy and the impact of physical climate events as global temperatures rise."[32]

J.P. Morgan also positioned the sustainability initiatives of countries and cities like New York as a competition. Places that are most able to take "advantage of the advances in technology needed to reach net zero carbon emissions will be best positioned to flourish in this environment."[33] As the financial capital of the world, New York City is a particularly symbolic and practical place to meet the moment.

Notes

1. https://www.bloomberg.com/graphics/2021-cities-climate-victims/.
2. https://www.researchgate.net/publication/261718817_How_much_of_the_world%27s_land_has_been_urbanized_really_A_hierarchical_framework_for_avoiding_confusion.
3. https://www.un.org/development/desa/en/news/population/2018-revision-of-world-urbanization-prospects.html.
4. https://www.baltimoresun.com/maryland/bs-xpm-2012-07-12-bs-md-backstory-underground-wires-20120712-story.html.
5. https://www.eastcoastundergroundllc.com/post/new-york-utilities-went-underground-in-1889.
6. https://www.nhc.noaa.gov/data/tcr/AL182012_Sandy.pdf.

7. https://www.japan.go.jp/regions/resilientjapan/flood.html.
8. https://www.cna.com.tw/project/20200416-metro-english/page1.html.
9. https://english.dorts.gov.taipei/News_Content.aspx?n=07AD51A0326 C05A8&s=EB778A52E17E85DF.
10. https://www.nytimes.com/2018/02/12/nyregion/water-nyc-subway. html.
11. https://www.freethink.com/articles/subway-tunnel.
12. https://www.popsci.com/subway-flood-proofing-and-repairs/.
13. https://www.wired.com/2017/03/keep-riding-subway-means-know-not-green-think/.
14. https://parks.ny.gov/parks/shirleychisholm/details.aspx.
15. https://parks.ny.gov/parks/shirleychisholm/details.aspx.
16. https://oceanservice.noaa.gov/ecosystems/coastal-blue-carbon/.
17. https://www.researchgate.net/publication/261718817_How_much_ of_the_world%27s_land_has_been_urbanized_really_A_hierarchical_ framework_for_avoiding_confusion.
18. environment/climate-change-environment/cities-most-affected-by-climate-change.
19. https://www1.nyc.gov/assets/dep/downloads/pdf/environment/ education/10-analyzing-urban-heat-island-effect.pdf.
20. https://www.centralparknyc.org/articles/park-city-healthy.
21. https://www.researchgate.net/publication/225594951_New_York_ City_property_values_What_is_the_impact_of_green_roofs_on_rental_ pricing.
22. Carbon Emissions and the NYC Climate Mobilization Act (pillsburylaw .com).
23. https://www.scientificamerican.com/article/how-to-set-a-price-on-carbon-pollution/.
24. https://hvcnyc.com/green-roof-legislation-nyc/.
25. How Much Will My Building Be Charged for Emissions Under Local Law 97? (ny-engineers.com).
26. https://www.nytimes.com/2021/01/11/arts/design/moynihan-train-hall-review.html.
27. https://www.nytimes.com/2016/10/02/realestate/is-new-york-ready-for-solar-power.html.
28. https://zeroirving.com/wp-content/themes/zeroirving/_content/ ZeroIrving_eBrochure.pdf.
29. https://markets.businessinsider.com/news/stocks/10-reasons-to-care-about-esg-investing-bank-of-america-2019-9-1028557439#1-esg-can-generate-alpha-1.

30. https://markets.businessinsider.com/news/stocks/10-reasons-to-care-about-esg-investing-bank-of-america-2019-9-1028557439#1-esg-can-generate-alpha-1.
31. https://am.jpmorgan.com/dk/en/asset-management/liq/investment-themes/sustainable-investing/future-of-esg-investing/.
32. https://am.jpmorgan.com/dk/en/asset-management/liq/investment-themes/sustainable-investing/future-of-esg-investing/.
33. https://am.jpmorgan.com/dk/en/asset-management/liq/investment-themes/sustainable-investing/future-of-esg-investing/.

PART

II

How to Design and Implement Your Organization's Sustainability Journey

IN NOVEMBER 2021, Tom traveled to Glasgow for COP 26—the 2021 United Nations Climate Change Conference—to speak on a panel sponsored by the Scottish North American Business Council. During the Q&A session that followed, the owner of a local craft brewery stood up and said he wanted to do his part to fight climate change, but that the problem was just too big. "What can I do that will really matter?"

Tom answered bluntly. "Just do something. Start your journey in whatever way you can that is right for you and your organization at this point in time."

The attendee was the owner of a small local business with a few employees, but he still had plenty of options to make a difference, such as installing more efficient lighting and heating, using water and managing wastes more smartly, looking at incentives to install solar panels, maybe even building a renewable micro-grid. He could become a role model and climate champion for other small businesses in Glasgow. If every organization from small to large embarked on the climate action and sustainability journey with a similar sense of purpose, their collective actions would add up to substantial greenhouse gas reductions and could successfully hold global temperatures below their tipping point.

Fortunately, the *need* for these changes isn't really disputed anymore. Today, we're rapidly transitioning from questions about "why" to questions of "how." For example: How do organizations account for and steadily reduce their greenhouse gas emissions? How do they engage communities on climate action? How do they analyze their climate risks, vulnerabilities and opportunities? How do they make and implement a sustainability plan or climate action plan? How do they report out to investors and other stakeholders on their Environmental, Social, and Governance (ESG) programs and accomplishments?

As with the owner of the local brewery in Glasgow, the most important thing is not to be paralyzed by the enormity of the global climate challenge, but rather to focus at the task and project level by first selecting the right kind of thing to do, and then doing it right. Over the past three decades, various tools, rating systems, and other frameworks have been developed to help organizations do exactly this.

Even as more standardized frameworks become available and mature, though, organizations still need to plot their own individual courses, set appropriate and achievable goals, and identify and properly implement programs and projects that are fit to purpose. While there are evolving best practices in resilience, sustainability, and climate planning, there is no one-size-fits-all approach to identifying what are the right things to do or the right way to do them. Each organization has its own assets, risks, business models, growth projections, and other unique inputs. Understanding the megatrends most relevant to your organization is critical to creating a Future Ready plan that is best adapted to your organization at the current time.

The second section of this book is a practical guide to putting resilience and sustainability at the center of your organization's vision, mission, and climate action programs. It is not intended as a definitive manual to address every aspect of these programs. But it does define common terminology, explore major ideas, and arm readers with enough knowledge to ask the right questions and confidently set a proper organizational course. It shares insights from WSP's experts on sustainability and climate risk, mitigation, adaptation, resilience, and finance. This section also identifies common pitfalls, and explains how to develop and implement the right programs and projects for your organization.

6

Define, Measure, and Set Targets

BEFORE YOUR ORGANIZATION can even think about designing and implementing a plan, you need to understand your current baseline and establish appropriate—and, preferably, science-based—targets. New countries, corporations, cities, and states around the world are now making net zero pledges and other sustainability commitments on a daily basis. Of course, it's always great to see commitment from organizations that recognize the scientific, financial, and human imperative to address climate change. But committing to be "net zero" before you're even sure what that term means isn't helping anyone.

The first question is: net zero of what? There have been several other "net zero" initiatives that aren't necessarily climate or GHG-oriented, like net zero waste or net zero water. In most cases, though, net zero refers to balancing out organizational GHG emissions by removing an equal amount of GHG from the atmosphere. More specifically, as the United Nations puts it, *net zero* means "cutting greenhouse gas emissions to as close to zero as possible, with any remaining emissions re-absorbed from the atmosphere into oceans and forests, for instance."[1]

The second question is: net zero by when? The science-based timeline for achieving net zero sets 2050 as the deadline that is consistent with limiting global temperature rise to 1.5°C (2.7°F) above pre-industrial levels. In the private sector, companies as varied as WSP, General Motors, Microsoft, American Airlines,

Sinopec—Asia's largest oil refiner—and Nippon Steel—the world's fifth largest steelmaker—have all made firm commitments to reach net zero by 2050 at the latest.[2] In the public sector, cities, states, and countries, including the United Kingdom, European Union, and United States, have all made similar commitments. Of course, achieving net zero before 2050 is preferable, and several companies have committed to these more ambitious goals, including WSP, which set 2040 as its target for net zero emissions.

Measure to Manage: GHG Emissions

Once the goal of achieving net zero is defined, your next step is figuring out how much greenhouse gas your organization is currently emitting. This is not as simple as many people may think. Leaders often believe that finding the relevant data on and/or calculating their emissions will be as easy as figuring out the number of calories in a granola bar. In fact, it's much easier to take a granola bar to a lab and measure the calories that are printed on a nutrition label. There are well-established, scientific processes for this—and a small, standardized bar to analyze.

By comparison, finding the GHG emissions of the granola bar, or the company that made the granola bar, is much more difficult. This sort of accounting covers the emissions of the entire supply chain that produces, combines, packages, and delivers the oats, sugar, oil, nuts, honey, salt, flour, and baking soda. It also includes the GHG emissions of the electricity used by the equipment that processed those inputs and the emissions generated by the automobiles that the employees drove to the manufacturing facility. While that's just the beginning of GHG inventorying, it gives a taste of how much more complicated measuring greenhouse gases is than product information like calories.

Fortunately, international organizations from the private and public sectors have been focusing on the thorny and critical challenge of GHG inventories and net zero accounting for 25 years. In 1998, a partnership of businesses, governments, nongovernmental organizations (NGOs), and other groups developed the Greenhouse Gas Protocol Initiative (GHG Protocol). The data-driven GHG Protocol has since become the main global framework for carbon accounting. The standards it established have helped organizations quantify GHGs throughout their operations and across their value chain. Calculating a GHG inventory is an initial step in establishing company-wide reporting, setting GHG emissions reductions targets, and then tracking progress toward meeting those targets. It is an excellent way to identify and understand the largest sources of GHG emissions within an organization.

However, even the GHG Protocol's authority and standardization hasn't made measuring emissions simple. Our world is still based on a high-carbon economy, which means that any data-driven deep dive into organizational GHG emissions will find many more sources that are obvious on the surface. The best-known system established by the GHG Protocol is the one precisely designed to manage this web of emissions. The framework divides emissions into three different categories, or scopes.

Scope 1 emissions arise from direct combustion of fossil fuels such as coal, gasoline, diesel, and natural gas in facilities owned by the company—for example, a gas furnace or gas-powered company car.

Scope 2 emissions are indirect GHG ones that result from an organization's purchased utilities, like the electricity used to heat a building or the air conditioning to cool it.

The last category, Scope 3, is a sort of catch-all for every other GHG emitted from an organization's activity, including expansive global supply chains. It's generally divided into 13 categories:[3]

- Purchased Goods and Services
- Capital Goods
- Fuel- and Energy-Related Activities
- Transportation and Distribution
- Waste Generated in Operations
- Business Travel
- Employee Commuting
- Leased Assets
- Processing of Sold Products
- Use of Sold Products
- End of Life Treatment of Sold Products
- Franchises
- Investments

Though each of these categories produces measurable GHG emissions, locating accurate data for all Scope 3 emissions can be difficult. For example, if one of your suppliers hasn't done its own GHG inventory, then it won't be able to provide your organization with accurate data.

The ubiquity of missing data points has led what's known as spend-based carbon accounting. This technique uses an industry standardized "carbon emissions factor" and multiplies it by the economic value of the good or service to determine their GHG emissions, allowing organizations to accurately fill in missing data points. As useful as it is, though, spend-based carbon accounting doesn't sufficiently consider the complexity of some elements of the supply chain. As a result, entities such as the U.K.'s Chartered Institute of Building Services Engineers (CIBSE) have been exploring ways to integrate a complexity factor into this calculation.

Because Scope 3 emissions are more difficult to accurately assess—not to mention control and reduce—organizations often design different reduction targets around them. For example, Microsoft's ambitious sustainability plan calls for cutting its Scope 1 and 2 emissions to near zero by or before 2030, while reducing the Scope 3 emissions of its massive supply chain by more than 50% and then offsetting the remaining carbon to get to net zero. There are endless permutations on how aggressively organizations approach reducing their GHG emissions, but all the plans begin with effective measurement.

The biggest challenges with Scope 3 are often the boundaries that we draw, and how one company's Scope 1 and 2 often contribute to another's Scope 3. These conversations are complex and industry specific.

Also, not all Scope 3 emissions are traditional supply chain contributions. Sports teams around the world have recognized that the transit of their fans to and from games is arguably the largest component of their carbon footprint. Europe's governing soccer body, UEFA, is attempting to reduce fan travel carbon emissions by advocating for fans to use public transit, bicycles, and other low-carbon alternative transportation approaches as they journey to and from the event.

To effectively tackle your Scope 3 emissions, you need to understand your business, identify the biggest levers that can be pulled, and engage all stakeholders—some through direct control, others through education and demonstrated leadership alone. What is clear is that there is no silver bullet or one-size-fits-all strategy that can be deployed in all industries and all locations.

Straight Science: SBTi

Once the organization's greenhouse gases emissions have been measured, the next step is establishing a program to reduce those emissions.

The Science-Based Targets Initiative (SBTi) is a best-practice framework for emission reductions target setting, and one that is also compatible with the GHG Protocol. An international nonprofit, SBTi is designed to align corporate net zero and decarbonization goals with climate science. Targets are considered science-based if they align with what the most recent climate science says is necessary to meet the Paris Agreement goals—limiting global warming to no more than 1.5°C (2.7°F) above pre-industrial levels.

SBTi highlights three main categories:

1. What the decarbonization pathway should be, along with its boundaries of focus.

2. How much an organization should be decarbonizing annually and what it should be most focused on. Organizations are not going to decarbonize 100% of their activities. They should, instead, focus on the material issues and establish some rules and metrics—reducing 4% of organizational emissions every year, for example.

3. Where to find additional resources or activities to reduce residual emissions. Net zero is premised on the idea that companies should reduce their organizational emissions as much as possible, but that it will be nearly impossible to reduce their emissions to nothing. Instead, they will have to find resources that can absorb, or offset, the final 10–15% of greenhouse gases.

SBTi has advantages beyond simply providing a framework for emissions reduction. As GHG reduction strategies and disclosures become an essential part of business planning, it makes sense to participate in an externally validated process. The credibility of SBTi validation avoids accusations of "greenwashing," lowers transition risk, and boosts investor confidence.

Companies from every continent—ranging from financial institutions to auto manufacturers to chemical companies—have committed to SBTi goals, including over 500 companies in the United States. As it becomes an increasingly common and consistent standard, SBTi also allows companies to benchmark themselves against peers.

The SBTi process is straightforward. Companies that are interested in having SBTi-approved reduction goals send a letter of commitment to SBTi. After that, the companies have 24 months to assess their emissions—including Scopes 1, 2, and 3—and develop a roadmap to its intermediate target, usually in 2030 or 2035. The long-term organizational goal is net zero across Scopes 1, 2, and 3 emissions to be achieved by no later than 2050. SBTi provides materials and assistance in establishing goals, as well as assessing and approving companies' reduction targets. After a plan receives approval by SBTi, companies must continue to disclose their emissions annually and monitor progress toward their goal.

In 2021, WSP's commitment to achieve net zero emissions across its value chain by 2040 was approved by SBTi. Target-setting began with GHG Protocol accounting of WSP's Scope 1, 2, and 3 emissions. WSP then used science-based target-setting to commit to reduce absolute Scope 1 and 2 GHG emissions by 60% by 2030, from a 2018 base year. Over that same time, WSP will reduce Scope 3 emissions 30%. As part of its GHG reduction strategy, WSP is committed to sourcing 100% renewable electricity by 2030.

As a design organization, there is an argument that the impact of our business—our Scope 3 emissions—are far greater. It is for this reason that WSP is actively developing a strategy to enhance the operational and embodied carbon of the designs we deliver. A tiered approach, our teams will not only continue to work with those clients that are committed to a low carbon solution, but also work to rase the minimum carbon performance of all projects that we deliver. This is a scale play that takes advantage of our role of a global leader to build momentum and accelerate the actual GHG emissions mitigated.

Due to their operational dependence on fossil fuels, airlines face a tough challenge decarbonizing versus some other industries. WSP worked closely with American Airlines to design a company-specific target that is aligned with SBTi's pathway. In 2021, the airline made a public commitment to develop a science-based, intermediate goal for reducing GHG emissions. Over the next year, American developed a plan to reduce its carbon intensity, which means the GHG emitted per ton of payload, by 45% by 2035, versus a 2019 baseline. Because most airlines' emissions are from jet fuel, American pledged to reduce both the direct emissions from fuel used in flight as well as the emissions from the production of the fuel. American also committed to reducing the emissions from the electricity it uses 40% by 2035, against a 2019 baseline.

The company will accomplish those goals through various methods, including increasing the operational efficiency of its flights as well as investing in sustainable aviation fuel and next-generation aircraft such as electric planes. In April 2022, American announced that SBTi had approved American's 2035 goals, making it the first airline globally to have SBTi-approved science-based targets.[4]

Designing Forward and Backward

As with American Airlines, every company will have to develop its own specific net-zero pathway. There are several tools to help organizations design the best possible roadmap for their individual journeys.

One common approach to all sorts of performance forecasting is gap analysis, which can easily be adapted for sustainability journeys. Gap analysis defines an organization's future goals or targets, and compares them to its historical performance to determine if it is on the right trajectory. Based on the discrepancies between historical performance and its targets, an organization creates action items to align its future performance with its goals.

One way to visualize that sort of roadmapping is by using what's called a wedge diagram. On a chart, one line plots an organization's business-as-usual GHG emissions trajectory through to a target date, say 2030. A second line plots the trajectory needed to achieve its GHG emissions targets in 2030. For every net zero reduction strategy, the business-as-usual line will sit above the second, because it represents higher GHG emissions. As the lines move left to right, they increasingly diverge—the emissions reduction goals are intensifying. The shape created by these lines is a wedge.

The goal of the exercise is to completely fill in the wedge by finding the right mix of levers and dials to reduce GHG emissions from business as usual to targets. For example, HVAC upgrades at administrative buildings may fill in some of the wedge. On-site solar and renewable energy purchases could fill in a bit more. The exercise also incorporates cost-benefit analysis so companies can see the relative benefits of filling part of the wedge by, say, installing LED lights versus improving their refrigeration system.

As the wedge approaches its target date, the projected space between the business-as-usual emissions trajectory and the net zero trajectory grows, meaning more GHG reduction measures are needed to fill the wedge. In some cases, these additional reductions are projected to happen without any action by the company. For example, cheaper renewables will result in cleaner grid energy, which will reduce the GHG emissions of every electric-powered device the organization uses. On the other hand, many planned future reduction techniques will become increasingly speculative. For example, parts of the wedge may be filled in by technology that isn't fully functional yet—like cheaper, large-scale carbon sequestration or innovations in manufacturing. Finally, the last bit of the gap is filled in with high-quality carbon offsets.

The wedge diagram is a very useful way of visualizing pathways to net zero. Each reduction measure is color-coded, making it easy to spot trends in growth or phasing out of processes and technologies. Circumstance will change—the development of some technology may lag behind projections, or a grid may provide cleaner energy faster than expected. In each case, data is monitored, updated, and the roadmapping adjusted. Gaps may be filled by incorporating technologies that become viable sooner than projected, like green hydrogen, or weren't predicted at all.

On an individual basis, every company is going to have a unique-looking wedge with different solutions to meet its goals. Many organizations have hotspots—particularly intense GHG emission areas—that should be targeted early on. For example, some companies use sulfur hexafluoride, or SF_6, in manufacturing. SF_6 is one of the most potent greenhouse gases known—over a 100-year period, 1 kilogram of SF_6 is estimated to trap the same amount of heat as 23,500 kilograms of carbon dioxide. Although SF_6 is typically only used in small quantities, removing it from the manufacturing process might be an early focus of that company's roadmap.

Another individual factor is a company's growth projection—a business with very high projected growth is typically has a business-as-usual line that shoots upward rapidly, creating a very large wedge. If a roadmapping exercise reveals that meeting an absolute reduction goal during a period of rapid growth is unrealistic or too expensive, the company could pivot to a different target. For example, it might decide to reduce the carbon intensity per unit of its product instead of absolute emissions.

Backcasting is another unique technique for setting an organizational net zero pathway that takes a traditional forecasting approach and flips it on its head. Instead of starting in the present to plan and predict the future, backcasting starts in the future, at a goal like net zero, and then moves step by step back to the present. This unconventional backward journey is then used to identify challenges to reaching that desired future. Organizations leveraging backcasting accept that, while they *will* achieve their desired long-term net zero goal, it's not possible to lay out precisely *how* they will reach it from the beginning because of changes and innovations that will occur along the way.

Because it is an ideal technique for tackling multifaceted, complex problems with a broad scope and long-time horizon, backcasting is broadly applicable to any sustainability challenge, including meeting net zero goals. Backcasting also allows for a complete alignment with an organization's future sustainability and resilience goals. Then, by relying on flexibility, horizon watching, and alignment with a normative future, backcasting offers an alternative approach to setting organizational goals. Utilizing the multifaceted forecasting technique can also encourage a broader organizational transformation along the sustainability pathway.

In both cases, the technical credibility of the analysis is essential to creating a compelling and viable roadmap, achieving a solid level of stakeholder buy-in, and making sure that the report doesn't live on a shelf. The scale of a facility portfolio or the complexity of an organization can make this anything but complex. WSP's experience working with a broad spectrum of clients in the development of their decarbonization roadmap has identified three common traits of those roadmaps that have been successfully deployed and maintain relevance far beyond their initial development:

1. Adopt a methodology that works with a variety of data granularity—from typology EUI benchmarks to ASHRAE Level 3 energy audits, from manual spreadsheet data to real time smart building data points.

2. Engage stakeholders in the conversation and the creation of the roadmap to maximize stakeholder buy-in and ownership

of the end result—embrace real-time gamification in client workshops in lieu of periodic grand reveals.

3. Understand what is controllable and start there to build momentum.

Whole Product or Service: LCA

Life Cycle Assessment (LCA) is another useful framework for credibly and scientifically determining the impact of a product or service. There are several important differences between LCA and other frameworks we explored. First, LCA doesn't use the GHG Protocol for carbon footprinting, but another standard known as ISO standard 14067, which is based ISO standards 14040 and 14044 that more generally cover the wholistic approach that focuses on more than just GHG emissions. The ISO standards were developed by the International Organization for Standardization, which has developed thousands of other globally accepted technical standards.

Additionally, instead of focusing exclusively on GHG accounting and net zero emissions, an LCA also looks at other environmental impacts, from air and water quality to energy, water and natural resource consumption indicators.

LCAs are most used to understand the total impacts—environmental and otherwise—of a particular product or service, not an entire organization. But it plays an important role in achieving net zero by informing some decarbonization choices. For example, an LCA might assess the total impact of a car—the energy and materials that go into manufacturing and the tail pipe emissions when the car is driven for 200,000 miles, all of the tires and windshield wipers and fluids used and its end of life, among many other inputs.

The LCA results can be used to communicate to customers what the environmental impacts are, including water, waste, and GHG emissions. Then customers can make decisions about purchasing the product or service based on its water usage or its emissions—and by comparing it to other similar services or products. By creating this sort of credible information about GHG emissions of a particular product or service—where often none existed previously—LCA becomes an important tool in the decarbonization roadmap.

WSP developed a comparative life cycle assessment (LCA) for Perfect Day, a global biotechnology company and manufacturer of animal-free whey protein. The assessment compared Perfect Day's non-animal whey protein and the total protein in bovine milk to provide science-based evidence that Perfect Day's whey protein substantially reduces GHG emissions, primary energy demand, and blue water consumption compared to total protein in bovine milk. Perfect Day can now use these results to support its communications to downstream businesses and consumers about the environmental attributes of its non-animal whey protein.

Additionally, if a food manufacturer uses Perfect Day's proprietary whey protein to replace other ingredients, the results of the LCA can inform the manufacturer's own LCAs as well as Scope 3 GHG inventory. By conducting an LCA, Perfect Day became a more desirable supplier for downstream companies trying to reduce their own environmental impacts.

LCAs also reduce the risk associated with public sustainability claims that are likely to be scrutinized or challenged by competitors or consumer activists. ISO-conformant LCAs require external critical review by independent experts, which provide credibility to sustainability claims.

In a different case, WSP assisted Bank of America in a comparative LCA of its two statement delivery methods. For years, businesses—including financial institutions—have claimed that electronic statements are more sustainable than paper statements. However, before a high-profile organization like Bank of America made its own public announcements, it wanted scientific, data-driven evidence to support this claim. Bank of America was specifically interested in two categories: GHG emissions and blue water consumption, or the amount of surface and ground water made unavailable for other freshwater applications due to a product or service life cycle. WSP conducted a cradle-to-grave LCA comparing the environmental impacts of paper and digital statements focused only on the differences between the two methods—because the electronic generation and storage of statements is identical regardless of digital or paper delivery, this phase of the life cycle was excluded.

Paper statements emitted GHGs from several activities, including producing paper, transporting the statements from the paper mill to the printing site, printing, USPS delivery, and the end-of-life—either recycling of statements or disposing them in a landfill. The GHG emissions from the electronic statements came from a different set of inputs, including internet electricity to deliver statements, customer device electricity, and at-home printing—as well as end-of-life processes for printed statements. While both types of statements also have some sources of GHG emissions and blue water consumption in common, specifically the electronic generation and storage of the statement data, those sources were not considered since the LCA was designed to report only relative impacts, not absolute GHG emission or blue water consumption values for each statement type.[5]

Comparing the relative greenhouse gas contributions of each process illuminated some interesting details. In the case of paper statements, for example, the largest relative greenhouse gas contribution per statement was from paper production—58% of the total GHG contributions. In the case of online statements, though, printing at home (for online statement customers who also wanted hard copies) resulted in the largest relative greenhouse gas contribution per statement.

Because any analysis has uncertainty, the LCA also considered multiple different scenarios and their impact on GHG emissions and blue water consumption. In one scenario, paper statements were assumed to be shredded which means they cannot be recycled. Other scenarios assumed different percentages of customers—from 0% to 100%—as printing out their electronic statements at home. The assessment concluded that no matter which scenarios were run, electronic statements would have lower GHG emissions and water consumption relative to the paper statements. The LCA estimated that if all of Bank of America's statements that are mailed in a year—over 550 million of them—were instead delivered electronically, this would save roughly 37,000 metric tons of GHG emissions and 136 million gallons (over 514 million liters) of blue water. As a result, Bank of America could confidently make GHG and water reduction claims about its electronic statements compared to paper. Likewise, Bank of America's member companies and customers could be confident that switching to electronic statements had significant environmental advantages, including GHG emissions reduction.[6]

Another common use of externally critically reviewed LCAs is when positive environmental impact is central to a brand's identity. For example, The Urgent Company's mission is making it "easy for consumers to take direct action on the climate crisis." The Urgent Company and WSP partnered to conduct an LCA of its animal-free dairy ice cream brand, Brave Robot. WSP evaluated the environmental impact of Brave Robot throughout its supply chain. The assessment found that, compared to ice cream made with conventional dairy, Brave Robot reduced GHG emissions by 72%, blue water consumption by 23%, and nonrenewable energy use by 60%.[7] The Urgent Company was able to confidently support its sustainability claims and provide detailed GHG and other environmental metrics to any other company it supplies.

While the central goal of both the GHG Protocol and LCA frameworks is to create credible and useful environmental impact data, they can also describe organizations in thought-provokingly different ways. For example, the gathering and sharing of LCA also highlights the broad, circular nature of supply chains. For example, to develop an LCA for a car, the manufacturer has to go to a whole range of suppliers, including a range of glass manufacturers. The glass manufacturers, in turn, have several engineering companies as their suppliers. The engineering companies may very well be buying those cars at the beginning of the circle. Everybody needs information from each other. It's not even a one directional circle, the data flows both ways.

In comparison, when the GHG Protocol framework divides emissions into the Scopes 1, 2, and 3, it also reveals the elaborate web of emissions that are all related to a company's different activities, from onsite fuel use and purchased electricity to purchased goods and services, employee commuting, business travel, use of sold products, and even investments—even if these indirect emissions occur on the other side of the world. Calculating Scope 3 emissions is an accounting and data-gathering challenge, but it also reminds us of our global interdependence.

In order to create a quantifiably sustainable economy, every international supply chain—and thus every country—also needs to be on a sustainable pathway. The countries that have historically benefitted most from the GHG emissions of industrialization, like the United States and Europe, must lead the way on climate action. In doing so, however, the wealthier nations can't leave the rest of the world behind. We are in this together—the whole world needs to be on the sustainability journey for the sake of the planet, and the assured well-being of future generations.

Notes

1. https://www.un.org/en/climatechange/net-zero-coalition.
2. https://www.unpri.org/pri-blog/seven-major-companies-that-committed-to-net-zero-emissions-in-2021/9197.article.
3. https://sustainability.yale.edu/priorities-progress/climate-action/greenhouse-gas-emissions/scope-3-emissions.
4. https://news.aa.com/news/news-details/2022/First-in-flight-American-Airlines-is-leading-the-airline-industry-on-a-science-based-journey-to-net-zero-emissions-CORP-OTH-04/default.aspx.
5. https://about.bankofamerica.com/content/dam/about/pdfs/statement_lca_report.pdf.
6. Ibid.
7. https://braverobot.co/pages/impact.

7

Tools and Technologies

BECAUSE NET ZERO plans have to be specific to an organization's needs, each should consider and integrate many different technologies and tools that will vary due to regional availability, industry relevance, cost-benefit analysis, regulatory requirements, and other organizational needs. Among the most common are energy efficiency measures—LED lighting, daylight sensors, HVAC upgrades, insulated window upgrades, and connected smart building technology. These decarbonization technologies are popular for two simple reasons: they are commercially available at scale and make a significant difference in Scopes 1 and 2 GHG emissions.

Other industry-specific technologies—construction materials with lower embodied carbon, manufacturing technologies that reduce energy usage, and electrified supply chains—are coming online and will be integral to net zero strategies. Part I explores many examples of both off-the-shelf and cutting-edge technologies that will be essential parts of the decarbonized economy over the next 5–10 years. However, with current technologies and initiatives, the world is likely to meet just 60–70% of global net zero objectives.

To fill those gaps left after squeezing out as many GHG emissions of operational discharges as possible, several imperfect or as-yet unproven technologies and tools will be necessary to meet net zero targets. It's advisable for organizations to avoid designing sustainability pathways based exclusively on the current best solutions. When we're projecting 15 or more years into an uncertain future, decisions we make now will almost certainly need adjusting. But tracking megatrends in climate, society, resources, and technologies will help design plans that remain relevant and useful well into the future.

To stay on the cutting edge of new technologies, WSP partners with other private companies, research institutes, universities, and government institutions. Among the most used and rapidly developing are renewable energy, green hydrogen, Renewable Energy Certificates (RECs), Purchase Power Agreements (PPAs), carbon offsets, and Carbon Capture Usage and Sequestration (CCUS). Because of their potential—and the very narrow window we must dramatically reduce emissions—we should remain optimistic that all of these technologies meet their supporters' claims. However, understanding their shortcomings and potential stumbling blocks to implementation is critical for building a realistic, robust sustainability roadmap.

Renewable Energy Options: RECs and PPAs

Virtually every country generates electricity from a variety of sources, including natural gas, coal, nuclear, solar, biomass, geo-thermal, and wind. But once that electricity enters the grid, there's no way to differentiate between an electron generated by coal versus one generated by wind. As a result, when a company buys electricity from a grid, it doesn't know if the energy is from a renewable source. Companies that are pursuing lower GHG emissions, particularly Scope 2, could guarantee that they are using more or exclusively renewables by building their own on-site solar or wind capacity. But, for all the benefits of microgrids, they carry upfront capital costs and other logistical issues that make them less attractive or not the most cost-effective option for some organizations.

Organizations can, however, get credit for the environmental and social benefits of renewable electricity without the capital costs of building their own capacity by purchasing what is known as a Renewable Energy Certificates (RECs). Each REC is equal to one megawatt-hour (MWh) of electricity that enters the grid from a renewable source—roughly enough electricity to power 800 American homes for a year.[1] The party that generates that REC, like a wind farm, can then sell it to a buyer, usually a company. RECs are numbered, tracked, and contain other data about where, how, and when the electricity was generated. Once the owner of a REC claims any of the environmental or social benefits of the renewable electricity, the REC is retired from the system. RECs are an easy, and, historically, cheap way to reduce Scope 2 GHG emissions. RECs are also recognized by the GHG Protocol and meet the requirements of the SBTi.

However, there are significant differences between the two main types of RECs, unbundled and bundled. Companies that buy unbundled RECs are simply buying the legal right to claim the benefits of renewable production—they continue to power their operations with the same electricity from their same local grid. It's a simple solution and allows the renewable energy to be produced far away from the organization that buys the certificate. For example, a bakery in San Francisco could buy an unbundled REC from a solar farm in New Mexico.

However, unbundled RECs do have drawbacks in terms of decarbonization and other potential risks. The steady increase in electricity generation from renewable sources has pushed the prices of bundled RECs down so low that they are no longer a major revenue source for energy project developers. In fact, government grants and loans are much more likely to finance the construction of new facilities. As a result, unbundled RECs have faced criticism from the private and public sector for not creating additional renewable electricity capacity. Already, some organizations—including the U.K. Green Building Council—do not endorse or have taken steps to restrict the use of unbundled RECs.[2]

Bundled RECs are not subject to the same criticism because organizations that buy the legal right to claim the benefits of renewable generation also agree to buy the physical electricity. By buying the whole product, purchasers of bundled RECs create an additional revenue stream for the renewable developer. In fact, bundled RECs are usually tied to new build projects that help finance the growth of additional renewable energy capacity—what's known as additionality. Both types of RECs legitimately check the carbon reduction box on a sustainability report. Bundled RECs, however, accelerate the transition to a net zero power grid, which may provide co-benefits for local public health like reducing air pollution.

To further enhance the transparency of the REC markets, we are also seeing a move toward real-time RECs, which enable a more direct tie between the generation of the renewable energy and the consumption that it is being utilized to offset. Many of the Hyperscale Data Center operators, who are both major energy consumers and committed advocated for decarbonization, have embraced this approach to more credibly deliver carbon-free data services.

Purchase Power Agreements (PPAs) are a step up in commitment from RECs, but they can also offer financial benefits beyond meeting decarbonization goals. PPAs are long-term agreements in which an organization agrees to pay a fixed price for every MWh of electricity the renewable energy facility produces. PPAs can be off-site or on-site projects, depending on the energy needs of the company. In physical PPAs, buyers own the physical electricity, so they must be in the same energy market as the generator. Though companies generally purchase the RECs with electricity, they could decide to lock in a long-term price simply because they think renewable energy will be cheaper or more stable than energy generated by fossil fuel.

As with bundled RECs, the physical PPA also guarantees a revenue for project developers, which they can use to create additional renewable capacity. However, physical PPAs face serious impediments to expansion in the United States. For starters, some states don't allow PPAs. Additionally, local electric utilities operate as monopolies, meaning that renewable developers may not be able to sell their power inside those exclusive service territories. Nonetheless, PPAs are popular with tech companies like Microsoft, Amazon, and Alphabet. In 2021, for example, Amazon had PPAs with 44 renewable energy producers in nine different countries with a capacity of 6.2 gigawatts.[3]

Both RECs and PPAs can play important roles in an organization's roadmap to net zero, but they carry different costs and risks. Unbundled RECs are a relatively easy way to reduce a company's GHG emissions without any upfront capital costs. On the other hand, the criticism around unbundled RECs lack of support for expanding renewable capacity could signal more transition risk than bundled RECs or PPAs as part of a long-term net zero strategy. For one, they could be banned for the purposes of GHG accounting. Alternately, regulatory changes to the REC market could squeeze their supply—making them much more expensive to purchase. In contrast, PPAs require a substantial commitment of capital. But, as we have seen in various infrastructure solutions, that upfront spend may be cheaper over its life cycle—it's guaranteed to be transformative, is likely sheltered from future regulatory changes, avoids accusation of greenwashing, and provides a stable price for renewable electricity in volatile energy markets.

Putting a Price On It: Carbon Markets

For decades, putting a price on carbon emissions has been promoted by governments, NGOs, and the private sector to encourage decarbonization, help restore forests and other natural habitats, and accelerate investment in renewables. Today, there are a wide range of different cap-and-trade markets—regional, national, international—all of which rely on the same basic mechanism to determine what that price is. Under cap-and-trade schemes, which were originally developed in the United States to eliminate the toxic gases that cause acid rain, a regulator sets a limit for organizational GHG emissions. Because some companies will produce more than the limit—typically triggering a penalty like a fine—and others will be below it, a new market for carbon is created.

Carbon markets—often called emissions trading schemes (ETS)—create different opportunities for organizations on their net zero or sustainability journeys. Companies below the emissions limit can receive tradable carbon credits if they're located in jurisdictions with compliance limits. Companies with excessive emissions can reduce those emissions by buying the tradable carbon credits. Because a financial value is linked to GHG emissions, companies that produce services or products that reduce those emissions will find new customers, investments, and other opportunities.

Because the GHG emissions limit is set by a regulator or by an industry watchdog or simply because of internal corporate goals, cap-and trade supporters claim that the market mechanisms of emissions trading schemes are a more efficient method of setting prices than taxes or penalties would be, all other things being equal.

Today, however, there is no unified global carbon market, meaning that smaller country or regional markets each have their own regulations, and this results in a wide range of prices for carbon. Additionally, some markets are compliance-based, while others are voluntary.

The European Union Emissions Trading Scheme (EU-ETS) is the largest multinational GHG emissions trading market in the world. A compliance market, the program that caps the amount of carbon dioxide that can be emitted from heavy users of electricity, such as power plants, oil and gas, agriculture, and transportation sectors, as well as large factories.

Perhaps surprisingly, the world's largest carbon market is based in South Korea, which is also a compliance market, where over 600 or 700 industry players have to trade emissions per the environmental ministry rules. Largely due to domestic politics, the United States doesn't have a national emissions trading scheme, although California and Quebec run their own compliance-based market. Generally speaking, these compliance-based markets are larger, have a tax to induce market actors to trade, and tend to price carbon higher.

Voluntary markets are typically made up of companies and stakeholders that have unilaterally decided that they are going to reduce their emissions, either because they are good corporate citizens, or because their customers or shareholders are putting pressure on them. A number of nonprofits act as registries for voluntary markets. In the United States, one registry is called Vera, while a California-based registry is called the American Carbon Registry. In an exciting, relatively recent development, the aviation industry committed to net zero goals, which will be achieved in part by purchasing carbon credits. These commitments are voluntary, but, given the size of the high-profile industry, will drive substantial demand for high-quality credits. Organizations that want to pursue opportunities in the carbon markets first need figure out which emissions trading scheme makes the most sense. WSP works both with large clients that are interested in buying carbon credits as well as sellers.

In addition to helping achieve organizational net zero goals, emissions trading schemes also have positive material impacts on lives around the globe. In the developing world, for example, cooking with dirty and inefficient fuels—such as wood, kerosene, charcoal, and coal—is a major environmental and public health challenge. Dirty cooking contributes significantly to GHG emissions as well as local air pollution. In part, this is due to the sheer number of people who rely on inefficient, dirty cooking techniques—about 2.5 billion people worldwide do not have access to clean cooking. What's more, the toxic fumes from dirty cooking—many of which are emitted indoors—are responsible for up to four million premature deaths a year.

More efficient, clean, cook stoves, fueled by cleaner-burning biomass pellets and other more efficient combustion technology, can reduce the GHG emissions and the negative health impacts of air pollution, while also providing wide-ranging community benefits. For example, fuel wood is often scavenged or extracted from nearby areas, typically by women. Because the pellet-fueled cookstoves don't require gathering wood, women have more time for other purposes. The reduced need for wood gathering also reduces threats to local biodiversity and supports forest regeneration and reforestation.

However, the cook stoves face one major challenge: they are often priced out of reach of the people who would most benefit from using them. WSP developed a solution while working with a foundation to help support a Democratic Republic of Congo-based program and an Africa-based manufacturer of efficient cook stoves. WSP structured a loan that allowed the manufacturer to price their stoves much more affordably as well as capture the value of the resulting carbon credits. Because the stoves would be replacing dirtier, less efficient methods of cooking, their sale generated carbon credits, which were registered with a voluntary markets registry, the Switzerland-based Gold Standard, and marketed to North American buyers—primarily Canadian industry. The foundation's loan will be primarily repaid out of the sale of carbon credits, while WSP used the manufacturer's carbon credits as collateral.

Making the Final Push: Carbon Offsets

Carbon removal offsets are another option that organizations can use to "net out" the last bit of GHG emissions they need to reach net zero. For example, a company that squeezes its emissions down by 90% in 2050 could buy carbon removal offsets to net out the last 10%. They are market-based tools that guarantee to remove a certain amount of carbon, often measured as a metric ton of carbon dioxide equivalent, from the atmosphere. However, organizations should avoid being overly reliant on offsets, as well as understand their risks.

For one, the net zero standard stresses that carbon removal offsets should only be used as a final measure. This is, in part, because when companies rely too heavily—or entirely—on offsets, they are disincentivized from reducing their own GHG emissions first. This mindset disrupts the whole net zero ecosystem. When companies make reduction commitments, but don't invest in, say, innovations in construction materials, or energy efficiency, or deploying renewables at a massive scale, they hinder the global transition to net zero.

Additionally, organizations that are heavily reliant on carbon removal offsets to meet their net zero goals are betting on a nascent and under-regulated market. For years, some carbon offset project developers have made unreliable or unverifiable claims about the amount of carbon they truly remove from the atmosphere, and whether that carbon is re-released through leakage or project reversal. Despite the emergence of certification systems like the Voluntary Carbon Standard, the real-world impact of carbon offsets can still be hard to verify.[4] There are many new technologies, including direct air capture, biomass with carbon capture and storage, and carbon mineralization, that attempt to solve these concerns by removing carbon from the atmosphere and storing it through chemical, physicochemical, and other processes. In some cases, like bioenergy with carbon capture and storage, the atmospheric removal occurs through biological processes, and the capture through technological processes. However, very few of these technologies have reached the commercial stage, and those that have must scale up rapidly to meet upcoming demand.

These considerations aside, relying heavily on carbon offsets may not make business sense in the near future either. Because there are currently no global standards on offset quality, the market is saturated with cheap credits. Over the next few years, however, increased demand and the adoption of global and national rules—like those developed at COP 26—will begin to squeeze out the lower-quality credits, tightening the overall supply. Over that same period, more companies will likely attempt to meet their decarbonization and net zero goals, in part, through buying carbon removal offsets, sending demand soaring. The result of both dynamics could be a massive spike in the price of carbon removal credits.

For example, forestry removal offsets—which offset carbon emissions through reforestation that pulls carbon out of the atmosphere—currently run from between \$2–\$45 per metric ton carbon dioxide equivalent. By 2050, prices for carbon offsets are estimated to be as high as \$120 per ton.[5] As a result, companies with net zero roadmaps based on buying large amounts of cheap offsets will find those plans are ultimately much more costly. In a scenario in which the price of offsets balloons by roughly 20–25 times, the "more expensive" options aimed at reducing emissions—solar power, electrification, and efficiency—will be both cheaper and smarter investments.

Carbon Capture, Utilization, and Storage

Beyond nature-based solutions for carbon dioxide removal such as planting trees and creating new wetlands, commercial technology to remove carbon dioxide in the emissions from industrial sources has been under development for over 50 years, but progress has been irregular and often slow. Today, there are fewer than 30 carbon capture plants in the world, most are still in demonstration phase, and they don't have nearly the capacity needed for companies, governments, or countries to meet their net zero commitments. Nonetheless, carbon capture is an important part of many organizations' net zero roadmaps, which means it needs to be scaled up rapidly. The International Energy Agency (IEA) calculates that the world needs to increase its carbon capture capacity by at least 40 times by 2030 to be on a 2050 net zero trajectory.

Fortunately, the currently underdeveloped technology is undergoing an unprecedented degree of expansion. Some sources see the global market for capture and sequestration growing from \$2 billion to \$7 billion in 2028.[6] In recent years, investment has driven substantial improvements in hardware as well the liquid solvents that isolate carbon dioxide from other gases, bringing down costs by 70%.[7] The Inflation Reduction Act passed by the U.S. Congress in August 2022 also provides massive government incentives for the carbon capture industry. Previously, the government offered a tax incentive of \$50 per metric ton for capturing carbon dioxide from polluting sources like factories, an amount that only drove limited investment.[8] Most of the projects were "easier"—capturing carbon only at facilities with the highest concentrations of carbon dioxide. By pushing the incentive up to \$85 per metric ton, carbon capture at a wider range of industrial facilities will be more financially viable. The Inflation Reduction Act also provides a tax credit of $180 per metric ton of carbon dioxide for the nascent technology that sucks carbon directly out of the atmosphere, as opposed to at industrial sources.[9]

In brief, the technology—which is used most commonly at large emitters like power plants or factories—sucks carbon-heavy emissions into ducts, where it is exposed to solvents that isolate the carbon dioxide from the rest of the emissions. Once isolated, the carbon dioxide is compressed for transport through pipes or into tanks. Ideally, the carbon can be stored in locations like repurposed underground oil or gas reservoirs.

A small amount of this captured carbon dioxide is not stored underground but reused for various purposes. Carbon dioxide can be used to carbonate beverages or naturally boost crop yields in greenhouses. A more substantial, industrial solution is curing concrete with carbon dioxide, a process that permanently locks away the carbon in a building or other structure. However elegant these circular solutions are, though, none of them yet provides the kind of storage capacity needed to meet global net zero goals. While the technology is not yet ready for a scaled rollout, the urgency of rapidly deploying carbon capture has generated huge government incentives and private sector investment, which should accelerate its development.

Some critics of carbon capture claim that focusing on the removal process discourages organizational investment and commitment to lowering the amount of GHG they emit in the first place. It's true that reducing emissions operationally should always be organizations' first goal. However, carbon capture will remain part of some organizations' net zero plans out of necessity, particularly fossil fuel intensive energy companies. Ultimately, we all have a stake in the ability of new investments in carbon capture to produce breakthroughs. Even if we achieve net zero goals globally by 2050, our atmospheric levels of GHG are still historic on a geological scale. Because some greenhouses gases, like carbon dioxide, remain in the atmosphere for centuries, a certain amount of global warming will still be baked into our climate future. However, technology that can remove or draw down carbon dioxide from the atmosphere more quickly could reverse the impacts of climate change in a faster timeframe.

Returning to Earth

To date, the most effective sequestration technologies are natural—found in places like oceans, wetlands, forests, and soil. The Earth's natural contribution of carbon dioxide emissions is much larger than that of human activities. However its impressive carbon sequestration capacity effectively nets out these natural emissions. Our planet's rising levels of carbon dioxide are almost entirely due to the extra contributions of human activity—we don't re-absorb our carbon emissions as effectively as nature. Given this, it makes sense that new sequestration technologies should leverage some of these natural processes.

One fusion between natural processes and human technology is ocean alkalinization. Oceans absorb a large amount of carbon dioxide from the atmosphere, but, after they reach saturation, the water becomes acidic. Introducing alkaline minerals or industrial products like lime to the ocean converts the carbon dioxide into stable molecules, clearing the way for the ocean to absorb more carbon dioxide. Ocean alkalinization could offer at least one co-benefit—reversing the acidification of the ocean that is damaging to marine life, including coral and shellfish. However, the minerals used for large-scale alkalinization will likely require mining and energy intensive processing, which creates additional GHG emissions. There are also unknown consequences of dumping industrial amounts of alkaline materials into oceans.

Another process based on natural sequestration is restorative agriculture. Just like oceans and trees, natural soil is an excellent carbon sink. Due to intensive agricultural practices and land conversion, though, soils have lost 50–70% of their original organic carbon content.[10] By eliminating some of the most harmful modern practices, restorative agriculture processes create healthier soil, which is also able to sequester more soil. These practices include farming that is either no-till or low-till, and keeping cover crops or compost on fields instead of letting them sit fallow. Unlike ocean alkalinization, restorative agriculture doesn't rely on heavy industrial practices—it is a fully nature-based solution. Like other NbS, restorative agriculture has multiple co-benefits, including climate resilience against both droughts and heavy rainfall, as well as reducing the use of chemical fertilizers.

Regrowing clear-cut forests, restoring wetlands, and recreating living shorelines are other nature-based solutions that are very effective at sequestering carbon, while also providing economic and human health co-benefits, habitat restoration, and recreational opportunities. While we are developing cutting-edge decarbonization technologies, we should also deploy these solutions that combine sustainability, natural resilience, and multiple benefits at scale. One study suggests that cost-effective nature-based solutions could provide 20% of the mitigation needed to keep global warming well below 2°C (3.6°F) by 2050.[11]

Notes

1. https://www.nwcouncil.org/reports/columbia-river-history/megawatt/.
2. https://www.nature.com/articles/s41558-022-01379-5.
3. https://www.eib.org/en/essays/renewable-energy-power-purchase-agreements.
4. https://doi.org/10.1111/gcb.15943.
5. https://about.bnef.com/blog/carbon-offset-prices-could-increase-fifty-fold-by-2050/.
6. https://www.fortunebusinessinsights.com/industry-reports/carbon-capture-and-sequestration-market-100819.
7. https://www.cnbc.com/2021/01/31/carbon-capture-technology.html.
8. https://time.com/6205570/inflation-reduction-act-carbon-capture/.
9. https://time.com/6205570/inflation-reduction-act-carbon-capture/.
10. https://www.american.edu/sis/centers/carbon-removal/fact-sheet-nature-based-solutions-to-climate-change.cfm.
11. https://www.pnas.org/doi/10.1073/pnas.1710465114.

8

Reporting Risk and Assessing Vulnerability

REGARDLESS OF SECTOR or type, organizations have always faced some degree of risk from the natural world—earthquakes, volcanoes, hurricanes, ice storms. But over the past 5–10 years, the different types of risk related to climate change have become more widely recognized as serious threats to companies' assets, revenues, employees, competitiveness, and even viability. These categories of risks can be thought of and weighed against each other just as governments at all levels and some companies did during the COVID pandemic. First, organizations implemented and maintained ongoing assessments, including new waves of infections, hospitalization rates, and deaths. Organizations then used this data to inform a massive and delicate balancing act. On one hand, protective measures like wearing masks, getting vaccinated, and staying home could prevent large numbers of people becoming sick. However, when large numbers of people are home, many companies have to suspend at least some operations, which has a negative financial impact on the company, its employees, and society as a whole.

In the case of climate risk, there are two main categories, physical and transition, each of which impacts organizations in different ways and with various degrees of severity. Physical risk includes chronic, ongoing issues like temperature changes and sea level rise as well as acute events like heatwaves, hurricanes, wildfires, or floods that may occur with greater frequency and/or intensity. This is the public face of climate change—damaged buildings, interrupted operations, disrupted supply chains, and resource scarcity.

Transition risk doesn't specifically result from the damage caused by singular events like extreme weather, but rather from the cumulative long-term impact of the accelerating transition to a low-carbon economy—including policy and regulatory risks, technological risks, market and other financial risks, reputational risks, and legal risks. For example, a government-imposed high carbon tax could cause a petroleum or other carbon-intensive company to undergo an expensive carbon reduction program or face penalties, both of which could reduce profits and make the company less attractive to investors and shareholders. Changing consumer preferences for low- or zero-carbon products could also negatively impact companies with high GHG emissions and no credible sustainability programs or climate action plan.

However, such a transition also presents massive opportunities for a wide array of companies, like manufacturers of wind turbines or low-carbon cement or EV charging stations or green steel. In addition to ambitious and innovative GHG reduction plans, WSP assisted a leading technology company in launching a new product line—a cloud-based climate accounting service. Even oil and gas companies can find opportunities in this transition, like using empty belowground reservoirs to store captured and sequestered carbon or using its existing gas pipeline infrastructure to transport and supply green hydrogen.

This growing awareness that climate risk is also a financial risk can be seen in the high use and proliferation of standards and reporting frameworks. Shareholders, investors, partners, customers, employees, governments, and NGOs increasingly demand and expect corporations to disclose an array of nonfinancial data, often in the form of Environmental, Social, and Governance (ESG) reports. Although ESG refers to three broad categories, climate risk within the environmental category has been one of the primary drivers of ESG reporting's rapid rise. In the mid-2000s, demands for ESG disclosures were still mainly the domain of a few activist investors seeking transparency on issues that were considered nonfinancial—for example, workforce diversity, or air pollution, or potential conflict of interest on a board of directors. By 2025, however, ESG assets are expected to exceed

$50 trillion, which would represent over a third the projected $140.5 trillion in total global assets under management.[1]

Due to a lack of standardization, this explosion of ESG reporting was initially not as helpful as it could have been. Companies could issue their ESG reports at different times using different reporting boundaries, accounting methodologies, metrics, measurement units, and reporting formats. Organizations could also choose to feature a success in one area—say, an industry-leading percentage of female executives—and ignore another unmet challenge—like rapidly increasing total carbon emissions. The lack of standardization has meant peer benchmarking and decision-useful information can be somewhere between difficult and impossible. Over the past 5–10 years, a few frameworks have emerged as globally recognized leaders.

Spreading the Word: CDP, TCFD, and GRI

Organizations that want to disclose their carbon footprint, GHG emissions, or other nonfinancial metrics most frequently use several different reporting platforms, depending on what they want to communicate. CDP, formerly the Carbon Disclosure Project, is one of the leading frameworks. The group gathers data about organizational carbon emissions from companies and cities, scores it, and then posts the results. By disclosing information through an established and reputable third party, companies and cities can credibly communicate their activities to stakeholders, including investors, shareholders, and customers. Multiple studies have found that carbon disclosure is also linked to improved financial performance.[2,3,4]

A second well-known reporting framework is the Task Force on Climate-related Financial Disclosures (TCFD). Unlike CDP, TCFD does not gather or score data, but, instead, provides organizations with guidelines for reporting as well as developing indicators. TCFD is primarily focused on standardizing ways to assess climate risk and opportunities. Although TCFD was originally voluntary, the regulatory frameworks of multiple countries and regions, including the European Union, United Kingdom, Japan, Singapore, South Africa, New Zealand, and Canada are now integrated with or modeled on TCFD. In the United States, new disclosure requirements are being developed by the Securities and Exchange Commission (SEC), although the details continue to be politically debated. Many leading companies, including WSP, have already committed to voluntary disclosure as the right thing to do for their organization and investors—regardless of federal mandates.

The Global Reporting Initiative (GRI) is like TCFD in that it provides organizations with guidelines for both developing indicators and reporting. However, GRI is used to deliver ESG reports that are much broader in scope than just climate and GHG-related disclosures. To be part of a just and sustainable green transition, cities, companies, and other organizations need to measure themselves beyond their net zero playbook. For example, social indicators could include diversity goals for senior leadership, support for small and historically disadvantaged businesses, or director responsiveness to shareholders.

In addition to being the leading platform for corporations to issue broad-based sustainability reports, GRI supports and is compatible with other leading frameworks. For example, WSP's most recent annual ESG report, published in the summer of 2022, followed the GRI disclosure recommendations for Engineering and Construction Services as well as the Professional and Commercial Services. But the same report also included the disclosures recommended by the TCFD. Among annual highlights were an industry-leading CDP rating of A- as well as the announcement of WSP's SBTi-approved GHG emissions reduction target on Scopes 1, 2, and 3 emissions as defined by the GHG Protocol. The emergence of standardized programs has made peer benchmarking and target-setting much more transparent and useful.

Frameworks that provide guidelines for reporting organizational climate risk, as well as other social indicators and goals, are valuable as communication tools. But, by compelling organizations in assessing and reporting what's material to them, they can also foster organizational change, as well as provide tools for improving sustainability and resilience to climate risk at the enterprise level.

Plausible Futures

One key recommendation of the TCFD framework, for example, is using certain analyses tools to envision potential climate risks and opportunities. The American Society of Civil Engineers (ASCE) launched Future World Vision a few years ago as an interactive, immersive, three-dimensional tool that allows the development and visualization of different future scenarios by planners, designers, and others so that they can better communicate about and build the future.

Scenario analysis is a widely used process for predicting future risks and vulnerabilities. However, it isn't intended to forecast into a dynamic future to extract and develop a singular, best solution. In fact, scenario analysis is not intended to even represent just one entire future. Instead, it uses scientific data and climate projections to enhance critical thinking about *plausible* futures and what they would mean for the organization's resilience.

The process begins by inventorying an organization's assets and mapping out potential climate hazards. Second, organizations review their adaptive capacities—how they have retrofitted and upgraded from previous damage from climate-related hazards like windstorms or landslides. Once an organization has established a baseline in terms of current assets, climate risks, and adaptive capacity, then it can explore what impacts it may face in the future.

In response to extreme temperatures and wildfires that caused power outages, a company may have added backup power generators to cool its offices and critical information technology platforms. However, those adaptations may not be of much use if the office floods and connectivity is lost. Organizations may also face different risks if much of their workforce has transitioned to remote work since its adaptations. Organizations will need to consider how they continue to support their staff off-site by ensuring that employees can access comfortable working conditions and a secure online working environment.

To align this analysis with current climate science, multiple future scenarios are created based on Representative Concentration Pathways (RCPs). Among other scientific groups, the IPCC uses RCPs in its climate assessments. RCPs are modeled trajectories of greenhouse gas concentration adopted by the IPCC, and thereby indicate how much energy is retained in the Earth's atmosphere. Lower RCPs represent a faster drop in GHG emissions and lower temperature rises. For example, RCP 2.6, a low scenario, assumed that global annual GHG emissions would peak in 2020—a point we've unfortunately already passed. RCP 4.5, an intermediate scenario, assumes that global annual GHG emissions will peak around 2050. In contrast to what many people think, the numbers following RCPs are not indications of a temperature change. For example, RCP 8.5, a scenario on the high end, assumes that high emission trends continue to the end of the century, which will result in an increase in average global temperatures of 7.7°F (4.2°C) by 2100.

While the IPCC data is a valuable starting point for projecting plausible futures, every scenario plays out locally, so local data is critical for accurate scenario analysis. However, detailed and consistent data tends to be more readily available in wealthier nations. So, for example, a scenario analysis for New York City will likely have more complete data than the same analysis in Dhaka, Bangladesh. Even in the United States there is a discrepancy in the availability of useful data. Some states and other organizations—particularly in the Northeast and on the West Coast—have made measuring climatic changes more of a priority.

Preferably, a scenario analysis will start with an exact address and GPS coordinates, which can be used to map the organization's physical location into a climate risk tool. There are a number of good publicly available tools, including the Environmental Protection Agency's (EPA's) Climate Risk Index and the National Oceanic and Atmospheric Association's (NOAA's) state scenarios from the National Climate Assessment. GPS coordinates are useful because slightly different locations can result in big changes in expected vulnerability.

Other data to model scenarios can come from local sources, like city plans. Though FEMA maintains extensive maps of potential flood damage, they are often out of date—largely due to local politics and economic interests. As a result, they can't always be relied on for future projections. According to one 2020 study, FEMA maps underestimate flood risk to houses and businesses in the 48 contiguous states in the United States by 67%.[5]

Mapping Bumps in the Road

Caltrans (California Department of Transportation) is responsible for over 15,000 miles (24,140 km) of state highways in California, with varying climates and topography such as Death Valley, the San Francisco Bay Area, and the Sierra Nevada mountains. Like any highway system, Caltrans faces climate hazards such as landslides, ice, or washouts. Because of its extensive size and climactic variability, though, Caltrans is divided into 11 different zones.

WSP assisted Caltrans in assessing its future vulnerabilities. The department wanted to get out ahead of climate change impacts by envisioning their system's future vulnerabilities. Caltrans used three RCP projections—the low-emission RCP 2.6, the intermediate RCP 4.5, and the high-emission RCP 8.5. Caltrans also looked at these projections for three different years—2025, 2055, and 2085. The first scenario explored temperature rise and its potential impact on the highway system. Although global temperatures are expected to rise 7.7°F (4.3°C) by 2100, local temperatures were expected to rise between 10–11.9°F (5.5-6.5°C) in portions of the state.

Though a near 12°F (6.6°C) rise in average temperatures by the end of the century may sound incredible, it was dwarfed by a heatwave that covered much of California between September 1 and 9, 2022. Ten cities in California set or tied all-time temperature records, including Sacramento, Napa, and San Jose.[6] These records were far beyond the range predicted even by 2100 in an extreme scenario. Sacramento, for example, historically averages a high of 89°F (31.7°C). On September 6, the city hit 116°F (46.6°C), 27°F (14.8°C) above its average.[7]

One of the reasons for choosing the minimum and maximum RCPs is because of the impact of extreme temperatures on highway construction materials. Pavement binder—the "glue" that holds together the asphalt on highways and roads—is temperature-sensitive, so different binder mixes are used based on regional climate. If the weather is too cold, pavements can contract and crack. If it's too hot, roads can expand, leading to rutting. The scenarios for 2025, 2055, and 2085 showed increasing segments of the highway system exposed to temperatures that can cause asphalt binder to run and road surfaces to rut and otherwise degrade.

Another Caltrans scenario mapped changes in precipitation, snowfall, and rain across three different time periods and then overlayed that with the maximum daily precipitation in a 100-year storm event. One-hundred-year storm events are the standard around which Caltrans builds its infrastructure. For example, a bridge over a waterway must be high enough to accommodate the level of a 100-year flood. In different climate scenarios, however, that 100-year event could be very different. Again, each scenario showed an increase across the state in the amount of rain to be expected in a 100-year event. Several areas of California were predicted to receive as much as 30 inches (76.2 cm) of rain in a day during a 100-year event. For comparison, California's highest-ever total rain in a 24-hour period was 25 inches (63.5 cm). In fact, over the past 100 years, only three states in the continental United States have ever experienced a 30-inch (76.2-cm) rain event.

Caltrans' scenario analysis goes on to detail the changes in multiple other climate risks to operations. Wildfires can damage bridges, litter roadways, and create the conditions for more likely landslides. Sea level rise can cause sunny-day flooding onto highways. Storm surges can inundate and damage roadways. Cliff retreat can destabilize and undermine roadways.

The vulnerability assessment that Caltrans conducted was the first step in a much longer process, including conducting asset prioritization to determine which highways need a more detailed study as well as determining the state's adaptation options. Additionally, Caltrans can target incorporating resilience into project development. The vulnerability assessment can also be used to influence decision-making or to coordinate stakeholder engagement on climate risk-related community needs. The study provides additional benefits by creating additional tools—like a more informed cost-benefit analysis for future projects. Finally, the assessment is invaluable for training staff on the impact of climate change and adaptation.

Waterworks and Risk

Like California's highways, water utilities across the country are on the frontline of climate risk. People rely on clean water for drinking, bathing, showering, cooking, watering gardens and lawns, extinguishing fires, and industrial uses. Water is essential to the functioning of businesses, homes, hospitals, schools, offices, and the data centers that support the internet and the economy. However, climate-related phenomenon like extreme drought, heatwaves, and flooding are already stressing water resources in unprecedented ways.

In 2021, WSP co-authored a guidebook analyzing the enhanced climate risks water utilities will be facing. Written along with authors from Denver Water, San Francisco Power Utilities Commission (SFPUC), and consultants from Cadmus and the University of

Arizona, the guidebook is designed to help utilities understand how to incorporate future climate risk vulnerabilities and opportunities into their planning. For this guidebook, the framework and research developed in previous studies was refined into a series of tabletop exercises to promote awareness, critical thinking, and problem solving across the organization.

Tabletop exercises have long been used as planning and decision-making tools in the military, intelligence, and emergency management communities. This guidebook leverages those techniques and applies them to the challenges and opportunities presented by climate change. While these exercises were designed for drinking water utilities, their approach could be applied to any other large organizations interested in exploring the way climate change may impact their operations. The exercises prompt discussions about how to improve the long-term resilience of infrastructure, enhance employee safety, promote more cost-effective investments, minimize both physical and transition risk from regulatory changes, and promote greater communication and collaboration.

After selecting the team that will be participating in the tabletop exercises, the guidebook suggests holding a "Climate 101" presentation to make sure all team members have a baseline understanding of climate change and the scientifically established projections of future climate risk. Participants in the tabletop exercise are selected primarily because of their roles at the utility, not because they necessarily have the most up-to-date information about climate risks. Providing good information upfront increases their awareness of the risk that could potentially impact their business function. The "Climate 101" initiative defines key terminology and encourages open communication before, during, and after the tabletop exercise. It's also an opportunity to empower trained climate champions within the organization.

In order to develop science-based scenarios, organizers need to establish time horizons and gather the relevant data from the most up-to-date scientific research as well as localized projections in the utility's operational areas. This data will be used to inform the exercise's four different modules.

Based on their experience, Denver Water and SFPUC offered some basic feedback on how to select the most applicable and useful scenarios. The first scenario should play out in the current climate, establishing a baseline before advancing to future climate scenarios.

The other three scenarios should avoid time horizons that are too far in the future as they may be distracting. SFPUC chose 2070 for one scenario year but found it hard to make useful projections. Instead of a specific year, Denver Water included "warmer" and "hotter" future scenarios. This was useful because both scenarios are possible depending on what trajectory global GHG emissions continue, regardless of the time horizon.

The scenario should also be built on more than just climate risk data. Like the Future Ready approach, holistic and accurate versions of the future include socioeconomic, demographic, technological, customer behavioral, and other trend information. These diverse data points help answer critical questions like: How many people will the utility be serving? How many households will be using water recapture systems or water tanks for drinking water? How many people will have access to cars? How many people will willingly follow water restrictions? How many people are expected to have illnesses or obesity that make them more susceptible to heatwaves or drought conditions?

The tabletop exercises took place over three days. Each module (scenario) was allotted roughly two and one-half hours, during which time an enormous amount of ground was covered. Among the issues discussed were employee health, state permitting processes, applying for resilience funding, decreased water usage impact on revenue, infrastructure cracking in heat, supply chain disruptions by rising sea levels, Clean Water Act compliance, and the threat of wildfires on water quality and delivery.

Participants are often eager to identify solutions as the risks are being mapped, so the modules provided time and space to identify solutions. This collaborative process often provided co-benefits across business functions—greatly improving the results. After the exercise, executive leaders should also review the scenarios. They may be able to identify gaps in the risks the utility is facing or could face in the future, as well as associated opportunities and solutions.

Inducing Failure: ADAP

Mobile, Alabama, sits just inland from the Gulf of Mexico and roughly 150 miles (241 km) east of New Orleans. About 9 miles (14 km) of the primary east-west highway, Interstate 10, is exposed to wind and/or sea surge as it crosses Mobile Bay. Identifying vulnerabilities in the bridge can be invaluable, but only if it leads to implementing solutions. A framework called Adaptive Decision-making Assessment Process (ADAP) was developed in a partnership between the Federal Highway Administration (FHWA) and WSP, in part, to ensure scenario analysis leads to solutions.

Unlike most other guidelines or frameworks for infrastructure design, ADAP is a risk-based tool that analyzes life cycle cost and shifting future climate conditions. ADAP produces a cost-benefit analysis, but the financial assessment is based on a broader, more nuanced, and future-looking set of inputs. One reason infrastructure owners have been so slow to move away from traditional design standards or frameworks and adopt a risk-based approach to infrastructure improvement is because they still frame their decision making primarily around capital cost. ADAP is an attempt to bridge the gap between existing capital cost and guideline-driven engineering practices, and a smarter infrastructure design that is grounded in climate risk and long-term asset management that is inclusive of operational impacts and maintenance costs.

Another stumbling block in transitioning to a more resilient infrastructure is that the risk-based planning process often stops after the vulnerability assessment phase. The problem is a common one in mapping out sustainability pathways: there is no widely adopted alternative framework to implement solutions at the asset level. ADAP aims to provide a process for identifying infrastructure design solutions that incorporate life cycle cost and are climate-risk–based.

ADAP is also designed to be flexible enough to apply to a wide variety of infrastructure projects. Broad acceptance of an alternate framework for analyzing and generating design options—whether ADAP or some other methodology—is a critical step in building sustainable, resilient infrastructure at scale.

ADAP has 11 steps, the first five of which are familiar elements of a climate-risk or vulnerability assessment:

1. Understand the site context.
2. Document existing or future base case facility.
3. Identify climate stressors.
4. Develop climate scenarios.
5. Assess facility performance.

However, ADAP departs from many vulnerability assessments by moving on to a design phase that identifies specific life cycle and climate-risk–informed solutions. These last six steps are:

6. Develop adaptation options.

7. Assess performance of the adaptation option.

8. Conduct an economic analysis.

9. Evaluate additional considerations.

10. Select a course of action.

11. Develop a facility management plan.

ADAP was used by the U.S. Department of Transportation (U.S. DOT) as part of a Gulf Coast study designed to provide detailed assessments of the performance of critical coastal infrastructure under specific climate change threats. The U.S. DOT's Gulf Coast study analyzed the structural vulnerability of several structures, including the elevated freeway ramp in Mobile, Alabama. Because Interstate 10 is exposed to severe weather, including hurricanes, the city and its transportation infrastructure are vulnerable to climate hazards such as sea level rise and intensified coastal storm surge.

The freeway ramp used in the case study sits on a small peninsula jutting into Mobile Bay. A detailed engineering analysis looked at possible ramp failure in three different modes. The first mode was designed to determine if the ramp would fail as a result of wave-induced uplift and displacement of the superstructure. Generally speaking, the superstructure is the part of the bridge that provides the horizontal span, including the roadway. The superstructure is supported by the substructure, or foundation. Wave-induced uplift refers to powerful waves striking the bottom of a bridge, potentially lifting the roadway and other parts of the span off their foundation. The second mode examined lateral-loading–induced failure of the substructure, often from the extreme speed and force of the wind and waves striking the foundation from the side. The third mode analyzed scour-induced failure of the substructure. Scour failure is a result of fast-moving water removing so much soil around the bridge foundations that the integrity of the bridge is threatened.

Each failure mode was also examined in three different scenarios. The first scenario was the Hurricane Katrina base case, or the actual conditions in 2005 when category 3 Hurricane Katrina came ashore near New Orleans. The second scenario shifted Katrina so that the hurricane made landfall in Mobile. The final scenario looked at Katrina shifted, intensified, and added in a sea level rise of 2.5 feet (.8 m).

Working from these scenarios, the study then analyzed adaptions to the bridge structure to improve resilience, including strengthening bolt connections, installing empty open grid decks, and designing the superstructure to break away from the substructure, limiting damage to the substructure. The study suggested that the bridge was unlikely to fail in Mode 1, but could be vulnerable in Modes 2 and 3.

Although vulnerability assessments such as this are primarily used to identify overlooked or novel threats to infrastructure as a result of the cascading impacts of climate change and other dynamic forces, the study also had some surprises. Among them was that the worst damage to the bridge was not a result of the worst-case storm. In scenario 3, which added substantial sea level rise to a direct hit by a category 3 hurricane, so much water ran over the top of the bridge that the destructive impact of water slamming into the bottom of the bridge was minimized.

The ADAP tool is not intended to change specific design methodologies—or remake bridge engineering from the bottom up. However, by adding climate risk inputs and using scenario analysis, the final design selected will be more cost-effective and resilient through the full infrastructure project lifecycle.

Saving Safety Harbor

The ADAP tool was also deployed in Pinellas County, Florida—a geographically distinct peninsula with nearly 600 miles (970 km) of coastline and white sand beaches. It had long been clear how vulnerable the area is to hurricanes—2022's Hurricane Ian largely missed Pinellas but devastated its neighbors down the coast. What was less certain was exactly how the county should approach the risks accelerated by climate change.

In May 2019, NOAA forecasters reported that sea levels were rising rapidly and would continue to accelerate through the end of the century, bringing with them even more destructive storm surges. Multimillion-dollar beachfront houses and mobile homes alike faced the increasing likelihood of rising sea water eroding nearby beaches, inundating streets, or even rushing into their living rooms.

In a sense, NOAA was just confirming what many residents of Pinellas County already suspected. For years, residents of St. Pete Beach complained about "sunny day flooding"—when sea water pours out of stormwater drains and floods residential streets. Some had adjusted their trips, waiting for low tide, so they could drive their cars to the grocery store.

While NOAA was able to provide hard numbers that confirmed residents' observations, it didn't solve Pinellas County's problems. What's more, NOAA's predicted sea level rise through 2100 covered a very wide range, from a low of 2 feet (.6 m) up to a high of 8.5 feet (2.6 m). In other words, at the core of the data-based report was a substantial variability that left many questions unanswered. What critical infrastructure was most immediately threatened? Could historic coastline be preserved by sea walls? Which mitigation solutions were most appropriate: coastal armoring, elevated development, managed retreat—or something else altogether?

WSP partnered with Pinellas County to produce an innovative Critical Infrastructure Vulnerability Assessment—the first climate risk model in the United States that focused on effects and consequences. The ADAP tool was used to analyze multiple pieces of critical coastal infrastructure, WSP tailored and applied the ADAP tool to help an entire community in the county to identify resilience measures from a cost-effectiveness, climate risk, and life cycle cost perspectives.

The model included future probabilistic floodplain development to analyze the county's increasing infrastructure risk. It also used future storm surge data from state-of-the-art modeling to forecast the effects of higher water levels, including surge and wave action. Compiled asset information populated a geo-referenced database to establish a third dimension of risk: impact, outage period, and repair costs. The geo-referenced data, in turn, helped determine the costs of climate change for at-risk transportation, and water and stormwater infrastructure.

Following the study, WSP worked with Pinellas County and other stakeholders to develop a county-wide asset database that covers thousands of assets, including potable water supply, wastewater management, transportation, and electrical and natural gas infrastructure.

An economist used the data from potential flooding events based on multiple sea level rise scenarios to estimate damage costs for each asset category. These costs weren't limited to repairing the asset, but also detailed the projected socioeconomic impact on surrounding communities, such as the costs borne by residents who are left without clean water or electricity. These costs are then used to score the vulnerability of an asset, assisting Pinellas County to identify and prioritize long-term capital investments as well as policy changes that facilitate adaptation and resilience.

The rapid expansion of reporting using CDP, GRI, and TCFD frameworks reflects the growing importance of climate risk in financial decisions for investors, shareholders, and other stakeholders. This reporting further expands awareness of climate risk, as well as prompting organizations toward developing sustainability plans, including net zero roadmaps.

However, recognizing the reality of climate change and its high financial risk needs to be accompanied by rethinking our solutions. First, they should be based on analysis across multiple scenarios to account for the uncertainty of future conditions. Second, solutions should perform well across all possible features. Third, cost-effectiveness is an important consideration, but accounting should be based on full life cycle accounting, not just upfront capital costs. The cost of designing for robust, long-term resilience, and sustainability is often low compared to outdated one-size-fits-all designs that are only appropriate for historic climate baselines.

Funding Your Plan: FEMA and BRIC

The search for programs to fund resilience and sustainability plans and projects can be frustrating for state and local governments. While there is a significant amount of federal money available, the sources span many sectors, agencies, and departments across the federal government, which makes the identification of an appropriate resource challenging, and can be a barrier for applicants—especially those without prior experience accessing federal programs. Often, project developers are not aware that they might qualify for funding from multiple sources. When this opportunity arrives, it lowers further the amount of community funding needed to complete a project's budget.

The key is to know where to look, and to be able to identify where such opportunities are possible.

One relatively new program was launched by FEMA, best known as the federal agency that moves in after hurricanes and other disasters. Since 2020, when FEMA started its Building Resilient Infrastructure and Communities (BRIC) program, the agency has been spending a substantial amount of money funding mitigation projects—a future-looking approach that provides a much better return on investment.

In 2022, the program had a total lending pool of $2.295 billion available as grants to states, local communities, tribes, and territories to undertake a wide range of hazard mitigation projects that promote flexible, resilient, and sustainable development and infrastructure. These grants provide funding targeting climate change-related risks such as wildfires, drought, hurricanes, earthquakes, extreme heat, and increased flooding.

The funding also has a mechanism to prioritize instilling equity as a foundation of emergency management. FEMA prioritizes project applications from tribes and economically disadvantaged communities.[8] In 2022, for example, Gastonia, North Carolina, received $3.1 billion to restore and stabilize the bed of Duharts Creek, which has experienced significant erosion as a result of increasingly severe rain events.[9] The funding will also realign critical water and power infrastructure.

On the other side of the country, in Kern County, California, FEMA awarded a BRIC grant to provide resilience to multiple years of drought. By upgrading pipelines and pump stations, the county can add storage for 30,000 acre-feet (37,000 megaliters) of potable water in a naturally occurring aquifer located below ground and will add production wells for water extraction during droughts. The project is also designed to provide culturally appropriate water conservation guidance that is useful to people from all income levels.[10]

Across the United States, other BRIC-funded projects include flood control, utility infrastructure protection, stabilization and restoration, mitigation reconstruction, retrofits, project scoping, and shelters.[11] But, although BRIC is providing substantial amounts of funding that is desperately needed, some states don't appear to be taking full advantage. In 2021, for example, Louisiana submitted 13 sub-applications, but FEMA determined that only five met the program's requirements. Other states had the opposite problem. FEMA approved all of Tennessee's and West Virginia's proposed projects, but the states only applied for $188,000 and $327,000, respectively, of their available $1 million.[12]

WSP's climate finance team has created resources that can help governments avoid leaving money on the table. For example, the U.S. Public Sources for Climate Resilience Investment (US-CRI) database helps organizations navigate a variety of federal programs to compare uses, sectors, and geographies, and determine the best fit for any given resilience project, plan, or initiative.

WSP monitors developments in federal resilience investment—such as the passage of legislation or creation of new programs—to update the US-CRI database. The database, which was geared for U.S. state, local, tribal, and territorial governments, contains over 100 funding mechanisms from 20 federal agencies and departments. The dynamic resource offers filtering and sorting capabilities, which can cull 100 federal programs to, say, a dozen of greatest relevance.

Two of the most significant pieces of legislation of the past few years have substantially boosted government funding for resilience projects. The Bipartisan Infrastructure Law (BIL) unlocked an unprecedented $47 billion for climate resilience beginning in 2021. The following year, the Inflation Reduction Act contained provisions that will amplify resilience investment. This money will expand opportunities for many important and innovative sustainability initiatives in smaller communities. However, local governments need to know both where to look for funding and how to best present their case for those opportunities.[13]

The American Society of Adaptation Professionals (ASAP) recently published the Ready-to-Fund Resilience Toolkit. The toolkit, which WSP also helped develop and which incorporates a snapshot of the US-CRI database, describes how local government leaders and partners can design more fundable projects by pulling specific policy levers, seeking key partnerships, and rethinking and redesigning internal processes. Geared for all levels of government practitioners working on climate resilience, this toolkit will help potential funding candidates operate within current finance and policy systems to better prepare themselves and their communities for climate resilience funding and finance.

The resource breaks down the funding, including federal sources, in a way that helps organize criteria as agencies prepare their project applications. The Ready-to-Fund Resilience Toolkit will help organizations with limited resources streamline their efforts to develop projects that protect vulnerable areas from high water levels, such as Virginia Beach, where WSP-designed tide gates have now been installed to control flooding.

Even with the database available, it can be time-consuming, costly, and challenging for some state and local governments with limited human capital and financial resources to commit the time necessary to create projects and apply for the necessary funding. Governments need to regularly track updates in federal climate funding and new funding opportunities. With federal funding opportunities increasing, the time is ripe for organizations to develop resiliency projects that can withstand frequent and severe climate impacts.

While the database provides valuable information and guidance, it requires periodic re-evaluation to ensure it is being applied using current standards and criteria. For instance, many new and continuing programs under the Bipartisan Infrastructure Act are set to announce application criteria and timelines later this year. Because of continuous changes in the way the funding is awarded, the database is updated regularly, responding to changes and announcements to provide more timely guidance.

Not only can't organizations hide from the risk of climate change anymore, they can't hide their own organizational risk from employees, investors, citizens, and other stakeholders. Assessing, analyzing, and communicating vulnerabilities—as well as funding projects to build resilience—makes sense from a sustainability and financial perspective.

Notes

1. https://www.bloomberg.com/company/press/esg-assets-rising-to-50-trillion-will-reshape-140-5-trillion-of-global-aum-by-2025-finds-bloomberg-intelligence/.
2. Wenting Lu, Naiping Zhu, and Jing Zhang, "The Impact of Carbon Disclosure on Financial Performance under Low Carbon Constraints." *Energies*, 14, 4126 (2021). https://doi.org/10.3390/ en14144126.

3. https://www.sciencedirect.com/science/article/abs/pii/S105752192
1000776.
4. https://onlinelibrary.wiley.com/doi/abs/10.1002/bse.2426.
5. https://www.bloomberg.com/news/articles/2022-09-04/climate-change-is-
overwhelming-us-flood-maps-fema-head-says.
6. https://www.theguardian.com/us-news/2022/sep/09/california-sizzled-
in-a-record-heatwave-this-week-we-mapped-where-it-was-hottest.
7. https://www.sacbee.com/news/weather-news/article265412691.html.
8. https://www.fema.gov/grants/mitigation/building-resilient-infrastructure-
communities/after-apply/fy-2021-subapplication-status.
9. https://governor.nc.gov/news/press-releases/2022/08/12/governor-roy-
cooper-joins-fema-administrator-gastonia-announce-resiliency-funding.
10. https://www.fema.gov/grants/mitigation/building-resilient-infrastructure-
communities/after-apply/fy-2021-subapplication-status.
11. https://www.fema.gov/grants/mitigation/building-resilient-infrastructure-
communities/after-apply/fy-2021-subapplication-status.
12. https://www.nrdc.org/experts/anna-weber/building-resilience-bric-bric-
summer-2022-update.
13. https://www.wsp.com/en-us/insights/2022-asap-ready-to-fund-
resilience.

9

Building Support Inside and Out

WHEN WSP INITIALLY rolled out its Future Ready program within the company, getting early wins was essential to building momentum and buy-in. Once employees could see that establishing a new and better solutions-oriented framework produced results—being selected by key clients for large and high-profile projects—even sceptics were likely to become converts. The same is true of any organization's climate action and sustainability plans. Quick successes, however small, build broad internal support and increase commitment—even excitement—around organizational goals.

Depending on an organization's starting point, there may even be some low hanging fruit to notch these first wins. Reducing waste, decreasing water usage, or increasing energy efficiency are a few good places to look for those early wins. However, taking a surface-level scattershot approach—installing recycling bins, LED lights, and water attenuators—without going deeper, communicating, measuring, and reporting on these gains is a misdirected approach. Employees notice glaring anomalies that undercut a company's communication strategy. For example, an organization that has installed recycling bins, but is still providing, say, plastic spoons instead of bamboo will find it more difficult to create a convincing narrative about its commitment to reducing waste. Getting a solid win—achieving excellent results in one area—is superior to half-measures and incomplete initiatives.

For example, a waste reduction plan could *start* with education about different types of recycling bins. Recycling can be confusing, so any new bin should be clearly labeled in terms of what can and can't be deposited. Going beyond basic options—providing recycling for e-waste or plastic bags as well as composting food—also sends a strong message. Finally, organizations can move to full circularity where waste products become input for new products. Food compost can be spread on plants and landscaping, or the company could host a textile recycling bin.

Organizations can educate, impact, and communicate on a more individual level too. For example, replace waste baskets at desks with recycling bins or make reusable water bottles available for any employee and install drinking bottle refilling stations. For conferences, small measures like providing reusable lanyards and name tags are helpful. Avoiding the ubiquitous giveaways in favor of more sustainable options such as donations to green causes reinforces the idea that sustainability is interwoven into the fabric of the organization. And even though recycling and other waste reduction measures have experienced challenges that have reduced their overall effectiveness, the individual education and mindfulness elements are very important building blocks for broader success.

Regardless of what early measures are taken and the degree of success experienced, educating people to increase mindfulness, and sharing goals and metrics will help create a sense of mission and immediate engagement with a longer sustainability journey. Organizations should ensure that the metrics are easily understandable and relatable. For example: "LEDs we installed have reduced greenhouse gas emissions equivalent to removing 50 cars from the road as well as saved the company $10,050" or "Together, our recycling efforts have prevented over two tons of waste from ending up in a landfill."

Each organization needs to play to its individual strengths for early wins. Some businesses may be able to switch to electric automobile fleets relatively easily, others can quickly reduce their water and/or power consumption, while other companies can begin to transition their manufacturing process away from chemicals that emit particularly strong greenhouse gases. Even more importantly, though, organizations need to avoid cherry picking isolated easy wins that aren't part of a consistent bigger plan and organizational journey. Any climate action plan or sustainability plan is fundamentally a multiple-step, dynamic, long-term program that will necessarily include many tasks and projects.

Internal Buy-In

When organizations begin to look at formal goals and sustainability roadmaps, it's time to also consider their strategy for outreach and communication, both internally and to a larger group of stakeholders. The substantial transitions necessary for a meaningful climate journey are likely to run into a degree of resistance. The overall success of the project will require engagement and contributions from multiple constituencies, but internal skeptics need to be approached early on.

Winning over doubtful leaders and employees begins with establishing a baseline understanding of the challenge. Any communication— slides, speaker, emails—should seek to educate first and emphasize a few key points. First, climate change is a challenge that is here *now*. Second, climate change is a *global* problem. Third, it is already having *local* impacts—and those impacts will continue to change and intensify. Fourth, the organization is preparing to fight this challenge with a sense of urgency and purpose and needs *everyone's* help.

With the urgency of the challenge established, the next step is making the business case for a sustainability journey. This discussion can start by talking about the existing challenges that leaders, employees, and the organization already deal with. Some likely examples include retaining employees, maintaining brand image, monitoring performance, and uncertainty about future regulations. Vulnerability and climate risk assessments detail how climate change will exacerbate all these problems. In fact, investment in sustainability planning produces an excellent return. It increases a company's resilience against physical, regulatory, and other transition risks, and sets up an organization to succeed in a changing economy. Broad ESG reports, more specific TCFD-type reporting, and/or publicly stated commitments to decarbonization pathways and milestones attract and impress investors, employees, and consumers. Investing in sustainability is, by definition, investing in the long-term viability of the organization. Turn the question about the value of a sustainability journey on its head: Can you really afford not to understand your organization's climate-related risks and opportunities?

Another aspect of the business case is the actual savings or other types of increased benefits from implementing a plan. Emphasize how a life cycle approach simply makes better business sense than focusing on short-term costs. For example, organizations will have lower power bills from investing in energy efficiency and they can eliminate widely fluctuating gas or diesel costs by switching to an electric fleet.

As the process of developing a sustainability plan moves forward, it's critical to maintain communication with all stakeholders. A regular cadence of reporting on progress, particularly early wins, can also reassure both internal and external critics. The organization should identify a lead (or multiple but clearly defined leads) within the organization for people to approach with questions about the company's climate risk and opportunities. Organizations should be strategic about how they engage employees in the process, but they should provide regular updates with multiple opportunities for feedback. This is necessary to promote alignment, in general, and, specifically, with regard to getting buy-in from employees—while also giving them an opportunity to provide feedback and

Investors and other stakeholders will want to see a published plan of the organization's pathway. It needs to be consistent and clear, have targeted goals, with regular monitoring, reporting, and a way to hold management responsible, possibly involving its compensation.

External Buy-In

All climate action and sustainability plans, programs, and projects need to incorporate broad stakeholder engagement from the beginning. This is especially true for public sector organizations that need to make a special effort to engage their local communities—their programs are paid for by public money, need public approval for implementation, and will simply be more responsive, better designed, and provide co-benefits if they draw on local needs and knowledge.

Companies can decide how broad a segment of the public to engage, and what other external stakeholders require engagement beyond any nonemployee investors and shareholders that they may have. But public organizations always need to communicate their targets and strategies to a broad group that includes politicians, citizens, environmental groups, community organizations, business leaders, religious institutions, and nonprofits.

There are, however, multiple benefits to early and robust external engagement efforts. Speaking in a language that each group understands and listening to their concerns reduces social and reputational risk. Engagement at the front end fosters the broad support that is helpful, and sometimes essential, to move smoothly from planning to implementation stage. Disclosing specific measures and any additional co-benefits is critical to gaining buy-in from all stakeholders.

The positive impacts of external engagement are maximized when stakeholders are involved in a variety of ways through all stages of the project life cycle, from concept to delivery to decommissioning. Local and organizational-specific knowledge helps create stronger plans—ones uniquely attuned to the needs of the company, city, county, state, or region. The plan will also contribute to the creation of a better future for our cities, regions, communities, and environment.

While it is critical to engage multiple stakeholder groups, particularly robust efforts should be made in the case of the historically underserved communities and stakeholders that have suffered the most from unintended consequences of previous infrastructure projects and general economic growth. Even today, those shaping our built and social environments have often told marginalized people how they will be helped after decisions have already been made—rather than asking people early on what they need as a key input to making decisions. Since many potential solutions could create new burdens on those who could least afford to bear them, it is critical that we don't repeat the mistakes of the past. Quite simply, an inequitable, unjust climate transition will not be sustainable.

Despite the widespread recognition of external engagement's central role on a program or a project's ultimate success, it too often becomes a box to tick. The process of "engagement" may be limited to an announcement that precludes any meaningful feedback or real partnering with the community and other stakeholders.

The baseline assumption of engagement is inclusive, early, two-way communication. In addition to timing and looking to engage as early as is practical, some of the other key variables in facilitating this kind of interaction are time and place. A traditional public meeting is on a weekday, in the evening, at a government building. However, this setting doesn't make everyone feel safe or included—for example, it doesn't work well for single parents or people working two shift jobs. So, in addition to traditional meeting places, identify alternate locations that people are familiar with. Safe spaces could include a religious institution, a public library, a school, a community center, or a local business. Walking tours are another way to be present in the community that don't involve a fixed space—it's engagement that literally meets people where they are.

Hybrid workshops that people can attend in person or online are one way to expand attendance, particularly in a post-pandemic world in which immuno-compromised people still feel unsafe in large, public groups. Other ways to make people feel welcome might include free childcare or translation services during the events.

Creating community advisory groups in partnership with existing community organizations can also help reach a broader cross-section. However, to serve as true gateways into communities, these groups should generally not include any elected officials or consultants. It's better to have information presented by someone the community recognizes and with whom they have a standing relationship.

Presenting a clear timeline of engagement events from the very beginning is also vital. An external engagement plan tells people all the opportunities they will have to engage. One example of this type of commitment would be planning external engagement events at least on a quarterly basis across the life cycle of a particular project. These types of specific, upfront commitments lead to better participation than isolated meetings or one-off workshops.

One common pitfall at these external engagement efforts is inherent bias (whether conscious or unconscious) of technical experts who are important parts of presentations. As an expert, it's easy to think that one's work experience and technical knowledge always trump the lived experience of people in the community that an organization is trying to serve—as well as those of other stakeholders. However, true engagement requires valuing the lived experience as much as technical knowledge.

Of course, many presentations do need to provide technical information to help community members visualize potential project outcomes. In a project about street design, for example, experts can launch discussions by talking about different types of streets that already exist in that city, giving people familiar, concrete examples. The experts could also explain the technical guidelines they have to follow—the limits of space for bike lanes, sidewalks, walkways, and the trade-offs that exist. Then experts can listen to the priorities of the community in terms of mobility and placemaking.

Different ways of structuring engagement events will suit certain projects better than others—and determine what kind of participation there is. Some events might be about projects in which the solutions and outcomes have already been determined, like scheduled maintenance of a bridge or stormwater management. A suitable structure might be a community focus group that allows groups like small business owners a chance to give input on ways they might be impacted by possible traffic detours and safety considerations. On the other hand, a project like a multimodal mobility hub that includes affordable housing and public broadband is a good candidate for visioning workshops in which a cross-section of community members weighs on what they need and how the project could best serve their community.

Partnering on Bethlehem's Climate Action Plan

Bethlehem, Pennsylvania, is a historic city of about 75,000 located in the Lehigh Valley north of Philadelphia. Several years ago, Bethlehem decided to pursue an ambitious climate plan, including mitigation, emissions reduction, resilience, and adaptation. WSP was able to partner with the city as well as numerous community groups to develop a plan that leveraged community knowledge and galvanized substantial local support for the implementation process. This engagement started well before the action plan was conceived—WSP has a local office in downtown Bethlehem, so employees already lived in the area, knew the community, and were civically engaged.

The plan was guided by a broad coalition, including the Chamber of Commerce and other business leaders, local colleges—Lehigh University, Northampton Community College, Moravian University—the Nurture Nature Center, Sierra Club, the Sunrise Movement, and other environmental justice groups, nonprofits, and citizen advisory councils.

A series of interviews with local stakeholders provided a deeper understanding of the climate risks Bethlehem experiences today. The city's emergency management team informed WSP of its priorities in terms of resilience and adaptation. The Buildings Department provided recommendations on building codes as well as codes targeting net zero. Ultimately, every strategy in the plan was influenced by community and local stakeholder knowledge.

This information was complemented by support from WSP's national technical resources. Climate scientists, analysts, and engineers created detailed climate modeling to inform assessments of Bethlehem's local climate vulnerability, hazards, and local impacts. This highly technical climate modeling has helped shape the types of adaptation strategies the city's emergency management department and their health department will pursue. Additionally, that local data may end up getting used by other cities in the Lehigh Valley that want to increase mitigation or resilience, but don't have the resources to create such sophisticated climate modeling.

Industrial pollution is a key local environmental concern. The Bethlehem Steel Works were once the second largest in the nation, but they ceased most production in the 1980s and filed for bankruptcy in 2001. Although parts of the original building have been repurposed for arts and entertainment, the city's industrial legacy also includes toxic pollution, including numerous brownfields. As is often the case in the United States and other countries, much of this historic pollution burden has been born by Black and Brown communities.

Aware of this history, the climate plan was based on substantial input from the impacted communities. To be truly sustainable and resilient, the plan needed to be grounded in equity and justice. However, reaching communities that have historically been neglected, or not able to participate in similar public processes, often requires additional efforts or different engagement strategies. Outreach for the climate plan began in March 2020, the beginning of the COVID pandemic, creating an additional degree of difficulty. Public meetings were moved to webinars. The number of webinars were increased and held at different times for people working outside of a traditional workday. Through partnership with the Hispanic Center Lehigh Valley, the climate plan benefited from Spanish language engagement on the south side of Bethlehem, an area with a large Latino community.

This early engagement across different segments of the community resulted in feedback that reemphasized the appetite for an emphasis on righting historical wrongs. As a result, the climate plan includes a specific chapter on environmental justice and integrates environmental justice considerations into each strategy and action in the plan. Among the plan's goals is dedicating at least 40% of the funding toward benefiting marginalized frontline communities. The plan also creates a task force to ensure that there are no unintended consequences of actions and strategies that negatively affect frontline communities.

The extensive community engagement across Bethlehem, including education and a large amount of public input, also helped avoid an all-too-common fate of other plans. Even well-designed plans can end up sitting on a shelf and never moving to the implementation stage due to a lack of input and support from the community. However, by getting public buy-in, as well creating a clear path forward with key performance indicators, the plan gained public and political support and has moved into the implementation stage.

Communicating with, listening to, and winning over various stakeholder groups—including employees, local communities, voters, investors, shareholders, and partners—are essential elements for designing and implementing a successful sustainability project, program, and journey. Programs and plans that extend over decades will eventually falter if they aren't embraced across the entire organization. In the same way, effective external engagement with various groups will make these plans and programs more effective, more resilient, and more likely to provide additional stakeholder benefits and result in crucial buy-in more broadly.

10

Nature-Based Solutions from Coast to Coast

HIGHWAY 98 RUNS through Florida's panhandle region, hugging the coast from Pensacola to Alligator Point. In the 1980s, the road was known as the Forgotten Highway because it was left out of tourist brochures. These days, Highway 98 has made it onto maps, but the unassuming stretch of asphalt with views of the Gulf of Mexico still seems an unlikely place for the future of infrastructure to be taking shape. Just past Apalachicola, a small town punctuated by oyster bars, lies a peaceful, sparsely populated stretch of the highway that carries high infrastructure vulnerability. It is also the site of a remarkable program that brings together sustainability and resilience, while offering many other benefits to the community.

While every region of the United States is being impacted by climate change to varying degrees and in different ways, Florida's combination of extreme temperatures, flooding, and hurricanes regularly places it at or near the top of climate-risk rankings.[1,2,3,4] Headline-grabbing examples include the increasingly common sunny-day flooding in Miami Beach at high tide—when saltwater runs onto the streets from wastewater drains—and dire predictions that large portions of South Florida will be uninhabitable within a few generations.[5] But in Apalachicola, at the slower-paced, northern end of the state, the

213

impact of climate change and resource depletion has also arrived with disconcerting speed.

Shellshock

Until recently, Apalachicola was once one of the United States' oyster capitals, producing 90% of Florida's oysters and about 10% of oysters in the United States. The area's primary industries are still seafood harvesting and tourism. The two are interconnected since one of the main draws for tourists is eating fresh seafood. However, the oyster industry has been shrinking since the 1980s. Locals remember hundreds of oyster boats in the harbor just a few decades ago. Now you're more likely to see just a dozen boats at any time.

After the slow decline—a result of overharvesting, pollution, and other factors—the industry went into freefall about 10 years ago, following the Deepwater Horizon explosion that leaked 210 million gallons (795 million liters) of oil into the Gulf of Mexico.[6] As the massive oil slick began drifting north toward the coasts of Louisiana, Mississippi, Alabama, and Florida, harvesters were allowed to ignore state regulations and gather as many oysters as they could before the reefs became covered in tar.

As it turned out, the oil never made it to Apalachicola's coast, but the industry was nearly destroyed anyway. The reefs were completely denuded of oysters, killing off any chance of the shellfish quickly recovering to a healthy enough population to support the once-thriving industry. Some local restaurants—all of which feature oysters on the menu—have stopped serving local Apalachicola oysters, considering them an endangered species. In 2020, the State of Florida announced a moratorium on oyster harvesting in the area.

At the same time, the oyster population was also suffering from another type of environmental degradation. Oysters thrive in the inter-tidal combination of salty ocean and freshwater, but climate change and population growth have made this balance increasingly precarious. The primary source of freshwater that maintains the brackish mix runs into the harbor via the Apalachicola River, but the river originates hundreds of miles north in what is also a reservoir for Atlanta's drinking water. Since 2000, Atlanta has grown by over 2.5 million people, putting additional demands on its water resources. As a result, droughts in either Apalachicola or North Georgia can reduce the flow of freshwater into the bay. When the water becomes too salty, not only are conditions less favorable for oysters, but they encourage predators like the oyster drill, a small snail which attaches itself to oysters' shells, bores a hole through their valves, and then sucks out the insides.

The Apalachicola River also delivers pollution—the same agricultural fertilizers and industrial waste that have severely damaged oyster habitats around the world. A combination of pollution, overharvesting, predators, wetland loss, coastal erosion, ocean acidification, and drought has made oyster reefs one of the most imperiled marine habitats on earth. Over the past century, a stunning 85–90% of natural oyster reefs have been lost.[7] In short, the oysters just off the coast of an unassuming highway are battling for survival in the face of climate change and other environmental stresses.

It turns out, however, that Highway 98 itself could be just as vulnerable to environmental devastation as the oyster reefs. Hurricane Michael, a powerful category 5 storm, hit the region hard in 2018, destroying businesses, homes, forest land, and inundating, blocking, and wiping out portions of Highway 98—which is also the main hurricane evacuation route.[8]

Michael's wind speed was unprecedented for the area. Most of the time, the bay is calm and shallow, partially protected by Dog Island and St. George's Island. However, smaller but still powerful thunderstorms do roll through regularly. These storms increase wave energy and rainfall, which weakens Highway 98's shoulder, wears down hardened surfaces, and washes away the fill. The areas around the multiple concrete drains that funnel stormwater under the road and into the bay are particularly likely to erode. Since Highway 98 is part of the state's critical infrastructure, the Florida Department of Transportation spends a substantial amount of time and money repairing and then re-repairing the shoulder and roadway.

Oyster-Based Solutions

The plight of Apalachicola's oysters and the coastal erosion along the area's major highway might appear to be two separate challenges, each with its own solution. However, designing climate adaptation and hazard mitigation measures for the crumbling coastline ultimately led

WSP and its partners to a more holistic response. Healthy oyster reefs can serve as dynamic physical barriers that absorb storm-created wave energy as it approaches the shoreline, mitigating the impact of coastal erosion.

Oyster reefs provide varying levels of erosion prevention and infra-structure protection for assets like Highway 98, depending on a variety of environmental and human-made factors. However, once reefs are established, they provide multiple benefits for years. The reefs trap sediment, raising the elevation of the sea floor so that vegetation can establish itself and further stabilize the shoreline. Depending on how rapidly sea levels rise, oyster reefs may also be able to grow fast enough to continue to offer the same erosion mitigation benefits decades into the future.

Healthy oyster reefs also provide a wide range of environmental and economic benefits. For one, oysters are prolific water purifiers—a single adult oyster can filter up to 50 gallons (190 liters) of water a day.[9] The oyster reefs and grasses that are planted and build up around the reefs also provide habitats for all sorts of aquatic life. Sea anemones and mussels attach themselves to the oyster reefs. The irregular, shaded nooks in a reef provide nurseries for a wide range of commercially valu-able marine animals, including flounder, Spanish mackerel, blue crabs, and striped bass.[10]

Like hardened sea walls, the reefs can be damaged by storms, but they are also able to heal themselves naturally. If, however, the reefs are damaged beyond repair or fail to thrive for some reason, they don't require cleanup, hauling, or disposal. Oysters are part of the ecosystem, and, like all other nature-based solutions (NbS), have a much lower impact throughout their life cycle than other types of infrastructure. Their positive environmental impact and relatively inexpensive end-of-life not only makes oysters and other nature-based solutions more sustainable, but often more cost-efficient over their lifetime.

Cutting Edge Habitats

WSP approached the Apalachee Regional Planning Commission with a plan that deeply integrated resilience, disaster preparedness, sustain-ability, and the local economy. The project was ultimately approved and funded by a combination of grants and Deepwater Horizon settlement money.

Despite the large numbers of oysters that naturally flourished in the bay, the damage to the ecosystem meant that many hours of technical work went into establishing healthy habitats. What's more, there is no established best-practice manual or standardized design criteria for oyster reefs. Engineers have not definitively established which designs or guidelines are superior for, say, standing up to stresses of a hurricane or providing wave attenuation.

Despite a lack of consensus standards and techniques, a steady stream of reef-building technologies is coming onto the market. Over the course of 2020, a variety of different, sometimes bizarre-looking, products were field tested in the bay. One commonly used device is the reef ball, which resembles a concrete half-sphere cast with irregular holes in its sides. Another, known as an oyster castle tabletop, looks like mesh twine wrapped around a small table. Oyster castles are built out of concrete blocks small enough to be moved by hand that snap together like Legos to form artificial reefs of virtually any size or height. Other options included stick-like rastas, oyster catcher pillows—a mesh material loosely rolled into a log shape—and lollipops, which protrude from the water like the tops of giant screw eye hooks. Each product was taken through a feasibility study, rated on factors like cost, stability, and how well they recruited oysters.

The goal of the structures is not to last forever, but to jumpstart a natural process by encouraging sufficient oyster growth so that the reefs become self-sustaining. During the testing period, however, the oyster growth wasn't extremely high. In this particular environment, it turned out, the best option would be low-tech but high-stability piles of rocks. These stacks would host the oysters as they grew, organically expanding the shoreline stabilization year after year.

There was also a digital component to designing the environment in which oyster reefs flourish. A software suite called MIKE 21 provides a range of engineering elements essential for designing all sorts of offshore and port structures, including wave loads and currents.[11] The software analyzes water activity and detailed coastal modeling around the project area, including hydrodynamic, spectral wave, and sediment transport. Advanced Computational Fluid Dynamics modeling was conducted in order to better determine the degree of wave attenuation as waves pass through the various reef material.

Phase I of the project restores the oyster reefs, while also reducing coastal erosion, improving water quality, and providing commercially valuable seafood stocks. Although it is at the cutting edge of a new approach to engineering resilience and sustainability, it is—thankfully—not the only instance of these types of nature-based solutions.

First Line of Reefence

In September 2022, Rutgers University in New Jersey announced a $12.6-million project to develop an oyster-based shoreline ecosystem to help protect coastlines from storm damage, flooding, and erosion.[12] The project, an international partnership that includes universities, nonprofits, and WSP, is not funded by environmental or industry groups, but rather by the U.S. Department of Defense (DoD). The Defense Advanced Research Projects Agency (DARPA), an agency that can claim at least partial credit for high-tech innovations like weather satellites, GPS, voice interfaces, personal computers, and the internet, is now investing in developing oyster reefs to protect military infrastructure and personnel from storm damage, flooding, and erosion. Called "Reefense: A Mosaic Oyster Habitat for Coastal Defense," the project is investigating options beyond hardened shorelines. Reefense is, at least in part, motivated by conventional resilience solutions' well-documented record of causing ecological damage to marine plants and animals, as well as exacerbating storm surge damage.

The growing U.S. military interest in NbS is not limited to experimental measures. The Army Corps of Engineers, the United States' largest infrastructure builder, launched an initiative called Engineering with Nature that pursues innovative resilience solutions beyond the high-maintenance hardened infrastructure often used to protect DoD installations. Again, much of the impetus to rethink resilience and sustainability is the environmental damage consistently caused by previous non-holistic approaches. We can't turn back the clock on all the ecological damage previous solutions may have caused. However, the infrastructure of the future can learn from and leverage nature to create Future Ready, sustainable, and resilient solutions that offer multiple additional benefits.

For example, the Reefense habitats are expected to be made from biodegradable materials and low-carbon cement. Advanced biological technologies will also be used to create faster-growing, disease-resistant, but nongenetically engineered oysters. The habitat's modular design will also allow expansion of the structure if sea level rises faster than expected.

Despite the commitment to NbS by universities, nonprofits, the DoD, state and local governments, and parts of the private sector, there is still significant resistance to unconventional approaches to resilience and sustainability—especially if one is only looking at upfront construction cost comparatives rather than life cycle comparatives. Perhaps we've become accustomed to thinking that only huge slabs of concrete are going to offer any significant erosion mitigation, so much so that we are willing to ignore the high embodied carbon that makes such an approach unsustainable from a GHG standpoint. Oyster reefs, and NbS in general, are much more sustainable and also make better financial sense over their full life cycle. What's more, infrastructure and habitats around the world are facing the systemic breakdown of their environmental conditions. Nature-based technologies, tools, and processes offer holistic, systemic solutions for many different challenges.

The Two Ramonas

In 1941, a large, low-income housing development was built a few miles east of downtown Los Angeles on the northern edge of the expanding city's first freeway. Over the next 80 years, the housing complex, Ramona Gardens, and the freeway, Ramona Boulevard, shared more than just a name. Both have grown rapidly, with Ramona Boulevard transforming into the 12-lane Interstate 10, locally known as the San Bernardino Freeway, and the second busiest stretch of interstate in the U.S.[13] Over that same time, Ramona Gardens expanded to around 100 buildings and become LA's largest public housing project. The interstate and the housing complex also share something less desirable—the air pollution that originates from the tailpipes of vehicles on the large, congested road.

At the time Ramona Gardens was built, almost no one had any idea the damage caused by the fumes produced by internal combustion engines. In fact, on July 26, 1943—two years after the housing complex was opened—residents of L.A. were terrified and confused by a cloud of smog that enveloped their city. The fumes smelled like bleach, caused choking and tears, and was believed by many residents to be a Japanese chemical weapon attack.[14] A few days later, after it became clear that the smog wasn't a new front in World War II, city leaders quickly shut down a chemical factory, hoping to eliminate the noxious smoke. The plan didn't work and, while blame fell on various other industrial and electricity generating plants, the mysterious problem persisted.

It wasn't until the 1950s that scientists established the primary source of the choking pollution: cars. As we now know, exhaust from automobiles fueled by diesel fuel or gasoline contains a toxic brew of tiny particulates, ozone, lead, carbon monoxide, nitrogen dioxide, and sulfur dioxide. Since the 1970s, when the EPA was created and catalytic converters first required, automotive exhaust pollution in the United States has been reduced enormously. The combined emission of the six most-common pollutants has dropped by 78%.

Globally, however, the impact of air pollution, much of it from automobiles and other motor vehicles, is an ongoing crisis. The damage from motor vehicle emissions impacts people at every phase of their lives, resulting in pre-term and low-weight infants, childhood leukemia, and asthma onset, a lifetime of impaired lung development, cardiovascular disease, and premature death. Globally, the air pollution attributable to automotive emissions is estimated to have resulted in the premature death of roughly 385,000 people in one year. In the United States, the negative health impacts of vehicle emissions continue to be particularly acute for low-income and minority groups like the nearly 2,000 residents of Ramona Gardens, including 700 children.[15,16] Largely as a result of increased exposure to air pollution, Black and Latino children are at significantly higher risk of developing asthma.

Every day, hundreds of thousands of vehicles pass close by Ramona Gardens. As a result, residents of live in an area where the air quality is considered unhealthy 40% of the time—it is in the top 1% of most polluted communities in California.[17,18] Residents suffer disproportionately from serious health problems, not just because of roadway traffic, but also an adjacent rail corridor. To make things even worse, there is the urban heat island effect, local microclimate conditions, and other socioeconomic factors.

The health problems experienced by residents of Ramona Gardens are just one example of the negative side effects of one-purpose infrastructure solutions, like Interstate 10. The series of roads, bridges, overpasses, and tunnels that created the U.S. interstate system have been invaluable for domestic economic growth and allowing drivers to travel long distances much more quickly. However, that same interstate system has also been a main driver in the economic demise of some towns and urban areas, separating communities, and disrupting the walkability of neighborhoods.[19] It can also encourage, and, at the very least, facilitates more driving—an inefficient form of transport that contributes disproportionately to GHG emissions and the concentration of toxic air pollution in certain corridors.

Air Repair

Aware of the negative health impact of the freeway at their southern border, in 2015 community leaders secured a $400,000 grant to install an air filtration system at Ramona Gardens' local elementary school. While the treatment helped to protect students' respiratory systems in the building, it was too small to deal with a bigger systemic problem. After school ended, the same kids might go to the community playground, Ramona Head Start, the Boys and Girls Club, or the library— all of which sit within a few hundred feet of the polluting freeway. The community needed a broader solution for the freeway's air pollution, one generated by an infrastructure that was holistic, grounded in natural systems, and provided multiple benefits.

WSP was part of a team that developed a plan to install a living air filtration system between the freeway and new community outdoor space. If correctly positioned, using meteorological and air quality data, something as simple as trees, shrubs, and grasses are a very effective natural barrier and air quality improvement measure. They reduce exposure to particulate matter—tiny particles that invade lungs, causing asthma and other health risks—by as much as 50%. Unlike human-made barriers such as walls, trees can also help to clean up the air. Particles, odors, and gases like ozone, nitrogen oxide, and sulfur dioxide that settle on the leaves of trees are absorbed through tiny pores.

As with the oyster reefs, NbS such as this are dynamic and provide multiple benefits. When the trees grow higher, they will be able to better mitigate pollution and also provide a visual barrier and more shade to combat the urban heat island effect. The trees also remove carbon dioxide from the atmosphere while releasing oxygen, one of the essential cycles needed for life to flourish on Earth.

Virtuous Cycles

NbS is holistic by definition—deeply integrated into a larger ecosystem—and resilient, sustainable infrastructure incorporates whole-system processes throughout its design development. In fact, doing so is the only way to avoid the historic pitfalls of narrow, one-purpose solutions.

Take, for example, community engagement, which is critically important for public infrastructure projects, but often incompletely executed and/or undertaken after key planning and design decisions have already been made. For decades, the experience of many low-income communities has been one of neglect and disinvestment, leading to suspicions that future infrastructure investments are only a prelude to gentrification and displacement. However, robust and early-stage engagement—outreach, listening, responding, and brainstorming—will meet the specific needs of residents, incorporate local knowledge, lived experience, and gain broad support for projects. Engagement isn't a checked box in a linear process, but, when done correctly, is part of dynamic, iterative design process and best practice.

Part of the planning process for the Ramona Gardens project was a series of bilingual meetings and direct engagement carried out by volunteers and community groups. Residents learned about the planned project and shared their priorities, including a strong desire for a place to continue their weekly swap meet. The open-air market featuring vendors selling clothing, crafts, and food has been a community fixture since the 1990s. In 2016, it became the first fully legal and licensed market at a L.A. housing project. The park's final design accommodates multiple activities, including the swap meet.

Community engagement also revealed that among residents' highest priorities for the project was a sonic buffer from the constant buzz of the freeway and trains—traffic noise being yet another way that local communities can be very negatively impacted by infrastructure. As much as healthier air, residents wanted a quieter, natural place to escape the city. The ideal of nature as a place for reflection and relaxation is probably as old as the first urban center. Over the past few decades, however, scientists have begun to quantify the positive mental and physiological impacts of nature.

In 1984, a psychologist named Robert S. Ulrich published the results of breakthrough study in *Science* magazine. His study followed the post-surgical recovery of 46 patients in a suburban Pennsylvania hospital. Ulrich tried to eliminate as many differentiators as possible—weight, age, gender, attending surgeon and nurse, smoker or not. Because patients were immobile for much of their recovery, Ulrich was careful to make sure the study only compared patients in virtually identical rooms—going so far as to separate patients who convalesced in blue walls from those in rooms with green walls. All rooms had the same dimensions, layout, and furniture, ensuring that the bedridden patients spent much of their time facing windows with unobstructed views outside. The primary difference was what they saw: half the patients looked out onto a stand of deciduous trees, the other half a brown brick wall.

The results—a natural view helped improve post-surgical recovery—were consistent. The nature-facing group spent less time in the hospital and requested significantly fewer narcotics for pain. Nurses' reviews also showed that the brick-facing patients received three times the number of negative condition reports.

While even Ulrich admits the limitations of his initial experiment, his conclusion—exposure to nature improves health—has been instrumental in the creation of a new field called enviro-psychology. Over the past 40 years, numerous experiments have suggested benefits, including boosting creative functioning and sleep quality, increasing self-esteem, energy, patience, and life satisfaction, as well as reducing anger and cognitive decline. A 2015 study indicated that spending time in nature tended to increase what are called "natural killer" cells—a part of the immune system that attacks viruses. Of course, any designer who listened to the feedback from Ramona Gardens' residents would include natural space in their plans without needing to read the scientific literature about nature's parasympathetic nervous system component that reduces anxiety. Greater opportunity for natural seclusion is what the community was asking for already.

The final design for Ramona Gardens' park includes promoting the therapeutic effects of nature. A new 10-foot (3-m) wall will be erected between the freeway and park. Soil will be pushed up against the wall, creating a sonic barrier and a berm that raises up the trees planted there, increasing the amount of pollutants they capture, the shade they provide, and the visible expanse of green canopy. This nature-based approach aims to improve not only air and noise quality, but residents' quality of life by creating a model for public housing developments and low-income communities throughout California.

Public infrastructure design is at its best when community engagement is broad, early, and continuing in a virtuous cycle. Planners and designers need to provide substantial information early enough in the project development to get useful feedback that can guide future considerations for and iterations of design plans and construction.

Concrete Rivers

Many schoolkids' first science lessons often include the water cycle. In the classic, simplified version of the water cycle, water evaporates from the ocean, condenses into clouds, falls as precipitation on inland areas, runs over and through soils and rock formations, and, ultimately, runs through rivers back into the ocean. Without fail, the cycle irrigates crops, provides habitats for fish and other life, and delivers drinking water. It's an elegant, holistic system and a great example of circularity that we experience every waking moment of our lives—and one that humans have expended a lot of energy disrupting and breaking down.

For one, our great rivers no longer run uninterrupted and clean from the land to the sea. The Ganges, Rio Grande, Yellow, Mississippi, Jordan, Yangtze, Nile, Danube, and Indus rivers—flowing waters that are considered sacred, celebrated in song and literature, and essential for sustaining billions of people—have been dammed, channelized, overfished, and heavily polluted with a variety of fertilizer, antibiotics, industrial waste, and raw sewage. As a result, the cycle is no longer as dependable at delivering clean water for aquatic habitats, irrigation, or drinking water.

Climate change is further reshaping the water cycle into something new or barely identifiable. In the past several years, historic droughts and floods have plagued the American West, Central and East Asia, Australia, as well as much of Africa and Europe. Even when the water arrives after a drought, its timing and quantity are much less predictable.

This is not to say we can or should seek to eliminate traditional water infrastructure—the engineered solutions that provide essential resources like drinking water or wastewater management. Particularly in urban areas, this infrastructure will continue to be essential to healthy, clean, functional communities. But our traditional infrastructure development processes can still learn and benefit from the employment of holistic frameworks. L.A.'s expanding efforts to create a broader, more unified, and circular approach to rebuilding, restoring, and rethinking the relationship between its infrastructure and water resources is one such ongoing experiment.

In the mid-1800s, the Los Angeles River flowed approximately 50 miles (80.5 km) from the Santa Susana Mountains and into a wide floodplain passing to the east of what is now downtown L.A., through the marshlands near present-day Long Beach, and into the Pacific. Not only did the meandering river's course change over time, but its flow was extremely seasonal. It could slow to a trickle in summer, but it expanded to cover broad areas during the rainier months of winter.

The native Tongva, who had hunted and foraged along the river's banks for centuries, adapted to these seasonal shifts, but L.A.'s rapid growth in the 20th century permanently encroached on the floodplain, spreading concrete and asphalt. As a result, what had been the river's natural cycle suddenly became historically devastating floods. A few decades into the century, the city decided to undertake a massive engineering project to stop the flooding. The river was bounded by a massive concrete sleeve. The result—one of the most prominent examples of ordering and controlling nature in North America—worked well, the water flowed quickly past the city and into the Pacific without flooding. However, it was a one-purpose solution that transformed the river into a place more well-known as a movie set than a fishing or wildlife habitat. For half of the year, the dry, concrete L.A. River looked like an empty mirror of Interstate 10 to its east. The unnatural engineering also encouraged people to dump a wide range of waste onto the concrete channel, including oil, raw sewage, and shopping carts.

At least since the 1990s, environmentalists, citizen groups, urban planners, and engineers have been trying to figure out how to restore some of the river's previously rich plant and animal diversity. In the early 2000s, the city council signed onto cleaning up and restoring the natural river. Though it would be effectively impossible to return the river to its original state, the city could engineer a nature-modeled revitalization.

The People's Crown Jewel

Since 2016, one of the focal points of the larger river reimagining has been Taylor Yards, an abandoned railyard located adjacent to the L.A. River. The city bought a 40-acre (16-hectare) portion of parcel G2, which sits between the river and Rio de Los Angeles State Park, for $60 million.[20] Though the project area only covers a fraction of the overall flood plain, WSP has been one of the partners in the ambitious effort to incrementally reimagine the L.A. River in various capacities, including engineering, environmental remediation, design, and robust community engagement efforts.

The G2 site provides multiple opportunities, but designs must be bound by practical considerations. For one, Taylor Yards was the long-time site of Union Pacific's maintenance yard for virtually every Los Angeles-bound train until 1973. After nearly a century of rail operations, the plot had become a contaminated brownfield—any project would have to either isolate or clean up the site. Other considerations included a corridor of high-voltage powerlines running directly adjacent to the river's edge, a known flood risk directly upstream from the project site, various property rights issues, and overlapping jurisdictions of multiple agencies.

The future project also needed to consider one of the all-too-frequent shortcomings of large infrastructure projects: not considering what the construction would mean for the people most impacted. For example, encasing the L.A. River in concrete reduced residents' flood risk, but it also robbed them of a nearby natural resource in an intensely urban setting. So, rethinking this concrete sleeve needed to be more than an ecological project. It was an opportunity to engage with nearby communities, many of which have historically been underserved and lacked access to parks.

To design a robust engagement strategy, WSP worked closely with local partners, including Mujeres de la Tierra, a group with roots in the community that promotes environmental equity and empowers women and their children to own and act on issues affecting their historically under-resourced neighborhoods. Engagement was designed accordingly. At a baseline, engaging with the local community meant providing both English and Spanish language materials and speakers. Because many people in the community did not have ready access to the internet, face-to-face engagement was undertaken at family-oriented events like soccer games. In addition to holding traditional stakeholder meetings, the city and its project partners were asked to attend other community gatherings at places like churches.

The engagement was successful enough that a survey on residents' priorities for the park received over 1,300 responses. The number one request was for access to nature, including walking and hiking trails, ideas that were ultimately integrated into plans. Robust engagement like this should also be dynamic and cyclical, with designers sharing ideas, getting feedback, and then integrating local knowledge and priorities into future designs and checking back in with community members along the way.

In the early stages of rethinking the river, hydraulic analysis and modeling revealed that, though widening the river at Taylor Yards would create more habitat, slow the water, and allow it to infiltrate the ground and become cleaner, it would create major problems further downstream. Since the river flowed through concrete channels virtually all the way to the ocean, it is an engineering challenging to get the water back into a concrete channel after it flowed more freely through a naturalized corridor at Taylor Yards. However, it is made possible by integrating and adapting the river's artificial hardened edge along with, wetlands and a habitat corridor for coyote, steelhead trout, osprey, frogs, and other wildlife.

The visioning plan went forward with three primary options. The first was creating an island by directing part of the river through a channel in the Taylor Yards plot. The water flowing on either side of the island would provide multiple layers of new natural habitat. The second option was called "Soft Edge," which cut up the east bank into irregular inlets, promoting the development of natural habitats like wetlands. The third version largely maintained the existing riverbanks and encouraged natural habitat growth on and within them. Each design encouraged public use and enjoyment of the river, via a plaza, esplanade, trails, and/or nearby meadows for picnicking and other recreation.

The vision for the L.A. River project included multiple benefits like habitat restoration, access to nature, environmental justice, and passive recreation. However, reimagining an urban environment as holistic and sustainable as this requires a programmatic approach, as opposed to trying to do it as just one project. Though Taylor Yards G2 was called the "Crown Jewel" of a plan to revitalize the L.A. River, it is still just one piece of a bigger, more systemic and Future Ready solution.[21]

Recycle Everything

The most complete and holistic urban water infrastructure would include a circular system in which 100% of wastewater is recycled for drinking, irrigation, and other uses. As ambitious as that sounds, the need for such circularity has been increasingly obvious for over 100 years.

During the first few decades of the 20th century, the rapidly growing L.A.-area began tapping increasing distant sources for drinking water, first from the Sierra Nevada to the northeast, and then due east to the Colorado River, just on the other side of the Arizona border. The Colorado begins in the Rockies where it is filled with snowmelt as the weather warms. However, that valuable water resource, which Southern California shares with Nevada, Arizona, and parts of Mexico, is increasingly stressed and stretched thin.

Even before the summer of 2022, when Lake Powell and Lake Mead—the two largest reservoirs in the United States—shriveled to historic lows, the need for alternate sources of drinking water became abundantly clear. As climate change has squeezed Southern California's water supply, the region has eyed a new water supply source—its own wastewater.[22,23]

Orange County, to the south of Los Angeles, already runs the largest wastewater recycling facility in the world. Most of the water that runs down the drain and into the toilet ends up at the Orange County Water District's Groundwater Replenishment System where it is turned into 100 million gallons (378 million liters) of drinkable water a day. Further south, Pure Water San Diego, a program launched by the City of San Diego, will provide close to half of the city's drinking water by 2035.[24]

Los Angeles currently recycles about 30% of its wastewater, making the other 70% a valuable, untapped resource. Instead of pumping billions of gallons of treated sewage out to sea every year, the water becomes a model of circularity as part of holistic cycle in which it is recaptured and used to replenish reservoirs, aquifers, and even municipal water lines.

Operation Next is a roughly $16 billion plan from the Los Angeles Department of Water and Power to purify up to 100% of the wastewater processed by its Hyperion Water Reclamation Plant. The water cleaning includes multiple processes, employing microorganisms that break down toxic nitrogen compounds, membranes that can filter out particulate matter many times smaller than a grain of sand, and ultraviolet light for disinfection.

From Florida to California, innovative projects and programs are replacing one-size-fits-all approaches to challenges as divergent as coastal erosion, marine ecosystem collapse, vehicular air pollution, urban heat island effect, polluted runoff, and water scarcity. What they all have in common is building greater sustainability and resilience through holistic, multi-benefit, and/or nature-based solutions.

Conventional infrastructure design has disregarded the environment, destabilized resilience, marginalized communities, and—most profoundly—ignored the future. It's always been unsustainable to dump plastic into our oceans, or increase the human population by a billion people every 12 years, or maintain our frantic pace of resource extraction from the earth.[25] But today, those shortcomings have caught up with us. We live in a world with unsustainable inequities, pollution, and waste—as well an atmosphere bursting with more carbon dioxide and total GHG than at any time in at least the past three million years.[26]

Oyster reefs, trees, shrubs, and wetlands may initially seem like unlikely candidates to replace, much less improve on, tons of poured concrete infrastructure. However, it turns out that some of our most interesting, innovative solutions for our climate challenges come from the same natural world that we've been clearing, paving over, polluting, and taking for granted for far too long.

Notes

1. https://www.policygenius.com/homeowners-insurance/best-and-worst-states-for-climate-change/.
2. https://www.safehome.org/climate-change-statistics/.
3. https://www.cnet.com/personal-finance/these-us-states-are-the-most-vulnerable-to-climate-change/.
4. https://hazards.fema.gov/nri/map.
5. https://www.fox4now.com/wftx-weather-stories/noaa-report-sea-levels-on-track-to-rise-more-than-a-foot-by-2050.
6. https://homeport.uscg.mil/Lists/Content/Attachments/119/DeepwaterHorizonReport%20-31Aug2011%20-CD_2.pdf.
7. https://www.vims.edu/research/topics/diseases_immunity/ts_archive/oyster_reef_global.php.
8. https://www.nhc.noaa.gov/data/tcr/AL142018_Michael.pdf.
9. https://coastalscience.noaa.gov/news/water-cleaning-capacity-of-oysters-could-mean-extra-income-for-chesapeake-bay-growers-video/.
10. https://www.fisheries.noaa.gov/national/habitat-conservation/oyster-reef-habitat.
11. file:///Users/nathanmeans/Downloads/US_2018_OPEN_MIKE21FlowModelFMSW_HydrodynamicModelingUsingFlexibleMeshSpectralWave_UK%20(2).pdf.
12. https://www.rutgers.edu/news/rutgers-awarded-126-million-grant-create-oyster-habitat-coastal-resilience.
13. https://www.transportation.gov/briefing-room/new-fhwa-report-reveals-states-busiest-highways.
14. https://www.smithsonianmag.com/smart-news/1943-hellish-cloud-was-most-vivid-warning-las-smog-problems-come-180964119/.
15. https://theicct.org/new-study-quantifies-the-global-health-impacts-of-vehicle-exhaust/.
16. https://www.hsph.harvard.edu/news/press-releases/racial-ethnic-minorities-low-income-groups-u-s-air-pollution/.
17. https://www.transportation.gov/briefing-room/new-fhwa-report-reveals-states-busiest-highways.

18. https://www.foxla.com/news/inland-empire-commuters-enduring-traffic-nightmare-of-pre-pandemic-levels.
19. https://www.history.com/news/interstate-highway-system-infrastructure-construction-segregation.
20. https://news.yahoo.com/cost-la-crown-jewel-river-210028130.html.
21. https://news.yahoo.com/cost-la-crown-jewel-river-210028130.html.
22. https://laist.com/news/climate-environment/the-largest-water-recycling-plant-is-in-socal-and-it-plans-to-refresh-itself.
23. https://www.latimes.com/environment/story/2022-07-17/wastewater-recycling-provides-hedge-against-drought.
24. https://www.sandiego.gov/public-utilities/sustainability/pure-water-sd
25. https://ourworldindata.org/world-population-growth.
26. https://www.climate.gov/news-features/understanding-climate/climate-change-atmospheric-carbon-dioxide.

Conclusion: The Right Future, the Right Way

CLIMATE CHANGE IS now and tomorrow. It's local and global. It's risk and opportunity. It's too big to ignore—as a growth market, threat multiplier—but at the same time it can be very overwhelming, confusing, and even polarizing.

What is clear is the importance of rethinking how we design our future. New technologies, sustainability commitments, private sector investment, corporate initiatives, and government policies are all welcome and essential. But if the additional funding, resources, and programs are designed and implemented the wrong way, we'll end up losing valuable time in our decarbonization efforts—and perhaps even make the problem worse.

We've already discussed some climate maladaptation measures. Some sea walls, for example, damage local ecosystems and ultimately exacerbate flooding. But the severity of climate risk is so great that even more extreme climate mitigation measures have been debated. Take, for example, addressing rising temperatures by injecting reflective aerosols into the atmosphere. This form of geoengineering could bounce some of the sun's energy back into space before it can heat the

Earth's atmosphere. Though this process has never really been tested by humans, the planet has previously experienced a natural, and very effective, version of this phenomenon. Following the 1883 volcanic eruption of Krakatoa, atmospheric particulate matter circulated at high altitudes around the world. In the Northern Hemisphere, summer temperatures dropped by as much as 3.6°F (2°C). Injecting aerosols into the atmosphere artificially could potentially be a relatively cheap and quick way to reduce global temperatures—essentially turning down the heat.

However, the scale of potential negative side effects is massive and hard to predict. After Krakatoa, for example, Los Angeles experienced what is still its heaviest 12-month rainfall ever recorded, culminating in a massive cloudburst in February 1884. Two days later, the headline of the *Los Angeles Herald* read: "FURY OF THE FLOOD. Great and General Devastation. Railway and Other Bridges Swept Away. Hundreds of People Made Homeless. Temporary Suspension of the Telegraphs and the Railways. A Third of the City Under Water for Hours. Washouts, Caves and Demolished Bridges and Dwellings the Order of the Day. Southern California Up to Her Ears in Water."[1] In short, extreme measures like lowering global temperatures by injecting aerosols into the atmosphere isn't a panacea; it could have uncontrollable side effects. In fact, these extreme versions of maladaptation could accelerate precisely the same kind of damage from extreme weather that we are already experiencing, which requires urgent and very expensive climate adaptation programs.

Beware False Choices

Fortunately, that type of geoengineering is still considered an extreme, last-ditch option rather than a practical, one-size-fits-all solution to address global warming. All too often, though, we are presented with "either/or" choices and asked to come up with one-size-fits-all solutions. This is true of both organizational and infrastructure sustainability and resilience as well as climate action more broadly. The Taylor Yards case study described in the previous chapter is a perfect example—the challenge needed to be addressed programmatically as opposed to solved by a singular project.

Such false choices and polarizing debates overly limit our possibilities, ambitions, and creativity. Some of the most common false choices to guard against: a focus on climate adaptation and resilience because of the ongoing extreme impacts of climate change *does not* mean lessening or giving up on climate mitigation and the net zero initiatives that better address the root cause of climate change. A commitment to renewables *does not* mean an immediate end to oil and gas. The clean energy transition to electrification by leveraging of battery storage and proliferation of zero emission vehicles *cannot happen* without continued mining of natural resources. We *don't have to* make decisions based only on what exists and is 100% available, known, and required today; in fact, we must consider future trends, conditions, emerging innovations, as well as uncertainties before making such decisions. Finally, climate leadership *is not limited* to governments and nonprofit organizations—for-profit private organizations and investors have an essential leadership role to play and need to embrace it with necessary urgency.

Identifying the hurdles to an equitable, cost-effective, sustainable, and green transformation is just the first part of the developing and implementing of solutions. The more difficult and subsequent part is determining how to overcome such hurdles in a Future Ready way. You can do this by mainstreaming resilience and sustainability at the organizational level and building, restoring, adapting, and maintaining our bridges, parks, apartments, subways, airports, offices, and homes the right way—a better way. The truth is that there are no universal, one-size-fits-all answers to these challenges, but this book offers a structure for moving forward. First, pick the side of cautious optimism and shared purpose—we can all do something about climate change. Then, methodically identify the actionable projects or programs that you can and should develop, fund, and take on. Just as importantly, no matter how resilient or green a project or program is, it isn't the right project if it's not needed by our communities or appropriate as our technologies, materials, societies, and climate impacts rapidly evolve. As a baseline, develop the right projects or programs, and endeavor to do them in the most sustainable and resilient ways. Ideally, and frequently, you will find that these types of solutions also provide economic, environmental, and community co-benefits.

Read the Room

Understanding the attitude of the key decision makers—as well as to other more direct business metrics and goals—as early as possible in the process is often key to the successful deployment of a decarbonization roadmap, climate action plan, or ESG program. This book is full of stories of how such strategies, when delivered in a holistic manner, can often provide a broader set of direct business benefits—from basic cost savings to more complex operational benefits. In some situations, however, presenting these simply as secondary benefits won't close the deal, particularly when dealing with stakeholders that are not initially advocates of what you are seeking to accomplish.

When this happens, some things may temporarily need to take a back seat, which is sometimes hard for those passionate about sustainability and climate change. But we need to look to the end results. Whether your goal is sustainability or mission resiliency, or occupant well-being, or simply enhancing social equity, holistic strategies can be developed that achieve this and, at the same time, support the decarbonization of our society.

Beyond Doing the Right Thing

However, doing the right projects and programs and wanting to do them the right way still isn't enough—because it gives you "the what" while still leaving you to decide on "the how." Several of the case studies and successes shared in this book identified and implemented the how with the assistance of nationally and globally available tools and standards. Through long associations with several infrastructure-focused organizations and with the support of the Institute for Sustainable Infrastructure (ISI), Tom and others in WSP have been actively involved in shaping, refining, and applying one such tool: the Envision® sustainability and resilience framework and rating system. Consistent with WSP's philosophy and business model, this framework assists infrastructure owners and their consultants and contractors in delivering infrastructure of any type that tackles climate change, addresses public health needs, cultivates environmental justice, creates jobs, and spurs economic recovery. The driving principle behind the Envision framework essentially consists of two questions: 1) Are

Conclusion: The Right Future, the Right Way   237

you doing the *right* project? 2) Are you doing a project *right* (sustainably, resiliently, equitably)?

Imagine a scenario in which a public housing authority or private developer demolishes and disposes of outdated and energy-inefficient buildings. The apartments are replaced by a green, hyper-energy efficient building with modern electric heat pumps and smart LED lighting controls and other systems. In short, they are doing the new apartment building project right—deploying modern, green technologies and materials that provide utility savings for tenants—and maybe even getting a LEED platinum rating for the new buildings along the way. Unfortunately, they may not be doing the right project from a circularity and sustainability perspective. It turns out that the net impact of demolishing and disposing of the old building and then constructing a new one for the same purpose of providing apartments can actually be a worse option from a GHG emissions standpoint. In this case, it would have made more sense with a much lower total carbon footprint to retrofit the existing building with renewables, electrify its appliances, insulate it better, and otherwise update and maybe even expand it in a sustainable and resilient way.

One reason why WSP has enthusiastically helped develop and leverage the Envision framework is because of how well it dovetails with our Future Ready approach to planning, designing, and implementing infrastructure programs and projects. By analyzing megatrends, we can expand on the premise of doing a project right and doing the right project.

Meeting Our Moment

After decades of ignoring climate change, or, at best, responding with half measures, many companies and governments are finally energized and increasingly unified in their response to climate risk. Unfortunately, we've left ourselves a very short runway to avoid the worst consequences of a rapidly warming planet with increasingly frequent and severe extreme weather events. This is a moment that demands an urgent and fundamental rethinking of how we create solutions for a better world going forward. Ultimately, climate change is already forcing us to reconsider specific strategies, processes, techniques, and materials. The only real question left is how urgently and intelligently we will respond.

Rethinking everything means moving from a linear to a circular mindset. It means not building to yesterday's demands and specifications, but for what we need now—and what will need in the future. It means incorporating equity, biodiversity, sustainability, resilience, community engagement, and long-term value into every program and project where there is an opportunity to do so.

Over the course of this book, we've explored a range of proven and methodical ways to rise to meet the moment—not in the abstract, but through many real-world examples. Everyone and every organization can be part of creating more equitable, resilient, sustainable, and Future Ready workplaces, communities, and infrastructure. Our ultimate goal is educating, empowering and inspiring people and organizations to identify and implement transformational climate and infrastructure solutions. We believe that the world is up to the challenges ahead of us—if we choose to be.

Note

1. https://www.latimes.com/archives/la-xpm-2005-feb-26-me-record26-story.html.

Epilogue

When You Rethink Everything, Finance Will Flow

THIS BOOK DESCRIBES some of the many possibilities for creating organizations that are more sustainable, resilient, and equitable—primarily through the lens of our built and natural environment. Rethinking how to approach design, engineering, operational systems and functions, and indeed, organizational design are all critical to creating Future Ready infrastructure. We've looked at real-world examples of rethinking engineering in order to design critical assets such as transportation systems, buildings, homes, and energy and water infrastructure for a very different world—one in which our previous assumptions and solutions are rapidly becoming outdated. Equally important from an organizational level is developing long-term plans to realize climate resilience and net zero goals. But acting on these plans means moving from design to construction to operations, all of which requires investment.

Finance is the lynchpin in ensuring those plans and designs are executed, making it critical to realizing the Future Ready goals outlined in this book. Without funding and budgets, corporate net zero

239

plans will remain well-articulated ideas contained in a report on someone's shelf. Likewise, without policy and investment capital that directs developers to design and build-in sustainability and climate resilience measures, new infrastructure projects will not be prepared for the warmer, more volatile climate conditions that will exist during the life of those assets. So, while finance and investment are not the starting point for any corporate, organizational or infrastructure plans to become Future Ready, it is nearly impossible to have any of those plans realized without making serious investment, whether it is from a company's own account, or from outside sources, including public and private investors. To meet the challenge of climate change, financing alone is never sufficient, but it is always essential.

Funding and financing climate investment, be it resilience and adaptation or decarbonization and net zero, is multifaceted and complex. The topic requires a deep understanding of different sources of capital, different functions of those sources, including how much or how little risk those sources can bear, what financial product they invest through—such as debt, equity, guarantees, or other instruments—different time horizons for realizing returns, and other investment objectives. Investment decisions made by different sources of capital also operate within the broader context of financial markets, economic conditions, policy, and the existing utility of market mechanisms—such as carbon markets or RECs, in the case of clean energy—among other factors. When developing a financing strategy to realize a resilience and sustainability plan, it is important to understand the different sources of capital one might avail of to fund or finance an investment plan. But one must also understand an organization's context, including how its revenues are generated, as well as what its assets are worth, and how costs are borne by the entity, and the investor's own context and investment offering and unique investing goals.

A financial strategy for an asset, company, or infrastructure project can be simple or complex, is often developed with multiple important factors in mind, and often not merely a function of financial return on investment. Indeed, several sections of this book have referenced the need to undertake more comprehensive cost-benefit analysis—such as evaluating full life-cycle costs in a future marked by increasingly extreme weather—when designing a transaction. Integrating climate considerations into these financial models are all important and necessary.

Adequately covering this topic sufficiently in the context of a book focused on engineering for sustainability and resilience is nearly impossible. However, it is important to point out how investor views have changed over the last decade because of greater awareness that climate change poses not only physical and transition risks, but that these risks are proving to have tangible financial consequences. For infrastructure, specifically, there are specific, viable, and concrete actions that can be taken during feasibility and design that can have material consequences—both positive and negative—for transaction structuring and financing, and of course, operations.

Climate Finance Arrives

Investor views around climate change have evolved dramatically since Superstorm Sandy in 2012, where this book begins, in two important ways: risk and opportunity.

At the time of Superstorm Sandy, few investors viewed climate change as a financial risk issue, although some had started to perceive investing in climate-positive assets as an opportunity. Renewable energy projects at the time were roughly cost-competitive with other forms of energy production, and a handful of clean-tech private equity funds had launched in the early 2000s and were proving the investment case for investing in technologies and other approaches to addressing climate change. Nonetheless, in 2012, climate investing was still a bespoke and niche category. For the majority of investors, climate change was simply not registering as a mainstream issue, either in terms of financial risk or as a significant investment opportunity.

That has changed dramatically in the past decade, in part, due to market drivers, and in part, due to the observable changes in the global climate and the extreme climate-related weather events, which have resulted in billions of dollars in losses annually. This book references the Paris Agreement and the Task Force on Climate-related Financial Disclosures (TCFD), both of which were launched in 2015 and have brought greater awareness, clarity, and understanding to climate issues—precisely those climate-related financial risks that will become apparent if investors do not manage, mitigate, and transition their investment strategies.

TCFD was also groundbreaking, in part, because of the way it articulated for investors the direct linkages between climate risks and revenues, costs, and asset values. It put such risk in *financial terms*. Beyond simply recording losses when acute events—like Superstorm Sandy—occurred, investors have also started to understand and recognize that impacts from climate change are not only the immediate, direct impacts of storms, extreme heat, and drought, but also chronic and slow-moving physical impacts which can degrade asset values, increase costs, and impact profitability. As such, TCFD also gave rise to a greater understanding that some assets could lose value in the transition to a low-carbon, net zero world. In part, because of the language TCFD provided investors, and in part, because observable impacts from a warmer planet are more evident, the level of awareness among investors that climate-related financial risk needs to be incorporated into investment decision-making is higher than ever before.

Furthermore, key mechanisms that investors rely on to understand the riskiness of investments, namely, rating agencies, have all incorporated climate-data and analytics teams since 2015, and each of the three main rating agencies now integrate climate considerations—both climate-related risk, and whether an entity has a credible plan to address climate risk and build-in resilience—into some of their ratings, for example, sovereign bonds, municipal bonds, directly impacting the cost of capital for some.

Today, not only are investors of all types engaged in and seeking sustainable and resilient investment, but analysis shows that the investment opportunities to address climate change are significant. Globally it is estimated that the investment required to meet the Paris Agreements temperature and adaptation goals ranges between $3 to $6 trillion per year; according to the Organization for Economic Cooperation and Development (OECD), we will require $6.9 trillion annually in global investment in climate-smart infrastructure between now and 2030.[1,2]

Infrastructure investors and fund managers are sitting on trillions of dollars seeking new climate-smart assets, companies, and infrastructure to place their investment. They also understand that climate-smart investment is not simply about investing in the energy sector any longer. Over the last two decades, private investment in climate change has been dominated by renewables, but this is changing rapidly. Today investors are eager to get to work building the next generation of Future Ready infrastructure, and many of them understand that the net zero, climate-resilient investment opportunities involve much more than just the energy transition. Decarbonization will be required across all sectors and industries, and in all forms of infrastructure, including buildings, transportation, water, waste management, and energy systems, which need to be upgraded in terms of transmission, energy storage and distribution. Other investment areas attractive for investors include carbon capture and storage, recycling, hydrogen, electric vehicles, battery storage, and innovative technologies, such as climate data and analytics and direct air capture. In short, private finance is now ready to fund a green transition.

Future Ready Public Infrastructure

Notwithstanding the significant need for private investment toward climate and sustainability solutions, today 83% of infrastructure investment worldwide originates from, or is catalyzed by, public policy and involves some form of public capital.[3] About one-third of initial funding for those projects comes from government treasuries and ministries, and about two-thirds comes from state-owned enterprises, such as utilities.[4] This means policymakers have an interest in ensuring infrastructure investments are robust enough to mitigate economic vulnerabilities, which can be worsened by climate change. Policymakers also want to be sure that new infrastructure can withstand climate change shocks.

More specifically, investors today understand that strengthening infrastructure's resilience to climate change can yield more reliable long-term cash flow for public owners and private sources of capital, such as banks and investors, as well as improve service quality for users, and strengthen the economic and social resilience of communities. In addition to reducing value at risk, there are significant co-benefits, and integrating climate resilience against natural hazards yields an average of $6 of benefits for every $1 invested.[5]

With unprecedented impacts evident across the infrastructure development life cycle—including planning, design, transaction structuring, construction, and operations—as well as the clear imperative of the Paris temperature goals, governments have directed spending in recent years through fiscal stimulus packages that emphasize resilience in infrastructure investment. For many countries, the policy directions that underpin net zero goals have catalyzed important regulation on both sides of the Atlantic, with REPowerEU and the Inflation Reduction Act providing significant capital to help accelerate the energy transition of those countries. These policy drivers incentivize solutions that go well beyond utility scale renewables of solar or wind and could prove instrumental in decarbonization and sustainability transitions in transportation and water, among other sectors. For developing economies, the International Monetary Fund (IMF) has called for prioritizing sustainable, climate-resilient infrastructure investments in their funding package to drive economic recovery over the short term and support sustainable growth over the long term.

Infrastructure—whether financed, funded, or delivered by the public or private sector—can also be an important stabilizer in the context of rising interest rates. In many countries, public financing often plays a counter-cyclical role to attract private investments and ensure momentum is maintained in the climate-resilient, low-carbon transition. In many cases, governments are seeking to support "quality" infrastructure investments, and climate resilience will be a defining characteristic of quality.

Sustainable Design Drives Investment

One mark of the transformation in mainstream investors' perception of climate change, risk, and opportunity since 2012 is that designing climate-resilient infrastructure is now key to attracting funding and financing from a range of private and public sources. Given the realities of climate change, well-structured investments will both incorporate climate-related considerations and measures into infrastructure design and delivery of services over an asset's life as well as reducing investor risk. This also has the effect of reducing the cost of capital. Well-designed infrastructure that incorporates climate resilience and net zero measures will also increasingly be able to attract better financing terms, in part, because of the inherent ability of the asset to better manage climate risks, among others.

There are two primary determinants to understanding how climate resilience is achieved. The first is analyzing asset-level resilience to future impacts from a changing climate. The second is evaluating how an asset can contribute to wider societal resilience. In addition to being climate-resilient, existing, planned, and new infrastructure assets can provide a range of benefits that provide wider societal and community benefits.

The World Bank offers a similar, broader definition of how to build climate-resilience in infrastructure. First, building resilience in infra-structure is *resilience of* the project design—or simply, resilience of the project. This is the extent to which a project's assets have considered climate and disaster risks in their design. Incorporating approaches to address climate risk in the design of the project can help to increase investor confidence that investment outcomes will be achieved despite potential climate risks.

However, the second way to measure resilience in infrastructure is as a result of the asset's contribution to the resilience of wider communities and systems. This is *resilience through* project outcomes, or the potential for a project or program to enhance climate resilience through its inter-ventions. For example, improving watershed management in a flood or drought-prone area can enhance community-level resilience. These aspects of resilient infrastructure are particularly important for investors in municipalities, cities or communities where broader development is occurring. It may also become increasingly relevant for bond issuances that are raised to finance sustainable and climate smart urban development.

Integrating climate resilience and sustainability aspects into the financial transaction structuring will be dependent on how an asset is designed and engineered, and how the risks are addressed, planned for, designed around, or mitigated. To ensure net zero and climate resilient outcomes, climate considerations must be integrated throughout the infrastructure life cycle, including the enabling environment, upstream, and downstream stages, each of which can have a positive impact on an assets ability to raise capital from investors. The infrastructure life cycle reflects stages of infrastructure development. The "upstream stage" is typically characterized by 1) project scoping, 2) feasibility and design, and 3) transaction structuring. In contrast, the "downstream stage" is typically characterized by 1) financial/commercial structuring (if relevant), 2) construction, and 3) operations. Each of these stages includes actions and activities by different stakeholders, including policymakers, developers, engineers and designers, construction companies, operators, and of course, their funders and investors.

Many of the actions of developers, engineers and designers, and operators have been discussed in other parts of this book, including retrofitting approaches, ways to integrate energy efficiency measures to reduce costs, re-siting of infrastructure out of harm's way, and nature-based solutions that help to reduce potential impacts from climate change. Each of these has a very tangible impact on the overall financial profile of an investment, and these design efforts will be increasingly more material to the investment return of an asset. Sustainable and resilient engineering and design directly informs the financial model of the asset and can have a positive effect on the cost of capital, whether the borrower is a developer or asset owner, or a community or municipality raising funding to meet the infrastructure needs of a town or region.

Importantly, infrastructure assets can both be resilient themselves and contribute to the resilience of the populations they serve. From a broad perspective, ensuring the resilience of critical infrastructure is imperative to maintaining sustainable economic growth for broader communities, which will also have knock-on effects for the financial sustainability of the asset and potentially the perceived riskiness of the community. The positive benefits of this may be particularly impactful—financially, and for overall sustainability—in areas that are highly vulnerable to climate change. Effective responses to enhance climate resilience of communities through infrastructure will require activity at three levels including:

1. **Ensuring that infrastructure assets continue to perform well in a range of potential climate scenarios.** This requires having the right measures in place to reduce climate-related risks to acceptable levels, including the risk of damage to the asset itself, and negative impacts to others arising from asset failure, such as downstream flooding after dam failure. These include management changes like changing operating procedures as well as physical changes like changing the design to cope with adverse conditions.

2. **Strengthening infrastructure systems to ensure reliable and cost-effective service provision.** This goes beyond the level of specific projects to consider how climate change will affect

systems, such as road networks or electricity distribution. At this level, potential actions to strengthen resilience include building redundancy for critical links, demand management, and developing rapid response capabilities to respond to disruption. Working at the system level provides greater opportunities to target investment and build in flexibility.

3. **Ensuring infrastructure strategies and plans contribute to societal resilience to climate change.** Infrastructure reflects but also shapes development pathways. For example, providing protective infrastructure can encourage development in risky areas, whereas infrastructure that locks in high-carbon development will ultimately undermine societal resilience in the longer term. Ensuring that upstream planning considers climate impacts can be used to choose development pathways that ultimately enhance people's resilience.

Investors today understand well the investment opportunity at hand for building Future Ready infrastructure. Rethinking the design of the world's essential systems could include incorporating solutions like nature-based mitigation of coastal erosion, solar microgrids, more efficient HVAC in buildings, green hydrogen hubs at shipping ports, or public transit that combines electric vehicles with autonomous technology.

There are, of course, innumerable other possibilities for building a more sustainable, resilient, and thriving future. However, if you fail to take climate risk and opportunity into consideration when designing and engineering an asset, it may become more difficult or expensive to finance your investment. Conversely, projects and programs—whether driven by public policy, funded partially with public funding, or a purely privately financed, owned, and operated asset—that incorporate climate, sustainability, and resiliency considerations into infrastructure design will be increasingly attractive to investors. When you rethink everything, finance will flow.

—Stacy Swann
WSP's Executive Vice President of Climate Finance, ESG, and Sustainable Investment

Notes

1. Prasad, Ananthakrishnan, Elena Loukoianova, Alan Xiaochen Feng, and WilliamOman, "Mobilizing Private Climate Financing in Emerging Market and Developing Economies." IMF Staff Climate Note 2022/007, International Monetary Fund, Washington, D.C.
2. https://doi.org/10.1787/9789264308114-en.
3. https://ppi.worldbank.org/content/dam/PPI/documents/SPIReport_2017_small_interactive.pdf.
4. https://ppi.worldbank.org/content/dam/PPI/documents/SPIReport_2017_small_interactive.pdf.
5. https://www.fema.gov/sites/default/files/2020-07/fema_mitsaves-factsheet_2018.pdf.

Afterword
Ready, Steady, Breath...Go!

As you turn these final pages, I'm sure that you are filled with a mix of both excitement to get started, and apprehension as to how to start. The ideas, strategies, and stories we've shared will give you the tools you need to create your roadmap and commence your journey to be Future Ready. But, as you approach the finish line, the task of actually starting can still seem daunting.

Don't worry. That's normal.

My advice: it's time to take a breath.

The journey to transform your organization to be Future Ready is inherently complex, but like any good puzzle, you should start with the edges. Define the goals you are trying to achieve, the timeline you have to achieve them, and identify any immovable objects that you need to avoid. Know your stakeholders, their core values, and begin to understand how to make this journey personal to them. The quicker you get a handle on these factors, the faster you will get some wind in your sails.

Over the last 20 or so years, I have worked with organizations that span multiple sectors and have seen firsthand what has made these efforts successful—and what caused them to fail. To help you as you begin this journey as a Future Ready advocate, I want to share some of the guiding principles that have worked for me over my career to help you define the edges of the puzzle and get people personally engaged in completing it.

Guiding Principles to Be Future Ready

1. You don't need to be a carbon expert. Find expert partners who understand your business, and most importantly, embrace your culture. Let them be your CarbonSherpa and guide the way.

2. Spend the time needed to clearly identify your end goal and create the edges of your puzzle. Don't rush it.

3. Decarbonization doesn't need to be a compromise. Embracing holistic thinking can often de-risk your business, even create new revenue sources, all while achieving your bold climate goals.

4. Top down—bottom up. . . . The route to your decarbonized future is inherently complex. Embrace that complexity, for within it is the strategies that best align with your business needs.

5. Your decarbonization roadmap isn't a fixed route. You will find shortcuts, take detours, and may even make unscheduled stops along the way. Being open to these course corrections and maintaining focus on the end game is what will get you to the end goal.

6. Understand that sometimes carbon needs to take a back seat to get the deal done.

7. Expand your thinking on return on investment (ROI). Consider the entire life cycle of your decisions, include the cost of carbon in the analysis, and be open to using creative financing techniques to accelerate the deployment of your decarbonization plan.

8. Education is key. Stay informed and celebrate your successes with your stakeholders to build momentum.

9. Data is your friend. Don't be scared by it, or the lack of it. You can get moving on very little, and gain more as you go.

10. Being Future Ready always starts with the simple—quick wins build momentum.

11. And, most importantly, make it personal to your stakeholders.

—Aly MacGregor

Afterword

Why There's No *I* in *Team*—or *CRS*

WHEN I WAS first contacted by Wiley Publishing to write a book, I chose to ignore it. I knew that our rapidly growing climate, resilience, and sustainability (CRS) business was successful and making a real, material difference. When I regularly spoke at conferences, interviews, training sessions, and panels, I always hoped that sharing my experience and industry leadership activities within the sustainability and resilience space would be a force multiplier. But writing a book? I'd need much more time—not to mention more personal knowledge across the full spectrum of CRS issues, actions, and opportunities—to be able to do justice to such an urgent and vital project.

A few months later, the publisher called back. Fortunately, this time my trusted assistant Irene Altman implored me to at least have an introductory meeting. "What could it hurt," she asked, "to hear how the book might work based on the publisher's prior experience?"

As is usually the case with her, this was wise advice. During the exploratory conversation, I candidly shared why I ignored the first contact, then asked how we might use a team approach—something I have employed with consistent success and much enjoyment throughout my career. Happily, the response was yes—and the result is this timely and important book.

Though this was my first book writing project, I immediately recognized the value in the efforts of dozens of people—our writing, communications, and editing teams, author team, foreword and afterword contributors, project and case study contributors, and subject matter specialists, among others—who made this book a reality. Their teamwork was precisely the way organizations should look at and undertake their CRS journey, if they want it to be sustained and effective.

The truth is that no individual or department can build a Future Ready organization, community, or city alone. So, once organizational leadership is committed to undertake a sustainability journey, cross-functional champions (internal and/or consultants) need to be identified—and educated, as is often needed—across the CRS spectrum. If, as is very common, your organization cannot fund and undertake the whole journey at once, pursue your goals in increments using sequencing that is agile and tailored to your unique situation and capacity to meet the moment.

As my final words, I'll share a logical, sequential bucketing of core actions to frame your organization's CRS teambuilding and journey.

Bucket 1: Internally Controlled, Internally Facing

- Gathering your baseline-setting available data and inventorying it, with an initial internal report to leadership focusing on your organization's directly produced (Scope 1) and energy purchased (Scope 2) operational carbon emissions.
- Initiating an ongoing inventory verification and management program inclusive of at least your Scope 1 and Scope 2 emissions, and a commitment to ongoing reductions and controls of same, with purchased renewable energy credits or other carbon offsets to make progress toward reaching net zero in the future.
- Establishing initial, high-level goals and objectives (including a specific net zero timetable), with leadership buy-in that includes internal tracking, an accountability framework, and regular reporting.
- Developing and instituting an initial funding strategy—usually starting with internal sources (e.g., overhead allocation or

internal carbon pricing) and possibly evolving later to inclusion of external climate finance sources (e.g., CRS-related business, grants, and other public or non-governmental organization funding opportunities).

- Employing a cross-company, cross-function, cross-disciplinary education program, possibly including self-developed training but most often leveraging external resources, partners and frameworks such as USGBC's LEED, ISI's ENVISION, and several others available internationally.
- Evaluating, baselining, reporting, and managing nonoperational (i.e., embodied) carbon in the organization's properties, materials, equipment, and so on—as well as greenhouse gas emissions other than carbon (e.g., methane, nitrous oxide), if they are material.

Bucket 2: Internally Controlled, Externally Facing and Influenced

- Evaluating and leveraging improvement opportunities and innovations across your resource (waste, water, power/energy/ renewables, air, nature/biodiversity, materials/supplies), built environment (real estate and operations), supply (internal, upstream, and downstream), and value chains in accordance with good circularity (cradle-to-cradle) and organizational practices, including the employment of life cycle (versus capital cost-driven) benefit-cost analytics and decision-making with a future-focused mindset.
- Evaluating organizational governance and implementing CRS-related improvements.
- For climate mitigation and sustainability, progressing to inventorying, reporting, and reducing your indirectly influenced (Scope 3) emissions upstream and downstream of the organization's activities, products and deliverables, and supply chains.
- For climate adaptation and resilience, instituting a proactive disaster mitigation and preparedness program, as well as progressing to data-supported, future-focused, risk-based tools, assessments, planning, designs decisions, actions, and life cycle

operations, maintenance and recycle/reuse programs for managing properties, and other assets.

- Developing and instituting an evolved funding and due diligence strategy tied to your organization's strategic growth and/or action plan—inclusive of internal, organic, and acquisitive growth activities.
- Engaging in industry or other affinity-based organizations and initiatives regionally or internationally (e.g., the UN's Race To Zero and/or Race To Resilience, and the Science Based Targets initiative or "SBTi") through the best-fitting partnership program for your organization.
- Engaging in national—currently only mandatory in some countries—and/or voluntary, international risk and financial disclosure frameworks such as the Task Force for Climate-related Financial Disclosures (TCFD) and Taskforce on Nature-related Financial Disclosures (TNFD).

Bucket 3: Other Externally Facing and Influenced, Not Just Controlled Internally

- Evaluating organizational social responsibility activities and implementing CRS-related improvements in recognition of the fact that—when it comes to climate change's existential challenges—escalating impacts and opportunities as well as your organization's continued evolution and success will be influenced by how well the outside world is doing at community, national, and international levels to varying degrees.
- Based on this evaluation, developing and instituting an organizational social responsibility and stakeholder engagement program that is appropriate for your organization in recognition of the inextricable linkages between climate change, equity, environmental justice, and natural resource stewardship.

—Tom Lewis

Acknowledgments

JUST AS MANY people help drive all the ambitious projects we take on at WSP, many people have helped make this book a reality. Countless colleagues, clients, partners, and friends have offered expertise and perspective, and this book would not be possible without them.

Leaders set the tone, and we are deeply grateful to Lou Cornell and his team for their passion and direction and for supporting us in taking on this project. We'd also like to thank Alexandre L'Heureux and Andre-Martin Bouchard for their strategic vision and dedication to embedding WSP's Future Ready® process throughout our organization and ensuring that it walks the talk when it comes to climate, resilience and sustainability.

Despite their physical distance, the global WSP team members work together seamlessly and we'd like to recognize Rachel Skinner and David Symons in the United Kingdom for their contributions, which were particularly valuable during the brainstorming stage.

In the process of bringing this concept to life, we engaged with talented and insightful colleagues across WSP, who generously gave their time and perspectives on projects, ideas, and stories that span climate, resilience, finance, equity, sustainability, and other critical issues covered in these pages. Distilling their ideas to a few paragraphs was challenging, and many of them could have had a chapter or even an entire book to themselves. We particularly want to thank Heather Unger, Mike Flood, Anita Schwartz, Bernie McNeilly, Chin Lien, Dan Sobrinski, Eric Christensen, Dana Lowell, Darius Nassiry, David Earley, Denise Roth, Derek Fehrer, Michael Mondshine, Emily Wasley, Gabi Brazzil, Indhira Figuero, Jeffrey Irvine, Jennifer Brunton, Jenny Carney, Jerry Jannetti, John Chow, John Loughran, Jonathan Dickinson, Julie Sinistore, Kosal Krishnan, Michael Drennan, Mike Flood, Narada Golden, Phil Jonat, and Stephen Blair.

Today, WSP has more than 90,000 active projects in more than 500 cities and beyond. Once we narrowed down a lengthy list of potential case studies, we relied heavily on colleagues who spent time replying to emails, fact-checking content, and providing feedback. They include Amanda Schweickert, Amy Berline, Claire McCarthy, Erick Harter, Gabor Debreczeni, Mahaney Francis, Margaret Peg McBrien, Mathew Moore, Matt Burns, Nigel Temple, Pooja Jain, and Sarah Coleman.

We also recognize that our thinking has evolved in a broader professional context. We both help shape and are shaped by leading industry associations, researchers, planners, and do-ers across sectors who inspired us with their work every day. We would particularly like to recognize the influence of U.N. Climate Champions Race to Resilience and Race to Zero; Graduate School of Design at Harvard University; Institute for Sustainable Infrastructure (ISI) International Coalition for Sustainable Infrastructure (ICSI); LA Metro; Lexden Capital, LLC; MTA Construction and Development New York City; Resilient Coastal Communities Project at the Columbia Climate School; Resilience Rising Resilience First; The Disaster Recovery Contractors Association (DRCA); and The Environmental Financial Consulting Group (EFCG).

A large team produced this book and supported the logistics and planning that go into it all. A special thank you to Evan Ross for supporting the book's development at every step, to Kyle Wheaton for the incredible book cover design, and to Cory Dade for his initial implementation support. We also want to thank our marketing partners who help spread the word: On Purpose CEO Carol Cone, Talya Bosch, and Jennifer Aftanas. The team at Wiley has been an invaluable partner in this process. Our advisors, editors, and strategists include Jessica Filippo, Michelle Hacker, Richard Narramore, Sunnye Collins, and especially Nathan Means.

Finally, we thank our families, who inspire everything we do and support us during long hours of work on this project and many others: Tom's family, Christina, Alexa, Abigail, James, and Holly Lewis; and Alastair's family, Christine, Abigail, and Alexander MacGregor.

And thank you to everyone who has chosen to read this book, share it with others, and, most importantly, use it to further educate themselves and carve their own paths to becoming Future Ready®.

About the Authors

Tom Lewis IS a leading national and international climate, resilience, and sustainability consultant and business leader who has worked with WSP USA and WSP Global in various capacities inclusive of its Future Ready, innovation, and ESG programs. Prior to its acquisition and integration by WSP, Tom served as president of Louis Berger U.S. and a corporate board member, and prior to that, as its lead executive on environment, emergency management, disaster response and recovery, sustainability, and climate resilience working throughout the United States as well as globally. Across his 35-year professional career, Tom has also served on a variety of organizational and advisory boards and committees promoting sustainable and resilient infrastructure, environmental stewardship, emergency management, and disaster recovery. This specifically includes the International Coalition for Sustainable Infrastructure (as a co-founder), Resilience First, Disaster Recovery Contractors Association, and the Institute for Sustainable Infrastructure's Sustainability Advisory Board (previously the Zofnass Program's Sustainable Infrastructure Advisory Board at the

Harvard University Graduate School of Design). Tom holds both a B.S. and an M.S. in Civil Engineering and a J.D. with focus on environmental law/regulation. He is a licensed professional engineer (PE) and passed the bar in multiple states.

Alastair (Aly) MacGregor, Senior Vice President, leads the Property + Buildings national business line for WSP USA. Aly's 25 years of experience in high-performance design has ranged from individual net zero buildings to strategy portfolio analysis. His expertise includes sustainable, low-carbon, and passive building design; renewable energy and decarbonization strategy; operational resilience planning; smart buildings and smart cities; and digital solutions development. Aly has led sustainability strategy efforts across multiple markets, including global real estate portfolios; NASA's Net Zero, LEED Platinum "Sustainability Base"; Beijing's LEED Platinum World Finance Center; Spaceport America (the world's first commercial Spaceport), Jurong Lake eco-city, and a number of the world's most sustainable sports venues, including Golden1Center, Intuit Dome, and also supported the Los Angles 2028 Olympic bid.

Glossary

1.5° degrees Celsius: Scientists generally agree that global temperatures must be kept well below 2° Celsius (3.6° Fahrenheit), ideally 1.5°C (2.7° F), to avoid the worst impacts of climate change. Keeping global temperatures below 1.5C° was officially adopted as a central target of the Paris Agreement, a legally binding international treaty signed in 2015 by 196 countries. Meeting this target requires that greenhouse gas emissions peak as soon as possible and begin declining rapidly towards zero. The 1.5°C rise in temperature is measured against pre-industrial average global temperatures.

Anthropogenic emissions: Emissions of greenhouse gases, precursors of greenhouse gases and aerosols caused by human activities. These activities include the burning of fossil fuels, deforestation, land use and land-use changes, livestock production, fertilization, waste management, and industrial processes.

Blue water consumption: Freshwater, including rainwater and surface water, used to produce or incorporated into goods or services.

Biodiversity: The biological diversity of flora and fauna species on Earth, a complex web that underpins the natural life processes on the planet. Human-caused environmental damage, including widely used agricultural processes, reduces biodiversity. Creating healthy, sustainable societies requires increasing biodiversity.

Carbon: Shorthand for the carbon dioxide equivalent of all greenhouse gases. It's quantified as tonnes of carbon dioxide equivalent (tCO2e).

Carbon dioxide: A gas emitted in a variety of natural processes and human activities, such as burning oil, gas, coal, and wood. Carbon dioxide is the primary greenhouse gas emitted by human activities. Also written CO_2.

Carbon neutral: Achieving an overall balance between the amount of carbon dioxide an organization emits into the atmosphere and the amount it removes from the atmosphere.

Carbon Scope 1, 2, and 3 Emissions: Scope 1, 2, and 3 are methods of categorizing the various types of carbon emissions produced by a company in its own operations and throughout its value chain. Scopes were initially used in the Green House Gas Protocol of 2001, and they are still the foundation for required GHG reporting today.

Scope 1: Direct emissions from company-owned and controlled resources. These emissions are divided into four categories:

- Stationary combustion – fuels and heating sources that produce greenhouse gas emissions.

- Mobile combustion – greenhouse gas emissions from company vehicles (owned or controlled).

- Fugitive emissions – emission leaks from sources such as refrigeration and air conditioning units.

- Process emissions – emissions from industrial processes and onsite manufacturing.

Scope 2: Indirect emissions are those caused by the generation of purchased energy from a utility provider. In other words, all greenhouse gas emissions released into the atmosphere as a result of the use of purchased electricity, steam, heat, and cooling.

Scope 3: All indirect emissions not included in Scope 2 that occur in the company's value chain, including both upstream and downstream emissions. Companies focusing on reducing Scope 3 emissions focus on reducing business travel, encouraging employees to work from home, using climate-friendly transportation throughout the business, and reducing waste. Upstream activities include business travel, including employee commuting, waste generated, purchased goods and services, transportation and distribution, capital goods, and fuel and energy-related activities. Downstream activities cover invest-ments, franchises, leased assets, used sold products and end-of-life treatment.

Carbon sequestration: A process that removes carbon dioxide from the atmosphere and stores it as a liquid or solid. Also referred to as Sequestration.

CDP: Originally known as the Carbon Disclosure Project, this is a global nonprofit that runs an environmental disclosure system for investors, companies, cities, and governments to assess their impact and take action on carbon reduction.

Climate: The typical weather conditions of a region, averaged over time.

Climate adaptation: The process of adjusting to the actual and expected impacts of climate change through specific technologies, projects, and programs. *See* Resilience.

Climate change: Long-term shifts in regional temperature and weather patterns, in particular, those apparent from the mid to late 20th century onward and attributed largely to the increase in anthropogenic greenhouse gas emissions. Climate change-related events include an acceleration or more common occurrence of sea-level rise, prolonged high temperatures, wildfires, destructive hurricanes, drought, and extreme precipitation events.

Climate finance: Investment and financing options that are available linked to the outcomes of the investment program from a climate change perspective and are generally focused on investments, which result in 1) significant climate mitigation or greenhouse gas emissions reduction, or 2) climate resilience and adaptation improvement outcomes.

Climate mitigation: Taking action to reduce the probability and limit the extent of climate change, largely by removing or reducing the amount of greenhouse gases in the atmosphere. *See* Net zero emissions.

Climate neutral: A state in which human activities result in no net effect on the climate system. Achieving this state would require balancing of greenhouse gas emissions with emission removal.

Climate risk: Adverse consequences from the impact of climate change, including those on lives, livelihoods, health and well-being, economic, social and cultural assets, and investments, infrastructure, ecosystems, and species. *See* Physical risk, Transition risk.

Decarbonization: Programs, projects, and policies designed to reduce or eliminate the emissions of carbon dioxide and other greenhouse gases associated with electricity, industry, and transport.

Embodied carbon: The greenhouse gas emissions from the whole process of an asset's construction, including extracting raw materials, transporting, processing, manufacturing, installation, and end-of-life processes such as recycling, reuse, or disposal in a landfill. Embodied carbon from buildings represents 10% of total greenhouse gas emissions. *See* Operational carbon.

Energy Use Intensity (EUI):   When you benchmark your building in Portfolio Manager, one of the key metrics you'll see is energy use intensity, or EUI. Essentially, EUI expresses a building's energy use as a function of its size or other characteristics.

ESG (Environmental, Social, and Governance):   An umbrella term for nonfinancial factors used primarily by investors to evaluate an organization's performance and risks. Examples of data include levels of water pollution, carbon dioxide emissions, diversity initiatives, fair labor practices, or executive compensation.

Future Ready®:   WSP's trademarked global innovation initiative and process framework to bring clarity to a dynamic future by analyzing four categories of megatrends. These categories—climate, society, technology, and resources—each contain and organize a number of megatrends. For example, climate also includes drought, flooding, and sea level rise, among other climatic megatrends. Future Ready programs are designed to deliver a sustainable, resilient, prosperous, and equitable society for today and tomorrow.

Global warming: The increasing of the Earth's average temperature due to greenhouse gas emissions from human activity. Effects of global warming include, but are not restricted to, an increase in extreme weather events, decreased water security, and rising sea levels. *See* Climate change.

Greenhouse gas (GHG):   Atmospheric gases from natural and human sources that act like a blanket around the Earth, trapping the heat from sunlight and warming the planet. Since the Industrial Revolution, human activity—including burning fossil fuels for energy and transport as well as deforestation—has pushed atmospheric greenhouse gases to levels not seen in the past three million years. The concentration of GHG emissions is driving global warming and climate change. Significant greenhouse gases from human activity include carbon dioxide, as well as methane and nitrous oxide. *See* Carbon dioxide.

GRI (Global Reporting Initiative):   A global organization that helps organizations communicate their impacts on ESG-related issues. *See* ESG.

IPCC (Intergovernmental Panel on Climate Change):   A science-based intergovernmental body of the United Nations dedicated to researching and advancing knowledge of climate change. Internationally regarded as the leading scientific authority on climate change and the author of reports that advise policymakers on the impacts of, and solutions to, climate change.

Megatrends: Key trends used in the Future Ready program to better anticipate and plan for future conditions. Consideration of these trends from the outset improves the flexibility, longevity, reliability and accuracy of designs for programs and projects today and in the future. The four categories of trends are climate, society, technology, and resources. *See* Future Ready.

Nature-based solutions (NbS):   Actions to protect, sustainably manage, and restore natural and modified ecosystems simultaneously increasing sustainability and resilience while providing additional community and environmental benefits. An example is restoring and building wetland habitats to reduce flooding, store carbon, increase biodiversity, and improve human well-being.

Net zero emissions: The target of achieving an overall balance between the amount of greenhouse gas an organization emits into the atmosphere and the amount it removes from the atmosphere either directly or through offsets. Limiting catastrophic climate change requires organizations and countries to become net zero. Many organizational sustainability plans are based on achieving net zero by or before 2050. *See* Climate mitigation.

Operational carbon: The greenhouse gas emissions associated with the operation and maintenance of an asset. In the case of an apartment building, for example, this would include heating, cooling, and lighting. Operational carbon from buildings represents 37% of total greenhouse gas emissions. *See* Embodied carbon.

Paris Agreement: A legally binding international treaty on climate change adopted by 196 signatories in Paris in 2015. Paris-aligned targets are in line with what the latest climate science deems necessary to meet the goals of the Paris Agreement—to limit global warming to well below 2°C (3.6°F), preferably to 1.5°C (2.7°F) compared to pre-industrial levels.

Physical risk: Climate risk including damage to facilities and infrastructure, impact on operations, water and raw material availability, and supply chain disruptions. Physical risk includes both acute short-term events, like hurricanes, and chronic long-term changes in weather and climate, like droughts or sea-level rise. *See* Climate risk.

Resilience: The organizational and societal capacity to plan, adapt, recover, and thrive. In this book, *climate resilience* refers to these capacities with regard to climate change-related risks and vulnerabilities as well impacts from resulting from changes in society, technology, and resources. *See* Climate adaptation.

Science Based Targets initiative (SBTi):   The SBTi is a global organization that defines and promotes best practice in science-based target setting for greenhouse gas emissions reduction. The SBTi's goal is to accelerate organizational efforts to halve emissions before 2030 and achieve net-zero emissions before 2050. The group also offers resources and guidance to reduce barriers to adoption, and independently assesses and approves organizations' targets. The SBTi Net Zero Standard defines *net zero* as: 1) achieving a scale of value chain emissions reductions consistent with the depth of abatement at the point of reaching global net zero in 1.5°C (2.7°F) pathways, and 2) neutralizing the impact of any residual emissions by permanently removing an equivalent volume of carbon dioxide.

Sequestration: A process that removes carbon dioxide from the atmosphere and stores it as a liquid or solid. Sequestration can be achieved by human technologies or naturally by plants, oceans, wetlands, and soil, among others.

Site Energy: The amount of heat and electricity consumed by a building as reflected in your utility bills. Looking at site energy can help you understand how the energy use for an individual building has changed over time. Site energy may be delivered to a building in one of two forms: primary or secondary energy. Primary energy is the raw fuel that is burned to create heat and electricity, such as natural gas or fuel oil used in onsite generation. Secondary energy is the energy product (heat or electricity) created from a raw fuel, such as electricity purchased from the grid or heat received from a district steam system. A unit of primary and a unit of secondary energy consumed at the site are not directly comparable because one represents a raw fuel while the other represents a converted fuel.

Source Energy: The EPA has determined that source energy is the most equitable unit of evaluation for comparing different buildings to each other. Source energy represents the total amount of raw fuel that is required to operate the building. It incorporates all transmission, delivery, and production losses. By taking all energy use into account, the score provides a complete assessment of energy efficiency in a building.

Sustainability: The American Society of Civil Engineers (ASCE) defines sustainability as a set of economic, environmental, and social conditions in which all of society has the capacity and opportunity to maintain and improve its quality of life for future generations without degrading the quantity, quality, or the availability of economic, environmental, and social resources.

Sustainable development: ASCE defines sustainable development as the process of applying resources to enhance the public health, safety, welfare, and the quality of life for all of society and future generations without degrading the quantity, quality, or availability of economic, environmental, and social resources.

TCFD (Task Force on Climate-related Financial Disclosures): A global body that offers recommendations to improve and increase reporting of climate-related financial information. TCFD reporting is used to help companies and investors make more informed decisions about risk assessment, capital allocation, and strategic planning.

Transition risk: Climate-related risk that results from the transition to a lower carbon economy, and is related to policy and legal actions, technology changes, market responses, and reputational considerations. *See* Climate risk.

UNFCCC (United Nations Framework Convention on Climate Change):   The United Nations entity tasked with supporting the global response to the threat of climate change.

Index